Unforgettable

Unforgettable

Enabling Deep and Durable Learning

W. Michael Gray

RESOURCE *Publications* · Eugene, Oregon

UNFORGETTABLE
Enabling Deep and Durable Learning

Copyright © 2016 W. Michael Gray. All rights reserved. Except for brief quotations in critical publications or reviews, no part of this book may be reproduced in any manner without prior written permission from the publisher. Write: Permissions, Wipf and Stock Publishers, 199 W. 8th Ave., Suite 3, Eugene, OR 97401.

Resource Publications
An Imprint of Wipf and Stock Publishers
199 W. 8th Ave., Suite 3
Eugene, OR 97401

www.wipfandstock.com

PAPERBACK ISBN: 978-1-5326-0013-5
HARDCOVER ISBN: 978-1-5326-0015-9
EBOOK ISBN: 978-1-5326-0014-2

Manufactured in the U.S.A.   OCTOBER 11, 2016

This book is dedicated to my dear wife, Carol, and to our children, Heidi, Jenni, Will, Colin, and Melissa

Contents

Preface | ix

Acknowledgments | xv

Introduction | xvii

1. Teaching for Transformation | 1
2. Becoming a Clear-Thinking Teacher | 16
3. Thinking Like an Expert | 29
4. Developing and Clarifying Your Ideas | 61
5. Explanatory Power | 96
6. This Is the Way: Designing the Optimal Learning Path | 121
7. Student Flourishing | 145
8. Ask, Don't Tell | 173
9. Speaking Truth in Love: Assessment as Communication | 204
10. Averting Disaster | 247

Appendix 1   *The Logic of a Chef | 261*

Appendix 2   *Richard Paul's eight elements of thought compared with my approach | 263*

Appendix 3   *Gowin's Knowledge Vee | 266*

Appendix 4   *Socratic GPS | 267*

Appendix 5   *Assessment in Course Design | 268*

Bibliography | 269

Preface

My journey as a teacher began forty-five years ago when I entered a high school classroom with great apprehension about my adequacy for the task. As a high school student I was something of a nerd and a loner who loved learning. Now I was about to face my first class of students, and I realized most of them were likely not lovers of learning! Somehow I survived my first year and actually had some enjoyable teaching experiences. Later as a twenty-eight-year-old with a newly minted Ph.D., I entered my first college classroom filled with excitement and hope. I was also filled with passion for my subject and idealism about what could be accomplished in the classroom. *Teach Like a Champion*[1] had not yet been written, but such was my resolve.

Over the next decade my commitment was undiminished as I worked with intensity to craft an educational experience that would leapfrog what I had experienced as an undergraduate and even as a graduate student. But after ten years of college teaching, I began to have doubts. I still loved teaching and I loved "seeing the light come on" for students; but I had to admit that the light never came on for many students, and the lights that were lit were often low wattage.

Entering my second decade in academia, I was tired and unfulfilled as a teacher. I conducted a simple cost/benefit analysis that showed that my passion for teaching, my intensity as a classroom communicator, and an enormous investment of my time for a decade had scarcely budged the needle of student mastery. Even my most enthusiastic students seemed to have little to show years later for having been my students. At this point of potential disillusionment I entered a period of sober reflection. I shared my concerns and observations with two of my younger colleagues and with my department chair, who was ten years my senior, and I found that they all had similar observations and concerns.

1. Lemov, *Teach Like a Champion*.

As a new faculty member, I was fortunate to share an office with my department chair (who had been my favorite teacher during my undergraduate years). To realize that even he had deep concerns about his teaching effectiveness was enormously helpful. By this point in his career he might have reflexively adopted a skeptical stance that teaching couldn't be effective given the "dumb" or unmotivated students. Instead, he was passionate that durable learning was possible (even with today's students) but that we were missing something as teachers. It turned out that what we were missing was not simply an issue of technique but a matter of assumptions. Assumptions normally fly under the radar of our consciousness. They are things that we give no thought to—things that represent the starting point for our reasoning and that tend to resist rational analysis.

My own assumptions were rooted in a faith in the effectiveness of one-way oral communication. I had an implicit faith that teaching was mainly about transmitting information. In this, of course, I was not alone. Don Finkel suggests that "our natural, unexamined model for teaching is Telling. . . . [T]he fundamental act of teaching is to carefully and clearly tell students something they did not previously know."[2] The assumption that transmission of words equated to transmitting the ideas in my head was unjustified in my experience as a student. Despite energetic note taking and intense concentration on the teacher's lecture, I had often faced consternation in trying to decipher my notes. I also recognized how little long-term gain in knowledge I had experienced as a student who had been simply told things. Even when I "got it," I eventually lost it. As Robert Mager reputedly said in 1968, "If telling were teaching, we'd all be so smart we could hardly stand it."

The very act of questioning my assumptions about teaching was a significant step forward. An analysis of what makes a teacher a great communicator who effectively changes student thinking is not incidental; it is *primary*. To dismiss great teachers as mere outliers—people with extraordinary gifts—is to buy into the helpless view that teachers are born, not made. But if teachers can *learn* how to teach, dissecting the process should be the central focus of faculty development.

Glimpsing a Solution

Part of my academic journey around the same time I entered this period of critical reflection on my teaching effectiveness was to discover some important paradigm-changing books. There would be many of these in the years ahead, but one of the early ones was entirely unexpected. As a young

---

2. Finkel, *Teaching with Your Mouth Shut*, 2.

faculty member with a large family, I had bought a "fixer-upper." This was a house with potential, but at the time very real and pressing problems. One of these was the water piping, which we discovered belatedly was galvanized pipe about ten years past its life expectancy. When water flow to a basement laundry room was severely restricted by rust accumulation that constricted the bore of the water supply lines, I knew something had to be done. Short on funds and faced with imminent rupture of my pipes, I talked to my friends to try to find a solution.

Through the counsel of a friend in similar straits I discovered *Plumbing for Dummies*.[3] This was actually before the profusion of such books that flooded the market later. This book didn't provide idealized diagrams for purposes of imitation. I'd encountered such books before, and they definitely did not inspire my confidence in attacking problems that didn't match the ideal layouts in the book. This book actually explained the thinking of a plumber—the logic of plumbing. With the principles and logic of plumbing in my mind, I felt that I had a good chance of mastering plumbing while replacing all of my galvanized plumbing with copper pipes that would last much longer. The first principle to learn was how to use various fittings to make branches in the water supply lines, and the second principle was how to solder these fittings into place using a procedure known as sweating the fittings. The logic of these two principles and the way they related to each other was so clearly presented that I could make application to situations not specifically addressed in the book. I learned to think like a plumber! That was about twenty-five years ago, and I've had no problems with the plumbing in all of those years. Since then I've tackled other plumbing problems for close friends and plumbed a new house from scratch that passed the scrutiny of a plumbing inspector. My thinking was permanently changed as a result of a well-written book. I suppose I would have learned faster under the tutelage of a professional plumber, but I didn't have that luxury.

It may not be clear yet what plumbing has to do with teaching effectiveness. Let me lead you there by moving to traditional academics. A seminal text in my field is *Molecular Biology of the Cell* (*MBOC*) by Bruce Alberts et al.[4] The role of this book in shaping my academic thinking paral-

---

3. Fredriksson, *Plumbing for Dummies*. This book may have launched the "For Dummies" market. It is not a slick color-illustrated book but a window into the thinking of a professional plumber. Written in a somewhat cynical tone, it is full of wry humor and reflection.

4. Alberts, *Molecular Biology of the Cell*. This book launched a revolution because its clear writing extracted the central concepts and developed them succinctly yet thoroughly through the use of many visual illustrations. The book in its various editions has been the leading text in its field for the past thirty years.

lels *Plumbing for Dummies* in my life as a handyman. I was trained as a cellular and molecular biologist. Until the publication of *MBOC* in 1983, I sincerely believed that there were many parts of my chosen field that could not be simplified sufficiently for any but the most advanced undergraduates to understand. This was a problem, because molecular biology was becoming at that time much more than a slice of biology. It was, rather, an approach to thinking about biology as a whole. As an approach it was rapidly challenging more traditional paradigms and effectively displacing them. Molecular biology was a scientific tsunami that was poised to change the entire landscape of biology—and indeed that is precisely what has happened in the intervening years.

It is difficult to overestimate the significance of the 1983 publication of *MBOC* to the development of molecular biology. Many faculty with training like mine were emboldened to create undergraduate courses with the book as a centerpiece. I myself started a course at my institution in 1986, and it continues to be taught to this day. How can a textbook have so much influence? *MBOC* persuaded me over and over again that there is a way to explain even the most complicated concepts so that students can understand and apply them to solving problems. It unpacked the thinking process of a molecular biologist.

The Way Forward

What *Plumbing for Dummies* and *MBOC* did was to reveal and make accessible two very different ways of thinking. As a would-be plumber I didn't need information about plumbing; I needed to learn to think like a plumber. I didn't need step-by-step instructions to mimic. I needed an approach that was logical so that I knew why I needed to take the steps in that order and what each step contributed. I didn't need to know *about* plumbing, I needed to *become* a plumber (all right, maybe a novice plumber).

What I have just described in regard to plumbing should be true any time we learn anything. David Perkins in *Making Learning Whole* says we need to engage early and often with a "junior version" of the real game. In plumbing this was practicing with pipes and fittings, soldering them to gain facility with the process of "sweating" joints. This kind of thing "gets us past initial disorientation and into the game. . . . You may not do it very well, but at least you know what you're doing and why you're doing it."[5]

The pedagogy of *MBOC* was not different in principle from that in *Plumbing for Dummies*. The authors of *MBOC* were incisive in identifying

5. Perkins, *Making Learning Whole*, 9.

the core concepts of molecular biology and then developing the logic of those concepts and the ways in which they are logically related. Readers were engaged in the logic of molecular biology. The book focused on answering how and why questions rather than serving up information per se. It frankly admitted what we didn't know yet and speculated about possible alternative answers. This development took place in an environment abounding in real-game context. Applicable findings from the scientific literature were invoked in rich diagrams that invited the reader to think through the visualization seeking its logic rather than aiming for simple absorption. There was also a companion book to the *MBOC* text, *The Problems Book*, which contained problems derived from the scientific literature for nearly every chapter so that students could try their fledgling skills in the real game of molecular biology.

I have become convinced that the way forward for teaching is the need to become a Clear Thinking Teacher—a teacher who analyzes her thinking within her academic discipline in order to foster the thinking itself in her students. Traditional teaching aims to deliver the products of thinking but not to require students to do the thinking itself. Our aim should be to engage students in appropriating and using the thinking of a professional in an accessible junior version of the real game with an eye toward playing the real game. In this way we can harness our expertise for the sake of lasting learning by our students.

Whether you are a beginning teacher riding high on a crest of optimism and passion about making a difference in the lives of your students, an early career teacher critically evaluating the success of your teaching and searching for answers, or a more seasoned teacher who is contemplating a teaching "conversion," there is tangible direction in the story that will unfold in future chapters. Conversions require an epiphany—a revelation. Your eyes need to be opened to a problem much bigger than your classroom. It is not too much to say that higher education as a whole is experiencing a crisis. That reality will be developed in the Introduction.

Acknowledgments

Mark Twain said that "substantially all ideas are secondhand, consciously and unconsciously drawn from a million outside sources."[1] I have no doubt that Twain is correct about this. I have done my best to acknowledge my sources, but I can give credit only to those that I am consciously aware of. Chief among these are my comrades, Bill Lovegrove and Brian Vogt, who have taught with me in summer institutes since 2004 and sparred with my ideas for at least a decade prior to that. My debt to Bill and Brian is immense. Indeed for some of my core concepts in this book it is difficult to know how much of the idea is mine and how much is the refined product that came out of the crucible of our conversations. The synergy that occurs when we dialogue about the scholarship of teaching and learning is a marvelous thing.

Going farther back in my history, I have to acknowledge two exemplars who elevated my thoughts about what teaching could be and should be. Tom Coss was my favorite undergraduate professor although we crossed paths only during my first year as an undergraduate. Later, when I joined the faculty, Tom was to be my department chair. His generosity and transparency in sharing his teaching aspirations and frustrations were encouraging and affirming for me the rightness of my discontent with the teaching status quo. Tom and I worked together to make our teaching better through many an office conversation. He never talked down to me, as well he might have, in view of the vast difference in our experience levels. The other exemplar of extraordinary teaching effectiveness was Lyndon Larcom, who taught three of the molecular biology courses in my Ph.D. program. My favorite expression from Lynn's teaching is "it turns out that . . ." This always signaled an unexpected turn in the narrative and promised a resolution that would be satisfying because it was so imminently logical.

Two writers who have had a profound impact on my development as a learner and a teacher (in that order) are Richard Paul and Joseph Novak.

1. Twain, "Plagiarism."

I encountered Richard Paul's monumental 670-page book on critical thinking in 1992, and I later had the privilege of attending one of his two-day conferences in 1995. Paul's insights into the elements of reasoning that underlie all thinking are foundational to this book. Complementary to Paul is the work of Joseph Novak, whose book *Learning How to Learn* caught my attention as I was grappling with the role of concepts in Paul's elements of reasoning. Concept mapping was the tool that I needed to expose my own thinking to myself and to my colleagues.

Finally, I recognize the crucial role of the university faculty who have participated as students in the summer conferences I have directed for the past thirteen years. My students have always been among my greatest teachers and these peers have been invaluable in sharpening my thinking about teaching and learning. They have also encouraged the writing of this book. My writing has been financially undergirded by the Science and Engineering Endowment Fund, for which I am very grateful. I am grateful as well to my editors Grace Hargis and Suzette Jordan for their patience and their improvement of my writing. My thanks also go my nephew, Jeff Gray, for his professional illustrations, which help me to tell the story with greater clarity.

Introduction

Higher education is in serious trouble. We've fallen a long way from the vision articulated in 1852 by John Henry Newman in his seminal work, *The Idea of a University*:

> It is education which gives man a clear conscious view of his own opinions and judgments, a truth in developing them . . . and a force in urging them. It teaches him to see things as they are, to go right to the point, to disentangle a skein of thought, to detect what is sophistical, and to discard what is irrelevant. . . .
>
> He [the student] apprehends the great outlines of knowledge, the principles on which it rests, the scale of its parts, its lights and its shades, its great points and its little, as he otherwise cannot apprehend them.[1]

The student in Newman's university is becoming a critical thinker. The student in many present-day university programs is simply looking for vocational competence. He isn't engaged with great ideas from multiple disciplines; he is myopically focused on an occupational credential.

The parents of today's students are also impatient with learning that is not vocationally focused. They want their hard-earned dollars to buy an occupational future for their offspring. Never mind the reality that today's college graduates will change not just jobs but careers and need to be resilient to make these transitions. Parents and students are also frustrated with the increasing cost of a college education that has risen in the U.S. in the past thirty years at nearly five times the pace of inflation.[2] The average member of the college class of 2013 graduated $28,400 in debt while facing uncertain employment prospects.[3] And it's not as though not going to college is a viable option: almost 60 percent of the workforce have jobs defined

---

1. Newman, Discourse 7, Stanza 10, 178.
2. Anonymous, "Declining Value."
3. Anonymous, "Average Student Loan."

as requiring a college education.[4] The rest of the jobs are menial dead-end jobs that no parent wants for his child.

Many colleges shoot themselves in the foot with the low quality and irrelevance of their courses. This reality has become almost legendary and was the target of humorist Dave Barry back in the 1990s:

> College is basically a bunch of rooms where you sit for roughly two thousand hours and try to memorize things. The two thousand hours are spread out over four years; you spend the rest of the time sleeping and trying to get dates. Basically, you learn two kinds of things in college: Things you will need to know later in life (two hours).... Things you will not need to know in later life (1,998 hours). These are the things you learn in classes whose names end in –ology, -osophy, -istry, -ics, and so on. The idea is, you memorize these things, then write them down in little exam books, then forget them. If you fail to forget them, you become a professor and have to stay in college for the rest of your life.[5]

Who wants to pay a premium for courses that major in teaching you "things you will not need to know in later life?" And, for the students, who wants to attend such classes? What's the point?

The colleges of America give lip service to the importance of their teaching faculty but make little investment in teaching. Teaching is not valued. When was the last time you heard an institution proudly proclaim, "We are a teaching institution"? No, they all want to be "research institutions." Research produces publications, publications produce institutional and personal prestige, and such documented prestige leads to tenure for faculty and extramural funding for institutions. Ernest Boyer's call to recognize the Scholarship of Teaching and Learning[6] has gone largely unheeded by academia.

The breadth of human thought is contained in the liberal arts (which traditionally include the sciences). Mastery of the liberal arts has historically been the mark of an educated person. But the liberal arts have fallen on hard times since their apex in the 1960s. Fewer than ten percent of current college students are majoring in humanities or the liberal arts. In contrast, nearly one in four BA degrees granted is in business. Of 212 liberal arts colleges in 1990, about 35 percent had closed as of 2009. Many of the

---

4. Anonymous, "Value of a College Degree."
5. Choron and Choron, *College in a Can*, 104.
6. Boyer, *Scholarship Reconsidered*.

remaining schools are hybrids and offer vocational programs as well as their historical liberal arts majors.[7]

This is not an apologetic for a liberal arts education although I, a biologist, strongly believe that teaching biology in a liberal arts context is the optimal scenario.[8] My exasperation is with the ubiquitous pragmatism of vocational education, a pragmatism that produces in students a concomitant impatience with the thoughtful educational development of the theoretical base of *any* discipline. That's really bad news! It is through a mastery of big ideas rooted in theory that any discipline progresses.

College is supposed to be mind expanding. It is supposed to be transformative. It is supposed to take adolescents and transform them into adults. It is supposed to take those who have interest and raw ability in an area and transform them into professionals who are able to operate with facility in their chosen field and demonstrate expertise and mastery. Such professional competence is not mere vocational readiness or even an awareness of current "best practice." College should not be about training journeymen. A college education should open the mind to the world of ideas, and that world is not a vocational straitjacket. The industries, systems, and revolutions of tomorrow will come from the world of ideas and not the vocational givens of the present. Most significant problems require a multidisciplinary approach, and the ideal is that individuals be able to think in multidisciplinary and interdisciplinary ways. Most people will change careers several times, and multidisciplinary training then becomes almost a must. So much for the pragmatism of narrow vocational training.

Not Radical Enough

There are many solutions on the table to address the problems I have listed here. Some of them involve new models of what a college education should be. The *New York Times* declared 2012 to be "The Year of the MOOC." A MOOC is a massive online open course. What is massive? Try enrollments exceeding 150,000 students. Enrollments are massive because courses are free and have no prerequisites, so they are open courses. The classes are conducted entirely online and generally do not offer credit, although a certificate of completion is usually granted. Teachers of MOOCs are usually university faculty (or former faculty—some have started their own companies) who

---

7. Anonymous, "College English Major Pressures."

8. Cech, "Science at Liberal Arts Colleges," 195–216. Cech won the Nobel Prize in Chemistry in 1989. He was the president of the Howard Hughes Medical Institute 2000-2009. He is a graduate of a small liberal arts institution, Grinnell College, in Iowa.

were recognized on their campuses as effective communicators. As of 2013 the big name companies were Coursera, EdX, and Udacity. Together they enrolled more than 2 million students in 2012.[9]

MOOCs are basically online courses and have the same strengths and weaknesses as the rest of online education. Like more conventional online education, they are really only content delivery systems that aren't heavily invested in brick and mortar. What you'll hear if you sign up is a lecture—a well-scripted, lively presentation to be sure, but a one-sided lecture. The faculty member will not be able to respond to individual students—remember the course is massive. Your opportunity to respond will likely be to take online quizzes (with automated feedback) and perhaps participate in polls.

There is really nothing revolutionary about a MOOC when you get down to this level. It is a new *business* model for education that leverages the most effective lecturers of our day for massive audiences. It is really an electronic version of the medieval lecture when the limiting factors were the availability of teachers and books. The solution was the *lectio*. The teacher would read a book for the audience without interruption. Why, after six hundred years, are we still doing that?

The lecture is the centerpiece of an ineffective form of education. It is ineffective because it is based on a flawed view of how humans learn. It assumes that knowledge is a commodity that can be transferred from a subject matter expert to a novice by means of a monologue. There is no doubt that a lecture can be challenging and entertaining. Think about TED Talks and you will see what lecturing could be (but seldom is). On the other hand, education is about transforming minds, and for that you need interaction between minds, not words traveling from source to recipient. We are probably all familiar with the tongue-in-cheek definition of a lecture: "information transferred from the notes of the teacher to the notes of the student without passing through the mind of either."

Radically Rethinking College

The call to lay down the lecture will continue to be met with resistance from the professoriate. Lectures are their bread and butter. Lectures can be crafted in advance of class. Lectures are tidy. Lectures are an opportunity to showcase the professor's expertise before a captive audience. No doubt there is significant scholarship involved in producing well-crafted lectures that synthesize multiple sources and decades of academic experience. But such a synthesis can more profitably be delivered in a book or an online video

---

9. Pappano, "Year of the MOOC."

or a series of articles posted on a blog. When motivated students who want to learn sign up for your course, they don't sign up to hear you read (even with expression!) your ruminations—they want to interact with your brain. They don't want to just hear you deliver the products of your thinking. They want you to direct and critique their thinking processes and raise them to a higher level, preferably in real time. You can do this in only one way that I know of: through dialogue with them. You must probe their minds with significant questions and then patiently interact with what comes out. That is the truly radical proposal that needs to have the floor in discussions about the future of higher education.

This radical proposal doesn't sound so radical when we take stock of what the current lecture-dominated higher educational system has accomplished.

More than twenty-five years ago Paul Ramsden wrote:

> The message of scores of studies on student learning is unambiguous: many students are highly adept at very complex skills in science, humanities and mathematics. They can reproduce large amounts of factual information on demand; they have appropriated enormous quantities of detailed knowledge: they pass examinations successfully. But they are unable to show that they *understand* what they have learned. They harbor profound misconceptions about mathematical, physical and social [phenomena]. They have hazy notions of the accepted form of expression in the subjects they have studied.[10]

In 1995 Neil Postman predicted "the end of education" (in a book by that name) while also developing what he thought the "end" or aim of education *should* be. Postman said there are "two problems to solve. One is an engineering problem . . . it is the means by which the young will become learned. [We should not] . . . trivialize learning, to reduce it to a mechanical skill. . . . [T]o become a different person because of something you have learned—to appropriate an insight, a concept, a vision so that your world is altered . . . you need a reason. And this is the metaphysical problem I speak of."[11]

Derek Bok, past president of Harvard, in *Our Underachieving Colleges* singled out in 2006 the lack of progress students make in becoming proficient at critical thinking, writing, computational ability, and "moral reasoning" as cause for concern and action. He points an accusing finger at faculty who employ approaches in their teaching that have been proven to

10. Ramsden, *Improving Learning*, 13-14.
11. Postman, *End of Education*, 3-4.

be flawed. He also chastises administrators for assigning pivotal academic courses to inexperienced teachers.[12]

More recently Richard Arum and Josipa Roksa in 2011 published *Academically Adrift* in which they noted that,

> Three semesters of college education . . . have a barely noticeable impact on students' skills in critical thinking, complex reasoning, and writing. . . . [I]n the most optimistic scenario, students will continue their meager progress, leading to less than impressive gains over the course of their enrollment [four years or more] . . . leaving higher education just slightly more proficient in critical thinking, complex reasoning, and writing than when they entered.[13]

The common theme here is the lack of ability of the present higher education system to reliably produce students who understand ideas and can use them in critical thinking. Education as currently practiced is objective to a fault. Its focus is purely on an ability to reproduce factual information. We are like the schoolroom narrative envisioned by Charles Dickens in *Hard Times*: "In this life we want nothing but Facts, sir; nothing but Facts! [And we view our students as] . . . ready to have imperial gallons of facts poured into them until they . . . [are] full to the brim."[14]

I recently had a conversation with a humanities alumnus of my university. Ten years out from graduation he has a career that involves him regularly in creative big picture thinking in the business world. Knowing that I am an academic, he sheepishly confessed that he "hated college." Somewhat taken aback by his candor, I asked if he enjoyed learning. His reply was that he "absolutely loves learning about all kinds of things." He quickly explained that he found college overloaded with memorization of uninspiring facts—something he wasn't that good at (nor motivated to do). My university could have sharpened and intensified his learning as an undergraduate and accentuated his intrinsic love of learning instead of putting him "through the mill" of insipid irrelevance in pursuit of a credential.

"Business as usual" is no longer tenable in higher education. Changing the enterprise of higher education is not the place to start, however. Change has to begin with individual faculty members like you. I'll lay out in the following chapter a coherent vision for using your understanding of your academic discipline to serve the learners in your classes.

---

12. Bok, *Our Underachieving Colleges*.
13. Arum and Roksa, *Academically Adrift*, 35, 37.
14. Dickens, *Hard Times*, 2.

Chapter 1

Teaching for Transformation

Truly effective teaching changes students. "[It] reminds us of the primacy of *learning*, not teaching, in education. Learning is the end, teaching is a means to that end."[1]

DONALD L. FINKEL

Teaching and learning are necessarily interdependent and interwoven actions. Teaching may be done without learning occurring, and learning may sometimes be self-taught; but a very normal expectation is that teaching will increase learning. The fate of teachers is all wrapped up with the success of pupils. By success I mean not just producing a satisfied customer at the end of the semester—but transforming the customer.

Transformation is thorough and lasting. Students who are transformed by learning get more than they pay for. Their eyes are opened to new vistas with new possibilities. The life trajectory of transformed students is permanently altered. Life-long learning is the natural result of the pursuit of joy through the process of learning.

If you permit yourself reflection on your teaching, the hard question eventually comes, "To what extent does my teaching transform my students?" Asking the question requires humility before the evidence. We are all prone to cherry-pick. If you teach long enough, some of your students will excel in their professional lives. To what extent did you contribute to the success of a gifted student? A better benchmark would be found in your average students. Is it typical that they are transformed by being in your class? Perhaps your pool of evidence isn't encouraging. For many faculty sober reflection on their teaching effectiveness is the first step on a journey that opens their eyes to new vistas and undreamed-of fulfillment as a teacher.

1. Finkel, *Teaching with Your Mouth Shut*, 8.

Transformative learning is not mere fact acquisition; it is not even the ability of the student to recall in detail the pearls of your scholarship. Paul Ramsden points us to learning as "alter[ing] students' understanding, so that they begin to conceptualise phenomena and ideas in the way . . . experts conceptualise them."[2] Ramsden zeroes in on what is typically called higher-order learning as the thing that makes teachers indispensable. This is learning focused on not just knowing what but, more importantly, why. Such learning aims for deep understanding.

Ken Bain in his influential book, *What the Best College Teachers Do,* identified truly excellent teachers in two dozen universities across America. Bain's major criterion was that they "had achieved remarkable success in helping their students learn in ways that made a sustained, substantial and positive influence on how those students think, act, and feel. . . . We sought people . . . who constantly help their students do far better than anyone else expects. . . . Some students talked about courses that 'transformed their lives,' 'changed everything,' and even 'messed with their heads.'"[3]

Why the Best College Teachers Do What They Do

Bain's book is helpful because excellent teachers appear to almost reflexively do certain things that work, regardless of the academic discipline. As an admirer of Bain's work, I'd like to take it a step further and ask why certain mindsets and practices are characteristic of excellent teaching. Why do they work? By asking the question, we're trying to explore the logical foundations of the practices. We're trying to do higher-order learning of the process of higher-order learning. We're engaging in the "scholarship of teaching."[4] Those in higher education love the identifier of professor but avoid the label teacher, feeling it diminishes them. Yet, what the next generation needs most is teachers—*doctors,* to use an old term of honor that has been hijacked by physicians who, at best, give five-minute lessons to their patients.[5]

In higher education the Ph.D. is the credential that supposedly qualifies one to teach; students and their parents recognize this, and administrators insist on it. The assumption is that you don't have to have any formal

---

2. Ramsden, *Learning to Teach in Higher Education,* 7.

3. Bain, *What the Best College Teachers Do,* 5-10.

4. Boyer, *Scholarship Reconsidered,* 16. This was ultimately broadened into the phrase Scholarship of Teaching and Learning, eventually abbreviated as SOTL.

5. *Oxford English Dictionary,* s.v. "doctor" as noun, from L. *docere* meaning "to teach." The first meaning is "a teacher, instructor; one who gives instruction in some branch of knowledge, or inculcates opinions or principles."

training in how to teach at the college level. Teaching is what happens when you get up to share your expertise with your students. No wonder higher education is in crisis! The reality is that effective teaching at the college level requires both subject matter expertise and a deep understanding of how students learn to think in domain-specific ways.

To become a scholar of teaching and learning is going to take serious study and commitment. I've done a lot of study in this area over the past twenty-five years, and I'll help you go to the high-value thinkers in higher education through the footnotes in every chapter. Education is often dominated by jargon with a very short half-life. I'm a firm believer in holding vocabulary to the minimum necessary for clear communication. My argument in this book is not dependent on jargon. On this journey there will be deep satisfaction that what works actually works for sound reasons. You'll find here a logically connected causal narrative.

Education often seems to have a life of its own, independent of subject matter. The story in this book of how to maximize transformative learning will collaborate with what you know about your academic discipline. Indeed chapter 2 "Becoming a Clear Thinking Teacher" will start you on a quest that will improve the depth of your personal understanding of what you already know well. As you work to clarify and expose your expert thinking processes, you'll gain powerful insights that will enable your students to go farther than you thought possible.

Finding Mentors

Critical reflection on your teaching is intellectually difficult and can be dangerous. It can cause you to doubt without providing direction, and that can lead to disillusionment. The journey I'm inviting you on is always better when you have the fellowship and counsel of friends. I hope you can find such a circle on your campus, but I want you to make friends with some fellow travelers who have been candid about their struggles and who can point us to some solutions.

Richard R. Hake was a member of the physics faculty at Indiana University in the fall of 1980 when he began teaching a physics course for elementary education majors. "I gave the first examination. The results showed quite clearly that my brilliant lectures and exciting demonstrations on Newtonian mechanics had passed through the students' minds leaving no measurable trace. To make matters worse, in a student evaluation given shortly after the exam, some students rated me as among the worst instructors they had ever experienced at our university."[6] Hake's candor shows us a teacher who was facing painfully discordant data and was becoming critically reflective about the lack of effectiveness in his teaching. His response was to talk to other physicists he knew, and he ended up being directed to Arnold Arons, who taught physics to elementary education majors at the University of Washington. Arons had published multiple papers about his approach to teaching physics. "Arons . . . recommended that *I abandon the standard passive student lecture.*"[7] Hake ended up adapting Arons' methods to his course at IU and became an enthusiastic supporter as indicated by the title of his paper "My Conversion to the Arons-Advocated Method of Science Education."

This curious terminology is not unique to Hake and represents the magnitude of change required to move out of the reflexive "Teaching as Telling" methodology. Critical thinking authority Richard Paul puts it this way: "We must make a paradigm shift from a didactic to a critical model of education to make higher order thinking a classroom reality. This shift is like a global shift in our eating habits and lifestyle. It cannot be achieved in a one-day inservice or by any other short-term strategy. It must come over an extended period of time and be experienced as something of a *conversion*, as a new way of thinking about every dimension of schooling."[8]

Physicist Carl Wieman is an unusual exemplar of the ideal professor in higher education. Recipient of the 2001 Nobel Prize in Physics with Eric Cornell for his production of the Bose-Einstein condensate in 1995, Wieman was also the Carnegie Foundation's U.S. University Professor of the Year in 2004. This second award was among all professors (not just those in physics) in U.S. doctoral and research universities. Wieman started science education initiatives at both the University of Colorado at Boulder and at the University of British Columbia. He is also currently the Chair of the Board on Science Education for the National Academy of Sciences.[9] Wieman recounts his journey as a science educator:

> When I first taught physics as a young assistant professor, I used the approach that is all too common when someone is called upon to teach something. First I thought very hard about the topic and got it clear in my own mind. Then I explained it to my

---

6. Hake, "My Conversion to the Arons-Advocated Method of Science Education," 109.

7. Ibid.

8. Paul, *Critical Thinking*, 297 (emphasis mine).

9. "Carl Wieman," Wikipedia.

students so that they would understand it with the same clarity I had.

At least that was the theory. But I am a devout believer in the experimental method, so I always measure results. And whenever I made any serious attempt to determine what my students were learning, it was clear that this approach just didn't work. An occasional student here and there might have understood my beautifully clear and clever explanations, but the vast majority of students weren't getting them at all.

For many years, this failure of students to learn from my explanations remained a frustrating puzzle to me, as I think it is for many diligent faculty members.[10]

So what does Wieman recommend as a replacement for this failed approach? "A lot of educational and cognitive research can be reduced to this basic principle: People learn by creating their own understanding. But that does not mean they must or even can do it without assistance. *Effective teaching facilitates that creation by getting students engaged in thinking deeply about the subject at an appropriate level and then monitoring that thinking and guiding it to be more expert-like.*"[11]

Getting Inside Your Head

Most academics gravitated to a particular domain of academia because of innate (and uncommon) intellectual gifts. I'm not flattering you when I observe that you probably did not struggle to identify your expertise. To be sure, you had to work long and hard to perfect it, but you had definite advantages over the average learner. To serve the average learners in your classroom, you are going to have to "get inside your head." This process is sometimes called metacognition—thinking about your thinking. If this sounds hopelessly cerebral, the intellectual equivalent of navel gazing, please stick with me. It is doubtless hard work, but it is the only path to being able to helping your students think this way. If you can't articulate your own thinking processes, how can you teach them to anyone else?

One of my adult sons has undergraduate and graduate degrees in graphic design. When he was in college, he regularly expressed frustration that his teachers on both levels were not able to clearly articulate a path to improvement. Exactly what made some designs good and others great was something of a mystery, it seems. I don't think this is a problem just in

---

10. Wieman, "Why Not Try a Scientific Approach?" 10.
11. Ibid, 12 (emphasis mine).

the arts. Can you defend your evaluations of student work by referencing the concepts and reasoning used by experts in your domain? The fact that so much of our expertise relies on gut-level reactions rather than on clear and logical thought says that most of us need to grow in the clarity of our thinking. How can you teach your students to get better in their thinking and execution unless you can clearly state the strengths and weaknesses (or the logic and illogic) of their work?

You must expose your reasoning processes to clarify them and to have something tangible to teach your students. In doing this, you must learn what distinguishes your mode of thinking from the kinds of thinking that are used in other subject matter areas—other domains of knowledge. A useful tool for doing this is what I call a logic wheel. I'll develop this in depth in chapter 3 "Thinking Like an Expert." The foundation to your mode of thinking is to characterize the kinds of questions your discipline can answer. What was your discipline created to do? Does your expertise qualify you to answer questions relating to the structure of the U.S. government? How about what constitutes a healthy diet? What about the computational demands of self-driving cars? We might have an opinion about these questions, but for most or all of them we are laypeople and not experts. In conversation at a convention or a party you perk up when a question invoking your expertise is asked. Help your students at the outset of your course by letting them know the kinds of questions your class is going to equip them to answer.

In many cases you'll also have to help students understand what they will gain in being able to answer such questions. In doing this you're helping to address the question of motivation. Students who truly understand what motivates asking a question move naturally to engagement with the process by which the question is answered. In answering the question you will assume some things that you don't attempt to prove. You will also accept a certain body of factual information that any helpful answer must take into account. This body of facts represents conclusions that experts have arrived at as they answered earlier questions. Most college courses are focused on facts. This is very unfortunate because facts are relatively static givens. Facts give the impression that other people have made contributions to the field but students are simply bystanders whose job it is to passively absorb.

Students are not transformed by hearing how you would answer a question. Students are transformed by means of their own engagement in thinking through alternative answers and arriving at the best one. The main action in answering a question is to grapple with ideas. This is the arena of conceptualization. Concepts that might help to answer the question at issue have to be actively assimilated by each individual learner. Each learner has to wrestle with an idea to determine its boundaries and how it relates to other ideas the student has previously mastered. Because the history (and accuracy) of previous concept assimilation varies with the individual, learning is intrinsically idiosyncratic. Teachers (and student peers) help individual students by posing questions that cause the wrestling. Learners, in turn, generate their own questions during the wrestling and sometimes get stuck. Getting unstuck is usually going to require a push in the form of a clarifying question. In this whole process teachers and peers actively negotiate for shared meaning of concepts that they use to answer a question. Because the process of conceptualization is so central to answering questions, I've devoted chapter 4 "Developing and Clarifying Ideas" to this process.

Concepts (ideas) reside in mental networks. Concepts are logically tied to other concepts by propositional statements. Sometimes a student has put a concept in the wrong place mentally. The student has a misconception. The only way to unseat the concept and move it to the right place is through effectively challenging the logic by which it is currently linked in the student's mind. This puts questions in the driver's seat again. Questions are a central feature of a transformative learning environment. Some of the propositions that the student constructs will be exceptionally powerful and frequently used in answering the questions of the discipline. I call these principles, and I devote chapter 5 "Explanatory Power" to giving you the tools to recognize, formulate, and utilize them.

Exercising Your Core

Your class should be focused on engaging your students in discipline-specific thinking about the essential questions your academic domain answers. Principles are the essence of the answers that you and your students are seeking. (Some questions are answered by the application of more than one principle.) Besides answering questions, principles are used to forecast near-term implications and longer-term consequences of a particular course of action. Principle-based learning allows students to answer compelling questions and address real-world problems. The power of principles is very satisfying to students who learn to think in terms of them. For all of these reasons, principles should be the core of your course.

As you gain mastery over your own expert thinking using the tools in chapters 3-5, you'll gain a clarity that will help you design a learning experience for your students that is laser focused on principles. You want to make the main thing (principles) the main thing. chapter 6 "This Is the Way:

Constructing the Optimal Path" will help you to design your course from the ground up, based on principles.

As you design your course, you'll have to resist the tendency to let the textbook drive your course. Textbooks for the most part are comprehensive compendia of information, not sources of pedagogical insight. It will take a real force of your will to "stay the course"—to keep focused on principles. It is particularly likely that you will struggle to find instructional time to give to principles because of the content coverage model that has probably been your norm. Sacrificing content *exposure* for *mastery* of powerful principles should be a no-brainer since students seldom even remember content once the course is over. We academics do love our content, however, especially the fact base of our discipline. Facts reference a hall of fame of the movers and shakers in our discipline who came up with these seminal insights. How can we fail to honor our academic heritage?

Facts are not unimportant; they are just not the main thing. Facts hold our conceptualization and our principle formation (principialization) accountable. Seldom will students grappling with ideas call into question the credibility of the "inconvenient truths" of the fact base. When there is a collision, probably more wrestling with ideas is in order. What is the highest and best purpose of your class? It has been my experience that facts are remembered better and appreciated more deeply when they are tied to the concepts and principles that make sense of them.

You'll want to be thoroughly persuaded that principles are central to expert thinking and well grounded in using them before you try this out on a class of skeptical college students. To get to that point will take a good deal of consistent exercise. As with physical exercise, it will be much easier to be consistent and stay disciplined if you have an exercise partner, an academic peer with whom you are comfortable sharing and being accountable to. Whether with a partner or going solo, I suggest starting slowly by revising a portion of your course to be principle based, rather than throwing out the whole blueprint and starting over. For most faculty the best strategy is to successively modify more and more of your course each time it is offered until it is completely principle based. There will probably come a tipping point where larger-scale change is needed to finish the job and not send out mixed messages about where your priorities lie.

Mental Fitness Coach

As you're trying to unpack your own expertise and focus on principles, you might be tempted to take a shortcut with your students. You might be tempted to just deliver the principles you have unearthed and ask the students to "learn" them in the traditional manner. That would be a big mistake. Even if the principles you have unearthed are remembered, they haven't been assimilated unless the students have personally grappled with them in trying to answer questions and solve problems. Some students are naturally wired that way, but most are not.

Your course has to be intentionally designed to require each student to engage personally in the thinking of your expertise. I'm really asking you to teach "a mode of thinking"[12] rather than a body of content. "Teaching as telling" gives you the illusion that you are actually successfully transmitting a body of content. Telling falls flat immediately as a means of teaching a way of thinking. Students are the ones who have to do the thinking. It is what the student does that indicates whether she is thinking well.[13] You can't yet monitor brain waves to follow her logic.

In addition to moving to learning that is principle based, there is a second fundamental shift required to transform learning. You have to transition to the role that I call mental fitness coach. The teaching as telling model calls for the teacher to divide up the course content into a series of compelling lectures. In contrast, when you teach a way of thinking, the students are the thinkers and you help them to get better at thinking based on what you hear them say and do. Your work before the semester is the work of a coach rather than a TV producer. TV producers film episodes for delivery; coaches plan strategy and develop game plans that will flex with the realities of game day. Coaches develop physical fitness in their players as well as an understanding of the game that will help their players make good decisions on the field or on the court. Coaches study film with players and help them to see when they made good choices and what they failed to notice that led to a poor choice. In short, effective coaches construct scenarios that will challenge and develop their players' understanding of the game to maximize their performance in the game. Along with chapter 6, chapter 7 "Student Flourishing" and chapter 8 "Ask, Don't Tell" develop the strategies you'll employ as a mental fitness coach.

The reality emerging from cognitive science is that each student must build his own understanding of an idea through a process of logically justifying the idea in his existing conceptual framework. The logical justification is aided by the process of disciplined systematic questioning. Indeed, it has been noted by cognitive scientists that we learn perhaps exclusively through the process of questioning. (All of us are aware of the outburst of "why"

12. Paul, "Critical Thinking: How to Design Instruction."
13. Biggs and Tang, *Teaching for Quality Learning*, 19.

questioning that characterizes two- and three-year-olds who are trying to come to grips with reality.) One school of thought in cognitive science says that our brains index an idea as a logical answer to a question.[14] If that be so, it is no mystery that content delivery classrooms don't work because they deliver facts that are answers to questions that no one is asking. These bare facts typically float around disjointedly in short-term memory and are eventually purged because they can't be indexed.

An effective mental fitness coach needs to develop the ability to ask good questions. Compelling questions start a dialogue that exposes student thinking to the student and to you, the expert. A dialogue between you and the student presupposes a back-and-forth conversation employing a series of questions asked with the intention of clarifying and sharpening student thinking. Because you pose the questions, you guide the path of the thinking. In contrast, simply telling the student the answer to a question often aborts his thinking because "the expert" has spoken. Your goal is to develop student expertise rather than to display your own. You want to provide a stream of informative feedback to each student so that his thinking is constantly improving. I'll help you develop your ability to ask questions, monitor responses, and craft helpful follow-up questions in chapter 8. Eventually you'll conduct assessment that results in grades, but not until you've given your students a significant period of time to develop their thinking abilities. Assessment tasks can be aspirational for students and serve to cement their mastery. Assessment that is graded needs to center on substantive real-world tasks that document the acquisition of the thinking you've been trying to help your students develop. If you instead reward memory, you will sabotage your course. Most college faculty think they are testing for higher-order learning, but independent evaluation of their questions almost always says otherwise. Chapter 9 "Speaking Truth in Love: Assessment as Communication" will help you grow in this area.

Constructing Learning Environments

Traditional teaching as telling is done in defined class periods in which teachers implicitly tell students what they will need to remember ("know") to be successful on the tests and quizzes that will largely determine their grades. Rigor here often has to do more with the quantity of the material covered (the highest level being "drinking from a fire hose") than with the growth in thinking or long-term competence that students have gained.

---

14. Bain, *What the Best College Teachers Do*, 31.

How should class periods be used when you are teaching a way of thinking? To answer this question, think about what is the highest and best use of these limited opportunities. Jose´ A. Bowen, dean of the Meadows School of Arts at Southern Methodist University, says it well: "Class time should be reserved for discussion, especially now that students can download lectures online and find libraries of information on the Web. When students reflect on their college years later in life, they're going to remember challenging debates and talks with their professors. Lively interactions are what teaching is all about."[15]

Won't discussions compromise the breadth of your course "coverage?" Remember that your class should be principle based. You should be sharply focused in each class period or assignment on developing principial thinking. Deep development of a single broadly applicable principle is much more consequential for thinking than filling every class period with a fact fire hose. The truth is you can profitably think about your course in terms of a quiver full of arrows (principles). Mastery of no more than a dozen principles cuts to the core of most courses. Students with mastery of such a core will be far superior to students who have been fed a steady diet of content.

When you think about optimizing your course for learning, you need to think much more broadly than just what you'll do with the class periods. You need to be intentional about exactly what you expect students to be doing outside of class. How will the work outside of class prepare them for productive, engaged class discussions? How will you use web-based resources? How will assigned projects and papers develop their thinking? How will students get feedback on the quality of their work while it is in progress without creating an impossible workload for you? Will students work individually or in groups?

In asking these questions you are creating a learning environment. All of the elements of this environment should work synergistically to provide the greatest development of thinking ability for the greatest number of students. There should be no busy work—every component needs to contribute to your goal of real-world competence. There should be a recognition of the need for students to have accessible entry points into the elements of the learning environment. On the other hand, expected, achievable, incremental progress should allow successive entry-point competence levels to be raised as the semester progresses. The ability of students to accurately assess the quality of their own thinking should also grow over the semester so that course grades are not a surprise.

---

15. "When Computers Leave Classrooms, So Does Boredom," A1-A13.

Addressing the problems in higher education cannot be done piecemeal. We can learn by studying effective college teachers, but imitation of techniques is simplistic. Excellent teachers are effective because their practices are ultimately based on the way cognitive science tells us the brain learns. There is a logically coherent path we take whenever we learn. That synthesis of theory and practice is what this book was written to articulate.

Learning is ultimately about developing thinking. The starting point is for you to unpack your own thinking and get clear about the principles that are at the root of the answers you give to the essential questions of your discipline. Students then regularly encounter and use principles to answer compelling questions in the learning environment that you've constructed for them. You'll step into the role of mental fitness coach to maximize the personal growth of students by giving them regular feedback on their efforts and then pointing them to the next challenge that is now within reach.

Evidence-Based Teaching

The burning question at this point may be: "These are interesting ideas, but is there any evidence that they work in a real classroom?" You'd expect me to say yes, or I have no business writing this book. You don't need to know a lot about me, but you should know that out of my nearly forty years of college teaching I have been using some version of this approach for over twenty-five years, during which time I have taught thousands of students in major and nonmajor classes on all levels from freshmen through graduate students. What follows is a small sample from over three hundred unsolicited comments from these students:

"A teacher who cared enough about me to stretch my brain and teach me how to think for myself!"

"You have taught me how to reason logically and read critically."

"Thank you for presenting a challenge and a way to conquer it."

"You taught me to think."

"You created a need within each student to . . . master the ideas. You wanted students to think for themselves, piece together ideas, develop a conceptual framework that they wove themselves."

"The most important lesson you taught us: how to think and solve problems."

"There isn't a day that goes by in medical school that we [husband and wife both in medical school] don't use the reasoning and logical thinking skills you taught us."

"No overstatement: you taught us how to think." [Husband and wife both in medical residency]

Notice that each student emphasizes having learned how to think. This does not mean that I taught thinking only and viewed the course content as unimportant. I don't believe that it is even possible to teach thinking in the abstract. Students learn how to think only in the context of a real subject that serves to discipline their thinking. There are consequences to wrong thinking within the discipline (domain of knowledge). Misconceptions here produce inappropriate and even harmful approaches to solving authentic problems. The wrong experiments are run, the disease is misdiagnosed, the wrong questions are asked, the analysis is wide off the mark, the commentary is irrelevant. Once students discipline their thinking by means of a particular knowledge domain, they get regular feedback about the quality of their thinking. Their thinking properly predicts or accounts for what they observe, or it doesn't. If it doesn't work, they aren't thinking properly and that means their logic is confused or perhaps they have misunderstood a concept and are operating under a misconception. You can and should help them correct their thinking when you see evidence of this, but eventually this should become a self-correcting process that gives students power over their own thinking.

We have all heard that knowledge is power, but my students would rephrase that as "thinking is power." Thinking allows them to master even the nuts and bolts of the course much more efficiently than the transfer model ever did. In addition, however, students gain the satisfaction of learning how to think, and those lessons are seldom domain specific. My students regularly report using this approach profitably in content delivery courses in the humanities and liberal arts even though they learned to think this way in a biology course.

A final, and perhaps more important question from you, the teaching professor, would be this: "Just because the strategy you're going to explain in this book worked for you, how do you know it will work for anyone else?" That's an excellent question. Along with my colleagues Bill Lovegrove and Brian Vogt, I have developed these ideas by teaching them to over a hundred college faculty members in various summer institutes every summer since 2004. These summer programs range from three weeks to three summers of ten weeks each. My colleagues and I have taught faculty from the entire spectrum of academic disciplines. Representative comments from the faculty participants are listed below. Most of the comments are from veteran faculty who taught for many years before attending one of these summer programs.

"I feel like the scales have come off my eyes and I can understand clearly what my job in the classroom really is for the first time."

"My target course will now focus on a few big ideas . . . instead of a data dump of textbook facts."

"The most challenging aspect of [this program] is that it forces you to re-evaluate everything you've been doing in the classroom and you often come to the humble realization that it could be done better. Whether it's the curriculum structure or the way I interact with students, I constantly have to challenge myself to purposefully make my teaching as student-centered as possible."

"I am more committed than ever to bringing my courses to the level [that produces] understanding for students by clearer explanations, intriguing case studies, Socratic questioning, collaborative learning, and principled teaching. I want my students to develop a love for learning that carries beyond the classroom, so I must model the kind of thinking that I would want to sit under that would stimulate me to self-study."

"This year I have had the opportunity to have the first year's lessons reinforced with additional instruction that I believe will help me consolidate my gains and further move my courses to a question-driven format. Another area where I hope to make progress is in my ability to explain concepts. I need to slow down and build my explanations carefully, making clear my strong intention to help the students learn." [This faculty member was in his second summer of a three-summer program.]

"I am no longer in bondage to PowerPoint [presentations]. I feel that I am free to explore the principles, concepts, and big ideas that students need to grasp . . . so that they can, in turn, extrapolate and apply this understanding to new unfamiliar territory in their professional lives."

"My thinking about my purpose as a teacher was certainly revolutionized."

"I think it is critical that we [as teachers] understand our discipline. . . . but until we fully comprehend its core logic, we are ill equipped to teach our students to think as we do."

"The focus on the big ideas has helped change the way I think of my course content. I have deleted some content which I realize is not part of the major conceptual framework."

"I have already begun to restructure my target course to focus on concepts rather than facts. I am determined not to let content coverage drive my courses! I feel much more prepared to guide my students to deep, critical thinking about my discipline now."

"[T]he whole approach to my thought processes as I teach is different as a result [of attending]. [This program] was an inspiration and an eye-opener for me. My teaching has never been the same since, and I trust that my students are constantly reaping the benefits."

Chapter 2

Becoming a Clear-Thinking Teacher

Clarity of mind means clarity of passion, too; this is why a great and clear mind loves ardently and sees distinctly what it loves.[1]

BLAISE PASCAL

Academics are passionate about their sphere of knowledge. What they know is intrinsic to their identity. Everywhere they go, life is interpreted through the lens of their expertise. They crave an audience that appreciates it even half as much as they do, and they relish the opportunity to hold forth on the centrality of their academic domain. But academia makes strange bedfellows, and even faculty have difficulty understanding how one of their colleagues could possibly be passionate about *that*. The passions of faculty in other schools and departments seem quirky to those who are driven by different academic cravings.

Nobel Prize-winning theoretical physicist Richard Feynman reflected on the monochromatic vision that plagues many faculty:

> I have a friend who's an artist and has sometimes taken a view which I don't agree with very well. He'll hold up a flower and say "look how beautiful it is," and I'll agree. Then he says "I as an artist can see how beautiful this is but you as a scientist take this all apart and it becomes a dull thing," and I think that he's kind of nutty. First of all, the beauty that he sees is available to other people and to me too, I believe. Although I may not be quite as refined aesthetically as he is . . . I can appreciate the beauty of a flower. At the same time, I see much more about the flower than he sees. I could imagine the cells in there, the complicated actions inside, which also have a beauty. I mean it's not just

---

1. Pascal, Daily Quotes.

beauty at this dimension, at one centimeter; there's also beauty at smaller dimensions, the inner structure, also the processes. The fact that the colors in the flower evolved in order to attract insects to pollinate it is interesting; it means that insects can see the color. It adds a question: does this aesthetic sense also exist in the lower forms? Why is it aesthetic? All kinds of interesting questions which the science knowledge only adds to the excitement, the mystery and the awe of a flower. It only adds. I don't understand how it subtracts.[2]

John Pepper, the former chairman of Procter & Gamble and later of Walt Disney Company, is a history aficionado: "I love history because of the joy the acquisition of knowledge brings and because of what it teaches. There is joy in understanding the drama of lives and events unfolding; in seeing the connectedness of things; in the role of the individual choice and the contingency of events."[3] Pepper claims that his love of history was central to his effectiveness in business, yet most business professionals don't see this linkage with history. Many adults see history as a dull procession of names, dates, places, and events; it gives them no joy, but perhaps that's because they never really *learned* history.

Richard Reed, a meteorologist from the University of Washington, recounts the night he fell in love with meteorology through reading a meteorology textbook that he couldn't put down: "If there ever was a case of love at first sight for a scientific subject, I experienced it that day (and night).... The aesthetic feelings aroused in me by weather patterns and the fascination I felt for weather phenomena as physically evolving entities have always seemed to me inborn facets of my being. I cannot picture any other field of study having had the same emotional effect."[4] Weather is part of every person's daily reality. It determines how we should dress and even has the power to overrule our plans for the day. Sometimes we bless the weather, as when it rains on a Saturday we had planned to mow the grass. Sometimes we curse the weather, as when we have a week's reservation at the beach at the very time a hurricane is barreling toward our would-be Shangri La. Even if you are not addicted to The Weather Channel, you'd have to admit that at times you're in awe of a beautiful sunset or a glorious cloud formation. Maybe you're even curious about why the sky is blue?

Biologist Jennifer Frazier speaks of "Falling in Love with Biology" and of her "burning desire to share it with others. At its heart, my love of life on

2. Feynman, "Beauty."
3. Pepper, "Why I Love History."
4. Reed, "A Mini-Autobiography."

Earth is a love of shape, form, color, texture, and mechanism.... There's also a joy that comes from looking at a pine tree and understanding ... how that sucker works from root to shoot."[5]

An academic specialty viewed as one's beloved endowed with overpowering beauty and evoking joy, fascination, and deep emotional attachment is about as far away from the novice student perspective as it is possible to be. We academics run the risk of being viewed by our students as freaks who need to "get a life." How do we sell the notion of G. K. Chesterton that "there is no such thing on earth as an uninteresting subject; the only thing that can exist is an uninterested person"?[6] There seem to be a lot of uninterested people on my campus. Our students need to see the relevance of the corner of reality that evokes our passions, but most of them think they see adult academics who have "gone to seed" about the oddest things.

The first step to our seeing things from our students' perspective is to recognize the ways in which we ourselves are Philistines in regard to other branches of learning. We must adopt Feynman's perspective: "Nearly everything is interesting if you go into it deeply enough."[7] Other academic specialties get interesting if they are probed in depth. Learning disconnected facts is not satisfying in *any* discipline. We must evidence an enthusiasm for learning that transcends academic boundaries; our passion for life and learning must come through unmistakably to students who are used to jeering from the academic sidelines. When students see that our special passion for the arena of our expertise is simply part of a much larger life of passion and joy that relishes each opportunity for learning, they may catch fire just by standing close.

Establishing a Strong Foundation

We've observed that experts tend to be passionate, but we know by experience that they often can't convey either their passion or the reasons for it. Pascal said, "Clarity of mind means clarity of passion, too." The focal point is clarity of mind. Expertise involves solving appropriate problems "by tapping a well-organized system of connections.... experts rely more on structured knowledge than on analysis"[8] Don't be misled by the concept of structured knowledge into thinking that the expert who is capable of it uses it explicitly and consciously. Much of expertise is opaque to the possessor

---

5. Frazier, "Falling in Love with Biology."
6. Chesterton, *Heretics*, 23.
7. Feynman, "Nearly Everything is Interesting."
8. Ross, "Expert Mind," 66–68.

and is based on a hunch or a gut reaction that can't be articulated to oneself, much less to others. "Even when expertise undoubtedly exists . . . it is often hard to measure, let alone explain."[9] This means, simply, that experts don't necessarily have mental clarity about their competence. For an expert who is a teacher, that's deadly because the main thing he needs to teach is "a mode of thinking."[10]

What most teachers teach instead is content. Content is the "stuff" of our disciplines. It is the material we *have* to cover. It is the products of the thinking of the best of the practitioners of our discipline over the ages. It is usually catalogued in the massive textbook that we choose for our course, but we also have more content that we aim to shoehorn in. Like Gollum in the *Lord of the Rings*, "We wants it, we needs it. Must have the precious."[11] "The allegiance to content begins in graduate school, where long years of course work develop content expertise."[12] Notice that graduate school produces a type of expertise: it is content expertise. Faculty have minds full of content and, perhaps, a facility with *delivering* that content—that is the traditional aim and measure of a "good" college course.

I'm arguing for something quite different. Your aim must be to *engage* your students in thinking within your domain of expertise, not simply in assimilating its content. If students are going to learn how to play the junior game, the teacher must be accomplished in the adult game. When I say the teacher is accomplished, I mean adept at articulating the reasoning of an expert and at simplifying it without oversimplifying it. Simplification is necessary if neophyte students are going to become attracted and experience some success in working within your expertise. Simplification is the training wheels on the bicycle. Training wheels are meant to come off at some point. Oversimplification can be deadly if it limits the student by creating an inadequate foundation for future growth. Oversimplification can lead to academic hubris in students. It can lead as well to faulty problem solving and, ultimately, to lack of interest. There is a fine, moveable, and context-dependent line between necessary simplification and the distortion that is oversimplification. The ability to walk that moveable line is the expertise of a teacher.

Ernest Boyer argued that "the professoriate . . . [consists of] four separate, yet overlapping functions. These are: the scholarship of *discovery*; the

---

9. Ibid, 66.
10. Paul, "Critical Thinking," Workshop Syllabus, 7.
11. Tolkien, *Lord of the Rings, The Two Towers*. Gollum in a dialog with himself (Smeagol) contemplating the Hobbit, Sam.
12. Weimer, *Learner-Centered Teaching*, 47.

scholarship of *integration*; the scholarship of *application*; and the scholarship of *teaching*."[13] To most academics, expertise is thought of as generation of new knowledge in the field through research. This is *discovery*. Effective teaching must be informed by new discoveries in the field, but it must not be driven by them. The simple reason for this is that the significance and even the validity of discoveries is still in flux. This is addressed by the scholarship of *integration* and that of *application*. Integration aims to "give meaning to isolated facts, putting them into perspective. [It focuses on] . . . making connections across the disciplines, placing the specialties in larger context, illuminating data in a revealing way, often *educating nonspecialists too*."[14] Application "asks, 'How can [this] knowledge be responsibly applied to consequential problems?'"[15] Application endeavors to answer the question of society at large, "What is this knowledge good for?" Solid answers to this question serve to legitimize and motivate learning. Finally there is the scholarship of *teaching*. "The work of the professor becomes consequential only as it is *understood* by others. . . .[T]eaching both educates and entices future scholars."[16] Without effective teaching, every area of human endeavor would die out in a generation for lack of knowledgeable practitioners.

Higher education desperately needs experts in every academic discipline who are adept at the Scholarship of Teaching and Learning (SOTL).[17] Such expertise is focused on unpacking current thinking within the discipline to make it accessible to the next generation of scholars. A SOTL expert wants to make her thinking better—clearer, more concise, more memorable, more useable—so that she can make it clearer to her students. This is *the quest* for the clear-thinking teacher; and it is a formidable challenge to think about one's own thinking. I doubt you'll ever do anything more difficult (at least that's what the faculty in my summer institute programs say). You'll need tools to unlock and examine your thinking, and the rest of the chapters in this section will provide the major tools. I can't overemphasize how much is riding on your success. The clarity of your thinking is the limiting factor that will determine whether your teaching is actually transformed.

What makes metacognition (thinking about your thinking) especially challenging is that no one explicitly taught you how to do it before now. Your success in graduate school is an indicator that you are up to the task, but graduate education is not about metacognition. It is in graduate school

13. Boyer, *Scholarship Reconsidered*, 16 (italics in original).
14. Ibid., 18 (emphasis mine).
15. Ibid., 21.
16. Ibid., 23 (emphasis mine).
17. Ibid., 16.

that we develop our fascination with and mastery of the minutiae of our particular kind of content. In our graduate course work we were taught lots of particulars at an even more expansive level than in our undergraduate training, but likely there was no formal emphasis on putting this all together into a coherent picture. Engineer Daniel Schneck calls this an "inductive education." "Such an educational system puts the burden on the student to *integrate* (order, relate, synthesize) all of the isolated course material, and to work backwards (*inductively*)—going from the *specific* to the *general* in order to assemble the whole jigsaw puzzle from all of its individual pieces."[18] Physicist Carl Wieman expresses the same truth in this way: "A traditional science instructor concentrates on teaching factual knowledge, with the implicit assumption that expert-like ways of thinking about the subject come along for free or are already present."[19]

This kind of education works for a few students on the undergraduate level (and you were probably one of the fortunate ones who managed to impose intellectual order—at least in the area of your academic love—or you likely wouldn't be teaching it now). For graduate students this system appears to work most of the time, but this is to give the system marks that are much too high. There are two kinds of reasons for the high success rate in graduate school. The first is that typically it is the best and brightest of undergraduates who pursue graduate education and especially the endurance contest that is the Ph.D. Many of these students basically taught themselves as undergraduates. They had the ability to perform many of the inductive tasks, at least in their favored area, without formal assistance. The second kind of reason has to do with the process of carrying out academic research leading to the thesis/dissertation. In the research environment there is contact with a real-world academic problem about which they hope to write successfully. There is also available to them an accomplished advisor who can correct their thinking and direct them to fruitful ways of thinking about the problem. It is during the research quest that some course material finally begins to make sense because it connects with reality. Scientists in particular collide regularly with reality as they conduct experiments, and the dictum "data don't lie" serves as a corrective to their defective thinking. On some level the research experience is an apprenticeship and serves to crystallize productive thinking within models relevant to the research. This may give the student competence within a subset of the discipline, but seldom within the discipline as a whole. This is where narrow expertise is born, but the

---

18. Schneck, "Teaching Lessons Learned," 7.
19. Wieman, "Why Not Try a Scientific Approach?" 12.

fallback for those who must teach outside their immediate research expertise is to deliver content—someone else's conclusions.

Clear thinking is not exhibited in most textbooks (with some notable exceptions such as *Molecular Biology of the Cell*) because most academic textbooks are written by college professors who are drinking deeply from their academic discipline as a pool of content. Publishers are more afraid of leaving something out than any college teacher I have ever met. Every idea in the field (especially newly published ones) gets one or more paragraphs of fame, and books get longer and heavier. There is no significant pedagogy to most textbooks; they are simply compendia—reference books that don't aid or inspire learning. Organization is pragmatic and imitative of competitors, all of whom seem to find a way to put particular chapters in nearly the same sequence. In spite of all these shortcomings, most faculty relinquish pedagogical decisions to publishers. The decision to adopt a particular text takes care of nearly all of the important subsequent decisions about course structure and delivery (right down to the PowerPoint slides) for most teachers. Teaching becomes a simple calculation, e.g., 14 weeks to cover 20 chapters equals 1.4 chapters per week. Gentlemen, start your engines.

Unlike content, which faculty can look up in books and journals, there are no repositories of what it means to think like a linguist or a novelist or a biochemist. If we are to teach each class as a "mode of thinking," who is going to articulate what that thinking looks like? The unlocking of expertise will have to come from teachers who possess it (though likely subconsciously) and serve in some sense as intermediaries between the products of the academy and their students. Teachers are stakeholders because of what needs to take place in their classrooms. Teachers will have to unpack their expertise as the foundational act in the "scholarship of teaching." This will be pioneering work. Perhaps, in time, the products of these groundbreaking efforts will get the attention they will rightly merit. Perhaps, in time, the way will be easier for other teachers because certainly there is a fundamental unity to how historians (or any other group of specialists) think. Perhaps, in time, but that time is certainly not now. In any event, even future beneficiaries of this work will have to wrestle with it and make it their own. Certainly each discipline will profit and grow through this process, and students will be the beneficiaries.

No Turning Back

A potential reaction would be to point out how much has been achieved in the history of human thought with the content delivery model—as paltry as its gains may be for the average student. It might be tempting to think we can hold out longer before pursuing radical change, but the academic landscape is quaking with foreshocks of a convulsion to come. Here are *nine reasons the content delivery model can't continue.*

The first and most self-serving reason for the content specialist is the ready availability of content in this Information Age. There was a time when you *had* to go to a teacher for information; today there are many readily available sources. Today a second of searching the Internet unearths more than you can read in a year. Students can check your facts on their laptop during class; they can find conflicting facts and facts you haven't read yet. Are you ready to duel with them? Students are unimpressed with mere information since they are awash in it. They take ready access to facts as a given. Herbert Simon, winner of the Nobel Memorial Prize in Economics, pointed out in 1996 that the meaning of "'knowing' has shifted from being able to remember and repeat information to being able to find and use it."[20] As a teacher, you may be able to help students find information more efficiently, but you *must* help them to figure out why it is important and how to apply it when they find it.

The second compelling reason for most teachers is the ability to deliver courses by means of distance learning. The proliferation of MOOCs will eventually put the best traditional courses within reach of students everywhere. Why should students sign up for your distance learning course? More to the point of this book, how can you structure your face-to-face environment to transform student thinking in ways that can't happen in any distance learning environment? The distance learning community has the mantra "No Significant Difference,"[21] which marshals evidence that distance learning is equivalent to face-to-face instruction. Given the mediocrity of most face-to-face instruction, this is not a major accomplishment! College teachers everywhere need to seriously ponder these questions.

Reasons three, four, and five are the amount of information available, the growth of the "body of knowledge," and its complexity. Engineer Daniel Schneck explains it this way, which apply to all of higher education:

> The inductive approach to engineering education ... promises to fail in the more complex, 21st century because: 1) the number of pieces—*structure*—is rapidly becoming too much to handle.... 2). the jigsaw puzzle itself, i.e. the *synthesized* whole body of knowledge now required to function effectively in today's world keeps getting bigger and bigger. ... 3) the picture, too, keeps

---

20. Simon, "Observations," 5.
21. Russell, *No Significant Difference Phenomenon.*

getting more and more complicated and intricate, making one's ability to order, relate, and synthesize much more challenging.[22]

The sixth reason is that the delivery of content by telling is at odds with what we know about how students learn.[23] Telling puts information in short-term memory only. Only logical justification by the student transforms information into real knowledge and moves it into long-term memory, where it can serve as the basis for intelligent problem solving.

The seventh reason is that we are now in an era that is unprecedented in its demand for interdisciplinary problem solvers. These are people who can think in many modalities in contrast to narrow content specialization. The silo-based approach to education will have to give way to a richly interdisciplinary learning environment that produces workers who can contend with the complex problems they will encounter in a job environment. At the same time we must understand that staying life-long in a single career is unlikely for most workers. Therefore, the eighth reason is that education needs to provide graduates with the flexibility to move into careers that may not have even existed when they were in school. This flexibility is not available in narrowly focused vocational education. The ninth and final reason is related to number eight in that college is now expected for a historically unprecedented majority of the workforce. How will higher education make a practical impact on students who wouldn't have been viewed as "college material" just a few decades back? Methods that for the traditional college student are marginal at best will fail spectacularly for students who wouldn't have been admitted a decade ago.

As an advocate for profound change in higher education, I'm not dismayed by the failure of the content delivery model—I'm emboldened. The way forward is clearly to educate students in ways that transform their thinking, and transforming the thinking of the faculty who will teach them is foundational to that effort. Your expertise can confound or empower your students. It will be your ability to articulate clearly the core principles of your discipline that will be the key to helping your students learn thoroughly in a way that lasts. These are the goals of this book.

The Curse of Knowledge

Your expertise can confound your students. We've already seen how your passion for your discipline can perplex them unless it is part of a broader

---

22. Schneck, 8-9.
23. Bransford, *How People Learn*.

passion for life and learning. Given that your expertise is part of your identity, it is very difficult to step outside of it for the sake of your students, who are novice learners. The Heath brothers in *Made to Stick* call this aspect of your expertise "the villain of the book." "The Curse of Knowledge . . . says that once you know something, it's hard to imagine *not* knowing it. And that, in turn, makes it harder for you to communicate clearly to a novice. . . . When you open your mouth to communicate, without thinking about what's coming out of your mouth you're speaking your native language: Expertese. But students don't speak Expertese."[24] Even your vocabulary can be an obstacle to your students, and that's especially true of technical vocabulary. While the development in your students of an appropriate academic vocabulary in your domain is an important goal, it is certainly not the overriding goal. Avoid unnecessary technical jargon, and prune your academic vocabulary (and even your fluency with the English language) appropriately for the instructional needs of the moment. Richness of vocabulary can develop in the classroom over time.

While we are on the topic, technical vocabulary can actually mask ignorance, both in the student and in the faculty member. The appropriate use of a technical term can *hide* the fact that it is a label for something that is not fully understood or even something that appears to be needed logically, but has never been verified. As an illustration, let me use DNA methyltransferases, also called methylases for short. Textbooks for quite a while pointed out that there are two types of enzymes: maintenance methylases and *de novo* methylases. Maintenance methylases simply maintained a pattern of DNA methylation that was originally produced by *de novo* methylases. Many books a decade ago failed to mention that, at that time, no one had yet discovered an actual *de novo* methylase. This, by the way, is also an example of technical jargon that exceeds the instructional needs of the moment. Unless you are trained in molecular biology/biochemistry, this discussion was not helpful because I have not established an appropriate context. (Why should you care about methylases at all?) In a simpler vein, I recall my firstborn coming home from kindergarten bursting with enthusiasm that she could spell photosynthesis, which she then proceeded to do accurately. I unintentionally burst her bubble with my next question: "That's great honey, what *is* photosynthesis?" Her tears showed me that wasn't a fair question.

For teachers there are more sinister aspects to the Curse of Knowledge than a profusion of vocabulary. Vocabulary can be kept under control by simple awareness. A more intractable element is your inability to place yourself accurately in the role of novice learner. To be quite frank, you were

---

24. Heath and Heath, *Made to Stick*, 278.

probably never a typical novice learner in your area of expertise. Certainly now, however, many years after your first encounter with your academic love and in possession of academic credentials and scars, you are in no position to know accurately what your students are experiencing. There are aids available including a study of the literature of learning and the simple and direct approach of talking this over with your students. The humorous reflections of faculty shared in faculty lounges and on the Internet reveal how different student perspectives and faculty perspectives can be.

The most ominous part of the Curse of Knowledge is the difference in the value systems of the expert and the novice. They are almost completely in opposition. This was memorably laid out in *Made to Stick*. Here are some of the contrasts they found: Experts are "fascinated by nuance and complexity,"[25] but learners want to know the core message stated with simplicity and directness. Experts "fear . . . oversimplification"[26] and don't want to risk "dumbing down" by moving away from the complexity they treasure. Experts strive for accuracy down to the minute details (as though one of their colleagues will check up on them), but to the novice learners those unprioritized details may be "accuracy to the point of uselessness"[27] because they keep the learners from finding the core message. "Novices crave concreteness,"[28] examples or illustrations, while experts view concrete things as mere symbols of higher realities.[29] Experts treasure abstraction—indeed the ability to think abstractly is a distinguishing characteristic of the expert. In the teaching environment abstraction is a "luxury"[30] and puts the teacher at odds with the concreteness needed by the learners.

My first encounter with academic abstraction came when I asked my aerospace engineer father for help on my third grade math homework. After looking at the method my teacher had suggested, he told me there was a much better approach and tried to teach me the concept of an arc tangent. I was completely mystified by his explanation and flattered at the same time that he would think me capable of such abstraction.

The solution to the divergent agendas of teachers and students is for the expert to use his expertise to serve the novices, for this simple reason—experts were once novices, but novices have not been experts. This starts with the expert scrutinizing his thinking with the novice in mind. This

25. Ibid., 46.
26. Ibid., 46.
27. Ibid., 57.
28. Ibid., 106.
29. Ibid., 114.
30. Ibid., 104.

would especially be demonstrated by a concerted effort to cut through the complexity of his expert thought to find a small number of core understandings that constitute the course.[31] In the classroom this is reflected in using "a 'universal language,' one that everyone speaks fluently. Inevitably that universal language will be concrete."[32] Concrete language is not filled with needless technical jargon and is rich in everyday objects and accessible analogies. This concreteness is the servant of student learning; and once understanding has been demonstrated with sufficient depth, "concreteness [can be used] as a foundation for abstraction."[33] The effective teacher will thus move students from compelling core messages that have been made concrete to an appropriate level of expertlike thinking for the course. Since "the difference between an expert and a novice is the ability to think abstractly,"[34] your goal for your students remains as high as ever, but the means by which the goal is achieved is considerably different from the norm.

One of the main traits you want to develop as a teacher is the ability to explain with clarity. Our inability to explain concepts to our students primarily reflects on our personal lack of clear thinking. We can learn from Richard Feynman, who was not demeaned by the process of simplification, but rather took delight in it. "Feynman has been called the 'Great Explainer.' He gained a reputation for taking great care when giving explanations to his students and for making it a moral duty to make the topic accessible. His guiding principle was that, if a topic could not be explained in a *freshman* lecture, it was not yet fully understood."[35] Feynman was in agreement with another great thinker, Albert Einstein, who said, "You do not really understand something unless you can explain it to your grandmother."[36] (I've tried unsuccessfully to envision Einstein explaining relativity to his grandmother.) Clear thinking leads to elegant simplicity in our explanations. Clear thinking is an arduous discipline and a commitment to treat your students as you would want to be treated. I'm led back to Aristotle, who said, "Teaching is the highest form of understanding."[37] Perhaps, when teachers are regularly engaged in the titanic struggle for mental clarity, teaching will once again command the respect that it once rightly held.

---

31. Ibid., 28–32.
32. Ibid., 115.
33. Ibid., 106.
34. Ibid., 113.
35. Anonymous, "Richard Feynman."
36. Einstein, "Understand and Explain."
37. Aristotle, "Teaching and Understanding."

I promised you tools to use in clarifying your thinking, and those are coming in the next few chapters. The foundational tool is to gain clarity about the logic of your discipline, your special passion, and that will occupy us in the next chapter.

Chapter 3

Thinking Like an Expert

We teach a subject not to produce little living libraries on that subject, but rather to get a student to think mathematically for himself, to consider matters as an historian does, to take part in the process of knowledge-getting. Knowing is a process, not a product.[1]

JEROME BRUNER

The single most helpful proposition in my development as a teacher is this: "The spirit of critical thinking is 'there is a logic to this, and I can figure it out.'"[2] Critical thinking means different things to different people and has, at times, had a life of its own that its proponents insisted justified its *addition* to existing curricula. This is different. It insists that critical thinking is thinking about something else. The spirit of critical thinking is that each area of human thought has a logic that is, in principle, accessible. Critical thinking needs to pervade each academic domain rather than taking a place beside the various disciplines in the academic pantheon.

The concept that "there is a logic to this, and I can figure it out" creates hope in a single stroke by insisting that each domain of human thought at its root "makes sense." It doesn't mean that the figuring out will be easy. It doesn't mean that you don't need any help to figure it out, but it does mean that trying to make sense of it is not pointless. Thus reasonableness is intrinsic to the domain and is not something that you impose on chaos through the force of a mighty intellect. Thinking is not the engine to your muscle car that you like to rev to hear its thunder like the teenager down my street who doesn't yet have his license to drive. Thinking aims to uncover logic

---

1. Bruner, *Toward a Theory of Instruction*, 72.
2. Paul, "Critical Thinking: How to Design Instruction."

and put it to use. The discovery of a logic is intended to lead to appropriate application, which in turn leads to the solution of problems intellectual and practical.

The mastery that knowing a logic can provide is not limited to the academic realm. At their root even human behavior patterns are logical. There is a logic of introversion and extroversion. There is a logic behind adolescence as well as the temper tantrums of two-year-olds. To use the latter example, what could possibly be logical about temper tantrums? The terrible twos are terrible because children at that age are irrational, right? Not exactly. Please forgive my excursion as an amateur (but father of five) into child psychology.

Two-year-olds are cute little humans who are beginning to formulate a personal identity with themselves at the center of the universe. They don't like to be denied things they want, even if a loving parent knows those things would be harmful. Reasoning can go only so far with a two-year-old who is convinced she knows what is best. Based on the conviction that baby knows best, the child transforms herself into the most unpleasant personage she can imagine in order to control the situation—to gain the upper hand. The hope is that the parent will be cowed by baby's behavior into reversing himself. This has proven to be especially likely in public situations where the parent will be humiliated by an out-of-control child and decide to do damage control by acquiescing to her demands. The logic behind this behavior allows the parent to anticipate when this stunt may be pulled. The child is willing to imperil her relationship with a parent in order to have her own way. The solution ultimately is to break baby's perceived chain of logical cause and effect regularly. Baby needs to be shown that displays of this sort are a sure-fire way NOT to get what she wants. How this plays out in practice would be a different book.

In a previous chapter I explored the power that I gained when I learned (in some measure) to "think like a plumber." What I mean by that compact expression is simply that there is a logic to plumbing. If I have the equipment of a plumber, but not the logic of a plumber, my lack of judgment will quickly get me in trouble. If I understand the logic of a plumber, I'll be able to make reasoned judgments that will solve problems rather than create them. People in skilled professions have much more than physical strength and dexterity. The reason that you call for a licensed plumber is to assure yourself that the person who shows up thinks like a plumber so that he or she can solve the problem that triggered your call in the first place.

We hear a similar expression regarding ballplayers who "understand the game." Sure, they need to have physical skills, but standout players have more than physical attributes. They are students of the game, so during a game they are able to make good decisions. How much is there to understand? Games at collegiate and professional levels can be chess matches. Coaches who understand the game are sought after because their superior ability to think within the logic of the game allows them to "out coach" the opposing team even with inferior playing talent.

Each academic discipline is likewise based on a logic. Traditional teaching that focuses on content delivery and "mastery" usually leaves the logic of the discipline unexposed. As a non-historian I was completely occupied in my freshman history of civilization course by facts: who, what, when, where. Occasionally a unifying concept was a breath of fresh air that helped to organize some of the information, but no one spoke openly of the logic of history. As an outsider to the field, I was left to wonder at the competence of the teacher and some of the history majors I knew who seemed to "get it" with an ease I could only admire. Some faculty members in these settings like to assume the role of "high priest(s) of arcane mysteries," as Jerry Farber memorably put it.[3] By sheer force of intellect they have risen to their current level of mastery of the field, and it is enough that their students look on in adoring wonder.

The concept that there is a logic that demystifies a discipline is empowering to students. The quest of the student then becomes the discovery of that logic that will make sense of the disparate data and concepts of the field. The logic of the discipline is the key that unlocks the discipline and allows understanding to develop. How can the student capture the logic of an academic discipline? Certainly in most content-dominated courses they get precious little aid. To deal with that reality, Ken Bain has written a helpful sequel to *What the Best College Teachers Do* called *What the Best College Students Do*.[4] It shouldn't be solely the student's responsibility to work for higher goals than the recall of content. The thrust of my book is that unpacking the logic of your discipline and making it accessible to your students is your *primary* task in the classroom. How to unpack your own expert thinking is the particular focus of this chapter.

The power to make sense of an academic discipline that is gained through pursuing its logic encourages learners that the task is doable. They focus on learning the logic of the discipline, and the multitude of particulars comes along with that mastery. Lurking somewhere in the background, however, is the fear of too many different kinds of discipline-specific logic that need to be uncovered and understood. It is encouraging that it is

---

3. Farber, *Student as Nigger*, 143.

4. Bain, *What the Best College Students Do*. The first three chapters are particularly helpful for students who desire to rise above the current dysfunctional instruction that pervades higher education.

possible for you to learn to think as a historian because there is a common base of logic that all historians employ. But what about then having to master mathematical logic and psychological logic and sociological logic and chemical logic and, and, and . . . ? It still seems like too much! The unexpected good news is that there is a core similarity to all of the different logical systems, both in and out of academics. Learning how logical thinking functions in a domain-independent sense harnesses a unity to make sense of what otherwise seems like overwhelming diversity. That unity will be developed in this chapter, and then I'll help you to build the logic of your academic discipline.

The basics of the logic of a discipline can be pictured by thinking of an apple that has been cut in half. I'll be developing the three layers in the rest of this chapter.

The Logic of a Discipline

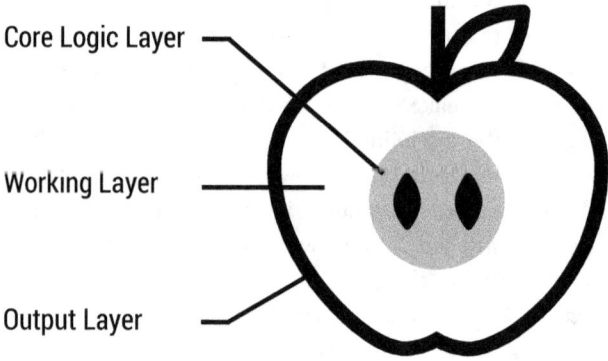

Logic and Discipline

The word *logic* may seem forbidding and stern. People who employ logic systematically are intimidating, coldly analytical people. Like grammarians who, we imagine, analyze everyone's sentences, logicians are looking to pounce on your thinking errors, gleefully pointing out a fallacy that you have just committed. In popular lore, logic is the domain of superior intellects who delight in showing their superiority. In reality we all seek logic over illogic. Illogic frustrates us and causes us to check out of classes and conversations and to stop reading books. We may not recognize where the teacher, the conversationalist, or the author stepped out of bounds, but illogic just doesn't make sense. Humans are rational creatures who are "as naturally sensitive to arguments as the eye is to colors."[5] We have a native ability to be rational, to construct reasoned arguments based on evidence and logic (which are two types of reasons), and to analyze and deconstruct the arguments of others (which may be only propaganda). Having a native ability doesn't mean that you are good at logic—only that you are capable of it. To develop your ability requires focus and discipline.

In the physical realm we know how to use focus and discipline to improve our fitness or our performance level in a sport. We have to schedule regular time to work out, we have to chart our progress and push ourselves to higher performance, we have to commit ourselves to accountability (such as signing up with a group to run a 5K), we have to have the right equipment (e.g., a good pair of running shoes), we have to learn about fitness and the activity (e.g., read *Runner's World* magazine). In the physical realm this is fairly well known, but how do we become more mentally fit? How do we root out illogic and sloppy thinking as we would declare war on a pot belly?

The first part of an answer is that you must put yourself regularly in situations where your lack of mental fitness shows. Lack of physical fitness shows in being out of breath, in copious sweat, in aching muscles and joints following the activity. Lack of mental fitness shows when you read something or hear something which is intriguingly presented and might even be life-changing if you understood and implemented it, but from which you walk away prematurely because it took too much effort. Mental growth happens when you purposely and regularly challenge your thinking with new and stimulating books, elective college courses, TED Talks, seminars, or whatever. Trying to follow challenging thinking often produces a level of frustration or confusion that is so natural that I call it "mental sweat" to parallel the physical sweat that invariably accompanies strenuous physical activity.

The second part of mental fitness is to involve other people as evaluators of your thinking. A challenging book may show you that you don't yet know how to be an analytical reader.[6] If that's true, you have lots of company. Why not get with other people and read through the same book together with the intent of uncovering and analyzing the author's logical argumentation? In academic circles you can bounce ideas off your colleagues.

5. Adler and Van Doren, *How to Read a Book*, 124.
6. Adler and Van Doren. Provides the best source I know of to provide a path to becoming an analytical reader. Parts 1 and 2 are enormously helpful in moving readers from a basic elementary and passive approach to reading to an active one characterized by dialog with the author as you search for his meaning and evidence.

If you're married, you can talk to your spouse. The point is that we humans don't evaluate our own thinking very well. We tend to self-assess ourselves as thinking more clearly than is really the case. In trying to articulate your own reasoning or the reasoning of an author to others, you may find that you have significant gaps in your understanding. Questions from others that appropriately probe your thinking can help you pinpoint problems. Identifying weaknesses in your thinking is the first step in becoming more logical and precise as a thinker.

I'm of the opinion that learning how to be an analytical reader is basic to becoming an analytical listener during classes and other presentations. As a reader you have the luxury of being able to reread passages as well as the ability to put the book aside and ponder the message you have just read. As a listener to a presentation, you seldom have the chance to alter the pacing of the talk. (In the best talks, however, there is an opportunity to ask questions and thereby to interact directly with the mind of the presenter to get clarification). Noting in writing during a talk both your agreement and disagreement with the speaker can be invaluable in helping you to clarify your questions. Listeners who take notes often write down what they understand. It is also helpful to write down what doesn't make logical sense to you, where you think there was a contradiction between two ideas or a contradiction with another source that the speaker didn't mention, where the evidence was weak or contrary evidence wasn't considered, and so on. This is all part of getting better at dissecting arguments.

Logic is sometimes confused with formal logic, which is an entire class on many college campuses. Is there any hope of being reasonable—that is, of thinking rationally using logic appropriately if you haven't taken a course in formal logic? The good news is absolutely yes! Actually training in formal logic doesn't appear to make trainees more logical in other academic domains and life situations.[7] Formal logic, and indeed many critical thinking classes, are too abstract and disconnected from reality in contrast to the real-world focus I've just laid out.

It takes discipline to learn to think logically at a high level, but there is a deeper sense in which the words *logic* and *discipline* are used in this chapter. When I speak of the logic of a discipline, logic refers to a systematized body of knowledge about a particular area of human thought—the discipline. This systematized body of knowledge, such as the logic of electrical circuits, is the accumulation of logical thought by many individuals over time. They all focused on this body of knowledge. They critiqued one another's ideas and the evidence supporting them with the intent of making their thinking

---

7. Van Gelder, *How to Improve Critical Thinking*, 539-48.

conform more closely to the realities of how and why electrical circuits function. Their thinking was not free to roam but was *disciplined* by reality. They tried to face reality and their helpful critics tried to make certain that they faced reality. This is why we academics talk about an academic unit as a discipline. Our disciplines hold us accountable to a slice of reality.

Great Expectations

As a teacher your very identity is tied to your academic discipline. I am a molecular biologist. I recognize and enjoy other academic disciplines, but molecular biology holds a special place in my mind and in my affections. I am knowledgeable and passionate about molecular biology. I see applications of molecular biology everywhere. To me, molecular biology is central to biology. It answers the how and why questions that I care about. What more could you ask of a teacher but this focused knowledge and passion?

The answer, simply put, is that none of what I have just said translates into my being an effective *teacher*. My knowledge and passion must be readily communicable to my students if I'm going to accomplish the mission for which I was hired. I'm not a specimen in an academic zoo: *Homo sapiens* subspecies *molecularis*. I'm not meant merely to represent a category of the academic world to satisfy an accrediting body. Like a good football coach, I'm successful only if my team is successful. My class of fresh recruits must be led from a position of raw native ability to a position of exemplary play on the field. They must show good instincts and good decision-making in real-world contexts. They must show that they understand the game. When my students participate in summer research or graduate school, or enter their first job, do they demonstrate an appropriate level of expertlike knowledge? Those are the criteria that indicate how effectively I'm doing my job.

Only a small subset of good football players become good football coaches. The reason seems to be that coaching requires an extraordinary understanding of the game coupled with both extraordinary analytical skills and extraordinary teaching skills. Not many players possess this combination, no matter how good they are at actually playing the game. Likewise, there are many accomplished molecular biologists who make significant contributions to molecular biology, but there are few who can analyze that body of knowledge from the vantage point of the would-be learner and then implement strategies that transform raw recruits into accomplished thinkers and doers in the arena of molecular biology. This is what I'm trying to help you do in your discipline because this is what a teacher is called to do.

An effective teaching professor is someone who combines Boyer's four kinds of scholarship (discovery, integration, application, teaching) with the analytical skills of a coach to come up with a successful game plan suited for the particular players on his team this season. I like the metaphor of a coach. Like a coach, a teacher can't play the game for his students. He can't teach to an idealized group of gifted students if the realities of his classroom are otherwise. To be effective, he must start with the abilities of his current students, diagnose their strengths and weaknesses, and develop an approach to coaching them to be all that they can be. Coaches don't have the luxury of resting on their laurels. There is always the next game and, periodically, the next season with a new group of players. With apologies in advance, are you a professor or a possessor? Do you merely profess to be a teacher or do you possess the heart and soul of a teacher? If you don't feel up to the task, do what a good coach does in the off-season. Work to become a better student of the game, a better diagnostician, a more effective motivator and teacher. That's what this book is about.

We're going to work on your analytical skills (in this and the next two chapters) and your teaching skills (beginning in chapter 6). Your analytical skills will be focused in this chapter on taking your expert thinking apart so that students can interact with it explicitly. (Later chapters will help you analyze the thinking of your students.) This is going to be challenging work, and there is no place to go to find the "right answer" after you finish. I encourage you to discuss the logic that you produce with your academic colleagues so that they can profit from it and offer constructive criticism for its improvement. The very process of creating the logic of your discipline will sharpen your thinking as you argue the logic into existence.

Your hard work is a means to the end that your students will learn with greater efficiency than you have learned. The logic that you produce won't (actually can't) be simply transferred to your students. They, too, will have to justify their logic, but their job will be made easier by your work. You have to argue it into existence, and they will have to do something similar until they understand the logical system in a deep, satisfying, academically sound, and yet personal way.

The transformation in learning in your course when students "learn to think like a ____" instead of being focused on simply learning the "stuff" of your discipline will be a joy and a wonder. Your students will be able to remember more of the factual content of your course than ever before, because it makes sense as answers to significant questions within your domain of thought. Moreover, students habituated in analytical thinking will ask deeper questions and learn with greater passion because the answers to their questions matter to them. You'll be able to set students to applying, analyzing, synthesizing, and creating as validation that they do "get it." Most satisfying of all is that your students' newfound talent for analytical thinking will start to transform their work in other academic domains. Since there is a core logic to all academic disciplines, analytical thinking gains in one area will jump the fence and cross artificial academic barriers. Imagine what could happen if every class purposely operated in this way—but that's a topic for the last chapter of this book.

Clear Thinking

Thinking is carried by language. It is difficult to imagine how someone could be said to think without words to transact the thought. You need to know what to call a thing. It will not do to have your own private vocabulary—we're social beings and a private vocabulary would leave you and your thinking isolated from others of your kind. You need to know what others who use the language call the same thing so that you can talk to them about that thing without ambiguity. Likely this is behind the rapid acquisition of vocabulary in small children. They have active and developing minds and, since minds are for rational thinking and the exchange of ideas, language acquisition is a limiting factor for expressing themselves and for the depth of their thinking. In adults who have moved from their native country to one where a different language is spoken, the ability to think within the new language without translation from the native language is an important acquisition.

Since language is foundational to thinking within your own head as well as transacting intellectual business with other people, the ability to use language to accomplish these ends accurately and efficiently ought to be highly prized. Instead, limited vocabulary and sometimes changes in language can separate generations. An overly limited vocabulary is a recipe for sloppy thinking since words are available in the language, but not to the individual, to express nuanced thought. More generic words or misused words are substituted for more precise words, and ambiguity or outright misunderstanding is inevitably created.

Mrs. Malaprop, a fictional character in *The Rivals,* a play by Richard B. Sheridan, gives her philosophy of learning in the first act:

> "I would by no means wish a daughter of mine to be a progeny of learning; I don't think so much learning becomes a young woman: for instance, I would never let her meddle with Greek, or Hebrew, or algebra, or simony, or fluxions, or paradoxes, or such inflammatory branches of learning; nor will it be necessary

for her to handle any of your mathematical, astronomical, diabolical instruments; but . . . I would send her, at nine years old, to a boarding-school, in order to learn a little ingenuity and artifice: then, sir, she would have a supercilious knowledge in accounts, and, as she grew up, I would have her instructed in geometry, that she might know something of the contagious countries: this . . . is what I would have a woman know; and I don't think there is a superstitious article in it."[8]

It takes a good bit of work even to attempt to make sense of this! We know of humorous personal examples of word substitution, but in daily adult life the results are usually anything but humorous. When "words fail me," it follows that thinking also fails me.

"Grammar . . . is 'a poor despised branch of learning.'"[9] Maybe that's how you feel about grammar too—many people do. Take care what you despise. Grammar is the logical structure of the language by which words are ordered to express precisely the intended thought. When the logic of the language is disrespected, people say all kinds of things they don't intend to say and perhaps things they don't realize they did say. I'm not recommending at this point either that you spend more time with the "Increase Your Word Power" section of *Reader's Digest* or that you review English grammar, but I am arguing that the roots of fuzzy thinking may go very deep indeed. There is already a logic of language (word choice and grammar) that constitutes perhaps the most basic discipline of all. How can we express ideas from other domains of thought coherently if we ignore the logic of language?

"Clear thinking becomes clear writing; one can't exist without the other. It's impossible for a muddy thinker to write good English."[10] Your lack of facility with language can limit your ability to express your thinking, but lack of clear thinking makes it certain that your communication, written or oral, will fail because you're not thinking well enough to have anything substantial to communicate. To diagnose why your thinking is sometimes muddy, we're going to need to take thinking itself apart and examine how it is supposed to function.

---

8   Sheridan, *The Rivals*.
9. O'Conner, *NY Times Book Review* of Fowler.
10. Zinsser, *On Writing Well*, 8.

Components of Thinking

What we're getting ready to talk about are universals. It doesn't matter what kind of thinking you're doing, these components are the moving parts of your thinking. I'm profoundly indebted to critical thinking authority Richard Paul for this transformative insight. Paul articulated "eight elements of thought" in his classic work *Critical Thinking: What Every Person Needs to Survive in a Rapidly Changing World*.[11] I modified several of Paul's elements in ways that made them clearer to me and to participants in summer programs that I led. In this chapter I will use my categories.

Rather than just diving into a list of the components of thinking (elements of reasoning), I'd like to recount a news story that occurred during the writing of this chapter that can provide a means of illustrating and probing the components of thought as they are introduced.

> Late Friday night, July 5, 2013 a train was parked about seven miles outside the small town of Lac-Mégantic in the province of Quebec, Canada. The train was comprised mainly of 72 tanker cars filled with crude oil from North Dakota in the United States which was heading for an oil refinery in New Brunswick, Canada. The 72 tanker cars of crude on this train were a small fraction of perhaps 140,000 that will be shipped by rail through Canada in 2013. Pipeline had been the preferred method of moving oil to Canadian refineries, but a boom in oil production combined with limited pipeline capacity has greatly increased rail shipments. This is part of what some feel justifies construction of the Keystone XL oil pipeline from Canada to the U.S. Gulf Coast, but so far that project has met stiff resistance from environmental groups.
>
> There had been some problem with the engines on this train that resulted in a small fire. The local fire department had been

---

11. Paul, *Critical Thinking: What Every Person Needs*, 28-30. According to Linda Elder, these elements are one of four "conceptual sets" that Paul developed from 1975 to 1990, and they constitute the bedrock of "Paulian Critical Thinking." See Linda Elder, "Richard W. Paul: A Biographical Sketch."

I used these elements under the direction of Richard Paul as one of his students in a 1995 Richard Paul conference to construct what I later began calling logic wheels. Examples of "logic wheels" for a wide variety of domains of thought including "The Logic of Anger" and "The Logic of Sociology" were provided in the conference syllabus. In the years after 1995 I worked within Paul's exact framework until 2004 when I launched my first very modest teacher development conference. At that time and in the intervening years I found greater clarity in the minds of the participants and greater applicability to articulating academic logical systems when I slightly modified Paul's original categories. A comparison of my categories with Richard Paul's is found in Appendix 2.

called and the fire was extinguished. As standard procedure in fighting such fires, the locomotive was shut down, thereby disabling the train's air brakes. In such an event, setting hand brakes on individual train cars would be standard protocol. The train was unmanned through the night as the crew took time off.

A few hours after the train was parked, a little before 1 am Saturday, it started moving down the long steep grade to Lac-Mégantic. Eventually reaching a speed of 63 mph, the train barreled into downtown Lac-Mégantic early Saturday morning and derailed. At least five of the tanker cars exploded, demolishing buildings and creating a huge wall of flame which vaporized objects and people in its path. The death toll is estimated at 50, but only 33 bodies have actually been recovered. The search for the 17 missing continues, but the intense heat of the fires may have consumed many of them. Firefighters worked first to get the blaze under control and then for several days to cool the remaining tank cars to prevent additional explosions. The vapors from the crude oil made breathing difficult for fire fighters and others and represented a continuing fire hazard. Hazmat workers were occupied with recovery of unburned liquid oil to keep it from getting into local waterways. The approximately 2000 displaced residents were allowed to return several days after the tragic fire. Lac-Mégantic Mayor Colette Roy-Laroche asked the government in Quebec to delay scheduled town elections for two years to allow elected officials the time needed to address the cleanup and rebuilding efforts.[12]

The first element of reasoning comes through loud and clear in this disaster and that is *Point of View*. The individuals and groups recounted in the news story represent many different perspectives. Out of empathy you would probably be able to try on various points of view represented in this story—to put yourself in their place. The various "stakeholders" are *primarily* thinking from a particular perspective. If you visited Lac-Mégantic in the days immediately after this tragedy, would your expertise particularly draw you into the reasoning about this event?

Contrast the following points of view:

12. Shingler and Gillies, "Canada Train Crash."
Koch, "Quebec Rail Disaster."
Anonymous, "20 Dead."
Anonymous, "Quebec Oil Train Disaster."
Wahba, "Bell Tolls 50 Times."

- The CEO of the railroad that operated this train.
- A communication specialist who is tasked with meeting the media for the railway.
- The engineer of the train who claims he set the hand brakes on 11 different tanker cars.
- The mayor of Lac-Mégantic.
- The owner of the bar in downtown Lac-Mégantic, which was packed with customers.
- A design engineer who designs brake systems.
- An oil well worker.
- A firefighter.
- A counselor.
- A physician.
- A coroner.
- A mortician.
- An environmentalist.
- A politician.
- A hazmat worker.
- A builder.

There are a variety of special interests here that would shape and color how each person views the event. They are all slices of a single reality, but each views his perspective as reality (as a fact). That "reality" may look very different when we compare any two groups. We adopt a particular perspective because of training and expertise, because of our upbringing, and because of geographical and socioeconomic factors. But reasoning from a single viewpoint can easily be a bias that keeps us from reasoning well. While as finite beings we have no choice but to reason within one point of view at a time, as fair-minded people, we should be able to try on other points of view. In fact, it has been rightly argued that we don't really understand our own point of view unless we can reason accurately from a different point of view.

The second element of reasoning is related to the first, but it is a question of *Motivation*. With regard to expertise, to domain-specific reasoning, "What is it that drives someone to pursue this field?" "What is someone with this expertise aiming at?" "What are they trying to accomplish with their thinking?"

In the Lac-Mégantic story not every possible kind of expertise is a direct stakeholder, but for those that are relevant we can ask, "What contribution might that kind of thinking make?" Here are my answers; what are yours?

Point of View	*Motivation*
Railroad CEO	Preserve the integrity of the railroad as a business
Railroad communication specialist	Manage the story that the media reports
Train engineer	Preserve my personal integrity
Mayor of Lac-Mégantic	Fulfill the obligations of my office
Owner of the bar that was destroyed	Rebuild my business
Design engineer	Develop better braking systems to prevent such disasters
Oil worker	Justify the mining of oil
Firefighter	Improve my ability to extinguish fires and save lives
Counselor	Help people work through traumatic experiences
Physician	Diagnose and treat injuries effectively
Coroner	Accurately determine the identity of dead bodies and the cause of death
Mortician	Treat the dead and their families with dignity and respect

Point of View	*Motivation*
Environmentalist	Preserve the diversity and balance of the earth's ecosystems
Politician	Balance competing citizen concerns to achieve the best ends
Hazmat worker	Remove and treat hazardous materials safely
Builder	Construct new buildings that are safe and durable in a cost-effective manner

    A third element of reasoning is related to both the point of view of the thinking and the motivation for thinking in this way. This third element of reasoning is to determine *Appropriate Questions*. What kinds of questions does this kind of thinking try to address? By implication there are questions that belong in someone else's domain of thought, but not in yours. For instance, teachers are not *directly* invested in the Lac-Mégantic tragedy. Their point of view sees students who need to learn something and their motivation is to provide effective approaches that will help them to learn. This expertise does not directly contribute to answering questions surrounding this disaster. I have deliberately chosen points of view that do answer questions that are relevant to this case. The table below shows examples of questions that are expertise-appropriate and germane to this event.

Point of View	*Appropriate Question*
Railroad CEO	How can I operate a profitable business in an ethical manner?
Railroad communication specialist	How can I balance telling the truth with the rights of my company?
Train engineer	How can I defend myself against my accusers?

Point of View	Appropriate Question
Mayor of Lac-Mégantic	How can I locate resources to rebuild our town?
Owner of the bar that was destroyed	How can I support myself now that my business has been destroyed?
Design engineer	How can I design a fail-safe system that will automatically engage brakes as part of shutting down a locomotive?
Oil worker	How can oil be efficiently extracted from shale?
Firefighter	How can oil fires be quickly extinguished?
Counselor	How can I help people to acknowledge trauma without being overwhelmed by it?
Physician	How can serious burns be treated to maximize the likelihood of survival?
Coroner	How can DNA forensics be used to conclusively identify burned human remains?
Mortician	How can my normal embalming procedures be made more time efficient?
Environmentalist	How can we rapidly transition to a way of life that is not based on oil?
Politician	How can I leverage this event to show the need for the Keystone XL pipeline?
Hazmat worker	How can oil-contaminated soil be efficiently remediated?
Builder	How can the debris of old buildings be removed to prepare for new construction?

This first group of three elements of thought (reasoning) are all interrelated to each other, and that sometimes makes it hard to distinguish them from one another. These three (point of view, motivation, and applicable questions) form what I call the *core* of logic. The core is so deeply buried that most people have significant difficulty making these elements explicit. These three elements are likely to be viewed by a person as reality rather than as perspective dependent.

This diagram may help you to see where we have been and where we are going:

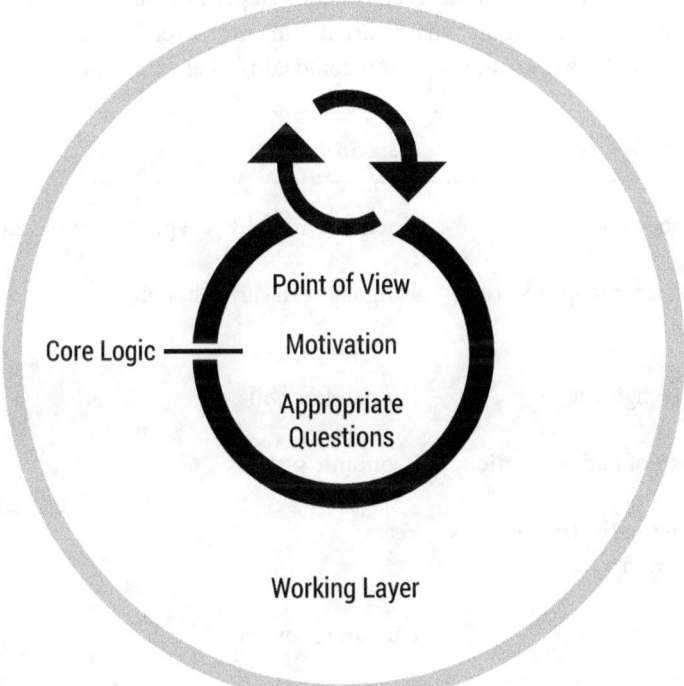

Notice that there are two arrows indicating flow in both directions between the core of logic and the next layer, which I call the *working layer*. The working layer is the area of your systematic domain-specific logic system where you actually *do* your thinking. This layer contains a component that is usually invisible to us as well as two components that we usually have some awareness of. The component that you are not usually aware of is your *Assumptions*. These are things that you just *assume* without proof.

Your assumptions may be things that can't possibly be proven such as the idea that matter has always existed. (Always is a long time. Many chemists, physicists, and cosmologists assume this starting point although it can't be proven or disproven.) Your assumptions may be things that your discipline doesn't provide the tools to investigate but that are the products of the thinking of people in other disciplines. Biologists often assume chemistry and physics in explaining how biological systems function. Chemists, on the other hand, don't assume chemistry or they aren't thinking logically. Chemists do assume other things, including physics. Making assumptions is not a flaw in human thinking. It is a necessary limitation of our finiteness. We have to assume some things, or our thinking could never get started.

What do the various kinds of thinkers we are investigating assume? I've listed an assumption for each point of view. Think about why each individual *needs* to assume what is listed. This may stretch your mind a bit. Think about other assumptions you could add—there are many.

Point of View	*Assumptions*
Railroad CEO	Chemical and physical properties of iron
Railroad communication specialist	Language can carry thought
Train engineer	Human free will
Mayor of Lac-Mégantic	Economic systems
Owner of the bar that was destroyed	Yeast
Design engineer	Human rationality
Oil worker	Geology
Firefighter	Chemistry of oxygen
Counselor	Neuroscience
Physician	Law of entropy
Coroner	Organic chemistry
Mortician	Law of entropy

Point of View	Assumptions
Environmentalist	Water (hydrologic) cycle
Politician	Sociology
Hazmat worker	Organic chemistry
Builder	Mathematics

If analyzing assumptions seems arduous, the next component of the working layer should be obvious. You should have no difficulty recognizing the role of *Information* in an area of thought. By information I mean things that you teach or work with at the low level of fact. This is stuff rather than ideas. To teachers, information is a good chunk of what they call content. To a biologist, information originates from observations within an experimental system including weight (mass), temperature, pH, light intensity, chemical concentrations, heart rate, respiration rate, food intake and other things that can be measured or estimated. The decision of what to categorize as information is discipline-specific. For instance, a financial statement is raw information (factual evidence) used by management in decision making, but the same financial statement is the *product* of the thinking of an accountant. The logic of accounting is focused on *producing* the financial statement, while management utilizes the statement as *factual input* into the decision-making process (which has its own logic).

With these distinctions in mind, I've listed below several things that fall into the category of information for each point of view. Information is evidence to support or confute higher levels of thinking. Depending on the nature of the factual information, we may have high confidence in the accuracy of the information, or we may recognize that it is limited in precision or repeatability or is outdated. So, for our CEO below, total tons hauled by his railroad company might not be absolutely accurate, but it is useful nevertheless. For some points of view, there are empirical things that are used much as academics and some others use information. An example would be firefighters using firetrucks. In the table below these things appear in parentheses.

Point of View	Information
Railroad CEO	Miles of rail line, number of locomotives, total tons hauled
Railroad communication specialist	Style manual; boiler-plate text; media contacts in TV, radio, newspapers
Train engineer	Liability law, contact information for legal counsel, contact information for bail bondsmen
Mayor of Lac-Mégantic	Number of lives lost, number of buildings destroyed, time-frame for hazmat operations
Owner of the bar that was destroyed	Annual sales, number of employees, inventory, insurance policy
Design engineer	Blueprints, catalog of circuit components, (CAD software)
Oil worker	Strategic petroleum reserve volume, price of a barrel of crude oil, OPEC
Firefighter	(Hook and ladder truck, fireman's axe, protective clothing)
Counselor	Neurotransmitters, antidepressants, manual of psychiatric disorders
Physician	Fasting blood work, pathology test results, vital signs
Coroner	Death certificate, vital signs, autopsy results
Mortician	(Embalming fluid, casket, interment charges, headstone)

Point of View	Information
Environmentalist	Environmental impact statement, Sierra Club, Earth Day
Politician	Legislative agenda, Office of Constituent Services, TV spot
Hazmat worker	Hazardous materials classification, environmental law, (personal protection equipment)
Builder	(Trusses, plywood, drywall)

So far in the *working layer* of our thinking we have *assumptions*, which we often fail to recognize, and *information*, which is tangible and obvious. Information is often used as evidence to support or challenge a case we are building. We are normally very aware of the extent and quality of our evidence.

Evidence (information) may be generated by others outside your area of thought. Physicians order tests on their patients, but the tests are usually not performed by physicians. Blood, for example, is often analyzed by a medical technologist or other trained professional, who reports the results to the physician. It becomes part of the patient's file to be used to buttress or rule out a diagnosis.

Evidence may be generated within your domain of expertise. Engineers profit from CAD (computer-aided design) software, which was generated by interdisciplinary groups that included engineers. CAD software was invented by computer engineers in response to the needs of the engineering community as a whole. These days there are incremental improvements in the features and capabilities of CAD, but it is no longer a breakthrough technology that engages the engineering community as it once did. CAD design is a fact, a given in the current engineering environment.

A third component in the working layer of thinking is the workhorse—your *Conceptual Framework*. This framework is constantly being added to and remodeled through the processes of conceptualization and logical justification.

The formation of a conceptual framework involves both inductive and deductive logic. You think inductively during the process of conceptualization in which you recognize or posit patterns. This is the result of careful observation of a number of specific items or instances that appear to have something major in common. You have been creating categories in this way since you first started to grapple with the world as a newborn (and possibly before that). Since you did it before you even recognized explicitly what you were doing, it is difficult for you to examine the process of conceptualization. Besides creating concepts, you also have to decide where to place the concepts within your conceptual frameworks. The concept could conceivably go anywhere, but there are actually only a small number of places where it fits. A concept "fits" when it has a logical relationship to the concept with which you are trying to link it. You think deductively as you try to find a place for a new concept in the framework of your existing concepts. This involves a process of logical justification of this form: "If _____, then _____." So, for example, a firefighter recognizes that the flammability of crude oil is directly linked with its temperature. His deductive reasoning would look like this: "If liquid crude oil is hot, *then* ignition is very likely." The concepts of flammability and ignition are closely linked to the concept of temperature.

Concepts are really ideas and obviously when you think, you think within the realm of ideas rather than facts. Concepts are so important that the next chapter will be devoted completely to them. No other element of thinking will get that kind of treatment. Facts can be more or less accurate; but if they are really facts, they are accepted as true. Facts are givens; they are just information. Ideas, however, are appropriately assessed and tossed around in the thinking process that goes on in the working layer. An idea may be inventive and attractive, but false. An idea may be interesting but in need of further testing. Ideas that have been around for a long while and thoroughly tested become part of the intellectual hardware of every practitioner in the discipline, but they might not be correct. Not all ideas are equally important. Individual concepts that are linked to many other concepts I call *big ideas*. Big ideas need particular emphasis as you teach the logic of your discipline because they are powerful and account for so much.

Conceptual frameworks are quite sophisticated, but to help you grapple with them (and because I am outsider to most of these fields), I've listed just two or three major concepts per point of view in the table below and I've not attempted to explicitly link them together into a framework. If one of these points of view is your field, you can surely do a better job!

Point of View	Concepts
Railroad CEO	Transportation systems, transportation infrastructure, preventive maintenance
Railroad communication specialist	Vocabulary (the importance of the right word), principles of clear writing
Train engineer	Liability, safety
Mayor of Lac-Mégantic	Intergovernment relationships, economic aid
Owner of the bar that was destroyed	Fermented and distilled beverages, business principles
Design engineer	Force, momentum, electricity/magnetism
Oil worker	Hydraulics, principles of boring, applied geology
Firefighter	Flammability, ignition, smothering fires
Counselor	Human minds can change their own thinking, conscious vs. subconscious thinking, support groups
Physician	Anatomy and physiology, pathophysiology
Coroner	DNA forensics, anatomy and physiology (autopsy)
Mortician	Decomposition, microbiology, preservation
Environmentalist	Ecosystems, food chains, energy pyramid
Politician	Economics, sociology, power theory
Hazmat worker	Personal protection, containment, remediation
Builder	Site selection/limitations, materials science, stress and load-bearing

The working layer is where the primary thinking actions are conducted. The components of this layer are quite different from each other, but all three are intimately interrelated.

Assumptions are usually unrecognized by the mind. ("I don't assume anything.") When they are acknowledged, they are taken as givens without proof. Assumptions are generally static although thinkers may grow in their recognition of how much they take for granted. Items of information, by comparison, are taken as true because they are the *result* of previous thinking (usually by a collaboration of an entire community of experts). There will be periodic subtractions as previous conclusions are invalidated and related "truths" are removed. There will also be periodic additions as new insights are gained and agreed on by the community of thinkers. Information is obvious to all practitioners and is sometimes perceived by students to be the whole of the discipline. However, concepts are where the real action is. Concepts are really ideas. Ideas are actively evaluated by the mind (and the community of minds) as true or false, weak or strong. Conceptual frameworks are actively remodeled by individuals, but are usually not explicitly known to practitioners.

The working layer of logic relates to both the core logic in the center and to the final layer, the *output layer*. The output layer is on the outside of this diagram, and it is where thinking is manifest both to the individual who is doing the thinking and to others (e.g., colleagues and students). It consists of two components: *Explanation* and *Implications/Consequences*. The relationship among the layers and the components of thinking can be seen in this diagram:

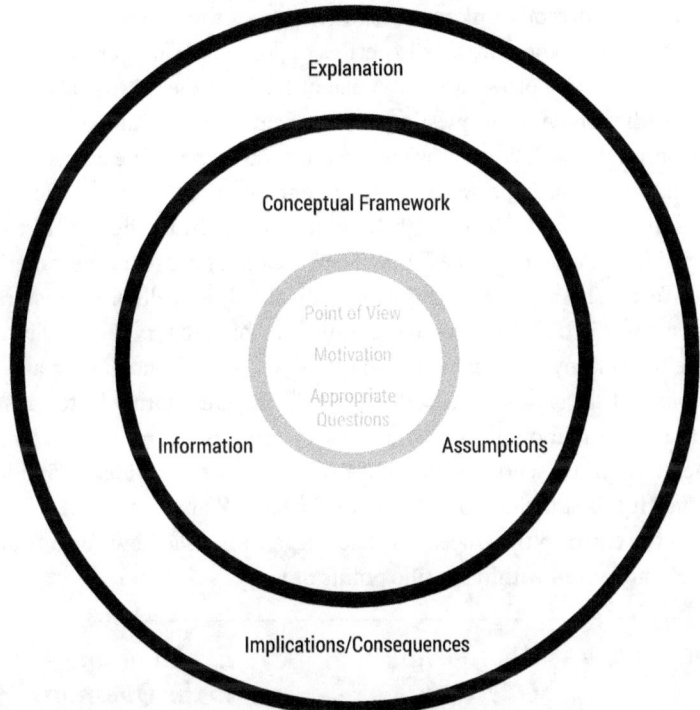

Explanation consists of answers to questions appropriate to the discipline. Questions are entertained at the level of core logic that embraces the question as relevant to the discipline or rejects it as not applicable. Thinkers "chew on" relevant questions in the working layer of their thinking using assumptions, information, and, especially, conceptual frameworks in a process of logically justifying an answer.

Explanation looks different in different domains of thinking. In some, it is a straight-forward cause and effect kind of explanation. This is true in the sciences where the explanation often invokes a mechanism. For instance, someone who is prone to migraine headaches might ask why her pain is so pronounced and includes light-sensitivity and nausea. The current answer is partly associational (there are poorly characterized genetic and environmental components) and partly mechanism-based (triggers such as stress cause chemical changes in the brain, which, in turn, cause changes in blood vessels which decrease blood flow to the cerebral cortex leading to a host of symptoms). Notice that this explanation is not ultimate. The chain of cause and effect gets longer as we learn more about the process, but we stop our thinking at some point because the answer to "and what causes that?" is unknown or currently unknowable, or it crosses the line into another domain of thought where we lack expertise to pursue the answer further.

Another way of looking at explanation is to view it as "accounting for" the phenomenon in question. In the field of accounting a reasonable question might be "Why did we lose money last year?" The answer an accountant might provide would invoke concepts such as transactions, accounts, inventory, overhead, cash flow, and so on. In the field of history a reasonable question might be "What were the major causes of the American Civil War?" The answer to this is still disputed, and different historians might answer in different ways depending on which theory they feel is most compelling. Many historians feel that the war was about slavery and the possibility of slavery in newly settled areas in the West. Other historians feel that the war was about states' rights and slavery was a comparatively minor element. Within a school of thought historians martial evidence and logic that they feel is sufficient to account for the Civil War.

Let's return to the tragedy in Lac-Mégantic to see how various questions are answered within specific points of view.

Point of View	*Appropriate Questions*	*Explanation (Answer to the Question)*
Railroad CEO	How can I operate a profitable business?	Unsafe operation leading to accidents jeopardizes company assets.
Railroad communication specialist	How can I balance telling the truth with the rights of my company?	Limit my comments to what legal counsel has approved in the press release.
Train engineer	How can I defend myself against my accusers?	Secure an accomplished attorney who will hear my whole story and decide the best way forward.
Mayor of Lac-Mégantic	How can I locate resources to reconstruct our town?	Use the current media focus to make the case for the magnitude of the reconstruction effort.

THINKING LIKE AN EXPERT

Point of View	Appropriate Questions	Explanation (Answer to the Question)
Owner of the bar that was destroyed	How can I support myself now that my business has been destroyed?	Check into what is covered by my insurance and file a prompt claim.
Design engineer	How can I design a fail-safe system that will automatically engage brakes as part of shutting down a locomotive?	Investigate the standard shut-down procedure and develop a device that delays powering down until air pressure actuates mechanical brakes.
Oil worker	How can oil be efficiently extracted from shale?	Our company should move out of strip mining of shale and into underground oil extraction from shale.
Firefighter	How can oil fires be quickly extinguished?	Find ways to rapidly cool volatile oil and simultaneously deny oxygen access.
Counselor	How can I help people to acknowledge trauma without being overwhelmed by it?	Construct support groups led by someone who has experienced a traumatic life event.
Physician	How can serious burns be treated to maximize the likelihood of survival?	Run cool water over the affected area, if possible, and wrap in sterile bandages.

Point of View	Appropriate Questions	Explanation (Answer to the Question)
Coroner	How can DNA forensics be used to conclusively identify burned human remains?	This requires extracting intact DNA from the remains and comparing the DNA with DNA from a comb, brush, or toothbrush used by the victim.
Mortician	How can my normal embalming procedures be made more efficient?	Eliminate bottlenecks in the existing procedure and look for ways to stage the bodies at alternative sites.
Environmentalist	How can we rapidly transition to a way of life that is not based on oil?	Determine which biofuel, such as natural gas, is closest to being a realistic solution.
Politician	How can I leverage this event to show the need for the Keystone XL pipeline?	Gather data to show projected rail traffic with anticipated levels of oil extraction and hold press conference.
Hazmat worker	How can oil-contaminated soil be efficiently remediated?	In view of the amount of contaminated soil, investigate the possibility of bioremediation after physical removal.
Builder	How can the debris of old buildings be removed to prepare for new construction?	Rent and bring in large scale equipment suitable for the magnitude of the removal task.

There is one final aspect of the reasoning process. You are not content merely to answer questions that seem to be fair game for your domain of thought. You want to move to asking new questions that haven't yet occurred to you. Clear thinking means that it occurs to you that "If _____, then _____." That means that one thing implies another. This is the beginning of an ever-broadening succession of ripples emanating from the original thinking. Some of these ripples will take you far away from where your thinking started to the long-term ramifications of this line of reasoning. *Implications* and *Consequences* are important outputs of domain-specific thinking. They often lead to intersections with other domains of thought that might be better equipped to deal with where the thinking is going. This is very healthy, because it helps you to break free from a silo mentality that can keep you from seeing a solution that is richly interdisciplinary. The situation in Lac-Mégantic is richly interdisciplinary and let's explore it to illustrate this final element of reasoning. I'll separate out the immediate implications and the long-term consequences.

Point of View	*Implications*	*Consequences*
Railroad CEO	I will need to fire some of my employees.	Railroad accidents of this magnitude have the potential to bankrupt my company.
Railroad communication specialist	If the public thinks we are trying to hide the truth, the demands for information can dramatically escalate.	Our company may be forced out of business because clients feel we are not ethical.
Train engineer	I need to go somewhere that the media can't find me, but that may make me look guilty.	If I don't find an accomplished attorney, I may spend time in jail.
Mayor of Lac-Mégantic	Once our situation is old news our chances of securing resources will diminish.	If I mishandle this catastrophe, it could cost me my job and force me to leave town.

Point of View	Implications	Consequences
Owner of the bar that was destroyed	If I don't get adequate insurance compensation, I could go bankrupt.	I may have to find a different way to make a living.
Design engineer	Safety can't be left solely to the operating crew of the train.	A successful fail-safe braking system could be mandated by railway safety agencies.
Oil worker	Public outcry about oil mining and refining could cause restrictive legislation to be passed.	Public outcry based on environmental concerns could stop oil production altogether.
Firefighter	What would the damage be if 72 tanker cars exploded instead of *only* 5?	Fire departments in railroad towns might be required to have sophisticated foam-based fire retardants like airports.
Counselor	Some of those who escaped loss will feel guilty.	This disaster will be memorialized because of the magnitude of the loss.
Physician	The death toll will likely increase as people succumb to their burns.	Some survivors will need long-term specialized care.
Coroner	Because of the intensity of the heat, there are no remains to identify some victims.	Some missing people will have to be presumed dead.
Mortician	My mortuary building will be insufficient to process the bodies.	Some bodies will be shipped to mortuaries in other locations.

Point of View	Implications	Consequences
Environmentalist	Oil deposits should not be mined.	Many cars and other forms of gas-burning transportation will need to be junked.
Politician	The Keystone XL pipeline will endear me to some groups and cause other groups to oppose me.	Construction of the Keystone XL pipeline will keep biofuels from being seriously considered.
Hazmat worker	Oil-fueled equipment will be used to remove the oil-soaked soil.	Removal of contaminated soil moves the problem to a different site.
Builder	Lac-Mégantic should seriously plan what the new downtown should look like.	Out-of-town construction firms will make bids for the work in Lac-Mégantic.

These eight elements of reasoning need to become part of the way you think. On some level they already are, because you're an expert in something. What needs to happen is that you become increasingly able to articulate your thinking process and connect, not just questions and answers, but all of the inner workings of your mind. What evidence do you have to support your answer? What are you assuming? What are the key ideas you're using, and what logical inferences do you make from those ideas?

Like a good football coach, you also need to become a good diagnostician as you interact with the thinking of your students. What are the academic parallels to these football coaching questions: What went wrong on that play? Was it a failure in blocking? Tackling? Were all of the players in position? Good coaches have a good game plan (strategy) and make good adjustments to their plan (tactics) once they see the game plan of their opponent unfolding. Your opponents in the academic realm are ignorance and lack of interest. The need to diagnose and correct thinking (in you and your students) is the essence of the game. Victory is students thinking at a level they couldn't have envisioned—solving problems with a facility that gives them fulfillment and makes them valuable to society.

We've covered a lot of ground in this chapter, but we did so by dissecting the elements of thinking. We learn best by doing, so it would be profitable for you to try one example on your own and then look at my solution (in an appendix). I love cooking shows and cooking and perhaps you do too. In consultation with a professional chef, I've characterized the thinking of a chef using each of the eight elements of reasoning I've developed in this chapter. I encourage you to take time out *before* moving to the next chapter. See what you come up with as you work through the thinking of a chef. Simply list each of the elements of reasoning in this chapter and articulate and develop the reasoning of a chef using this chapter as a guide. Compare your answer with mine (in Appendix 1) when you are done. With that practice exercise completed, you may then want to start tackling the logic of your particular discipline.

Clear thinking is an essential tool of effective communication, and teaching is all about communicating a way of thinking. You want to help your students learn to think within the logic of your expertise. Based on this chapter, I hope the big picture of your thinking process is starting to become clear. In the next chapter we will focus on the working layer and specifically on organizing your conceptual framework.

Chapter 4

Developing and Clarifying Your Ideas

> Anyone who pauses long enough to give the problem some serious thought cannot escape the conclusion that we live in a world of concepts, rather than in a world of objects, events, and situations.[1]
>
> DAVID P. AUSUBEL

Purists continue to insist that vinyl records have superior sound quality compared to digital recordings on CDs and MP3s. Interestingly this debate illuminates the problems that we all have with conceptual learning.

Sound is a wave that oscillates up and down a variable number of times per second depending on the tones (notes) that are being produced. In a live performance of speech or music this wave vibrates on your eardrum pushing it in as the crests of the waves pass and allowing it to rebound when the valleys of the waves pass. When the performance is recorded, the sound wave acts in much the same way on the diaphragm of the microphone. Vinyl recording methods are descendants of those originally used by Thomas Edison. Essentially the sound wave from the microphone vibrates a stylus, which cuts a path in a record master that physically represents the form of the sound wave. Vinyl records are produced by being pressed against this master. In all of these instances the sound is analog and varies continuously over time as a wave.

The digital recording method starts with analog sound since all sound waves are analog. The microphone diaphragm intercepts this natural sound wave as before and pulses in and out. The difference comes next. The analog sound wave is sampled many times per second and the results of the sampling are converted to numerical (digital) values. The wave is no longer a wave but a set of numbers that represent the wave and can be stored

---

1. Ausubel, Novak, and Hanesian, *Educational Psychology*, 88.

in a computer file as data. When you play the file, the encoded data file is used to *reconstruct* the wave (which would then be analog again) so that you can hear the performance recreated. The essence of what bothers some audiophiles is that digital files are only an approximation (albeit a very close approximation) that is *substituted* for the analog reality that was recorded and are the basis for the analog performance that results when you "play" the file.[2]

Like a digital computer file, your experiences in the physical world are encoded into a different form than you experienced. The events and objects are not recorded as such but rather are *encoded as concepts*.[3] As a result, your concepts are a schematic that approximates the events and thoughts rather than being an actual physical trace in the brain.[4] The memories of your past are recorded in the conceptual frameworks that you create. When you recall something, you actually recreate it in your mind by way of a rich network of concepts. You have been creating and refining concepts (conceptualizing) since you were born and perhaps even before. Most people conceptualize so effortlessly and uncritically that they don't recognize what they are doing.

The word *concept* is derived from the Latin *conceptum*, which in turn is derived from another Latin word meaning to conceive.[5] We conceive concepts in our minds and the process is even more mysterious than where babies come from. Individuals construct concepts based in part on how an object or an event is perceived. Perception indicates basic awareness and precedes cognitive processing. Both perception and cognitive processing, in turn, are idiosyncratic because of differences among individuals in terms of sensory thresholds, previous experiences, and expectations.

Problems in Communication

What keeps us from spiraling off in isolation into universes of one? The answer is that we share a common external physical world with other humans. Your conceptualizing deals with trying to mentally organize objects and events in this world that you share with over seven billion other human

2. Brain, "How Analog and Digital Recording Works."

3. This is not to deny that a few strong sensory experiences may leave such a recording in the brain, but this is not typical.

4. I'm not arguing at this point how the concepts themselves are encoded in the brain. There is a good deal of ongoing current discussion and research about how memory is stored, whether chemically or structurally or both.

5. *Oxford English Dictionary*, s.v. "concept" as noun.

beings. The fact that we all conceptualize about many of the same things is the basis for the ability to communicate. To be sure, my concept of any particular object or event is not precisely the same as yours, but it should be substantively like yours—at least enough alike to start the conversation. The conversation could lead to progressive refinement of my concept and/or yours.

Negotiating for shared meaning is a basic requirement for humans who attempt to share their cognitive worlds. When faced with disagreement or confusion, we move to more foundational concepts on which we can base shared understanding. When we recognize concepts as personal constructs, as individualized mental abstractions, we move away from thinking of our concepts as reality. There is a reality none of us grasps completely and perhaps none of us captures without some inaccuracy.

Notice how J.R.R. Tolkien helps us to enter the world of hobbits:

> I suppose hobbits need some description . . . they are . . . about half our height. . . . Hobbits have no beards. There is little or no magic about them, except the ordinary everyday sort which helps them disappear quietly and quickly. . . . They are inclined to be fat in the stomach; they dress in bright colours (chiefly green and yellow); wear no shoes, because their feet grow natural leathery soles and thick warm brown hair like the stuff on their heads (which is curly); have long clever brown fingers, good-natured faces, and deep fruity laughs. . . . Now you know enough to go on with.[6]

Tolkien is helping his readers to conceptualize a hobbit based on words that represent concepts we are all likely to already hold with reasonable clarity and universality. These would be things such as height, stomach (abdomen), dress (clothing), shoes, hair, and fingers. We formulate the concept of a hobbit by means of comparisons with other well-worn concepts. Hobbits are like humans in certain respects and different in others. Hobbits are good-natured and we like that (and "deep fruity laughs") in humans, so we're on the hobbit's side from the beginning of the story.

This process of comparison is particularly helpful when we embark on interplanetary adventures:

> They had a house of crystal pillars on the planet Mars by the edge of an empty sea, and every morning you could see Mrs. K eating the golden fruits that grew from the crystal walls, or cleaning the house with handfuls of magnetic dust which, taking all dirt with it, blew away on the hot wind. Afternoons, when

---

6. Tolkien, *Hobbit*, 2.

> the fossil sea was warm and motionless and the wine trees stood stiff in the yard, . . . you could see Mr. K himself in his room, reading from a metal book with raised hieroglyphs over which he brushed his hand, as one might play a harp. And from the book, as his fingers stroked, a voice sang, a soft ancient voice, which told tales of when the sea was red steam on the shore and ancient men had carried clouds of metal insects and electric spiders into battle.[7]

This account by Ray Bradbury about life on Mars contains reassuring similarities with human life and experiences on earth as well as things unknown, but not entirely new either. Books and insects certainly reference categories we all have, but singing books and metal insects are new and unexpected combinations.

When you converse with others, your spouse, your friends, your students, you interact with their conceptual frameworks. A good story is told in terms of language that references mental constructs in the hearers that represent, if not the same experience, at least parallel ones. It is through your concepts that reality is recorded, and these recordings are susceptible to regular refinement and possible revision as you interact with the concepts of others and the uses to which they put those concepts. When you ask students to learn, you are asking them to refine and revise their conceptual networks through extended dialog with you, with other students, and with the authors of textbooks and possibly audio or video sources over a semester. Through this dialogue old concepts are corrected, refined, and enriched, and new concepts are created and linked up with existing concepts. The opportunities for misunderstanding are legion, but this is the only way that lasting learning occurs. Real learning always involves messing with people's heads!

Labels vs. Concepts

Some years ago in the heyday of analog recording on tape, one manufacturer developed a catchy marketing strategy. A person would be put in a sound isolation chamber and music would be piped in. The person was supposed to determine "Is it live or is it Memorex?" In that spirit I would like to suggest that our students be assessed to find out "is it an idea or is it just a label?"

The difficulty with communication and especially with the communication of abstract ideas can be traced to just this kind of question. Words are

---

7. Bradbury, *Martian Chronicles*, 2.

the stuff of vocabulary as well as of ideas. Vocabulary can be memorized, used appropriately in a sentence, and then filed away to use in similar contexts. By contrast, ideas are the means by which *thinking* is done. The same word can represent either one!

Mother, for instance, is a label that we apply to a woman who has borne a child. A student might attach this label in a factually correct manner without being able within the logic of sociology to discuss current conceptions (concepts) of what a mother is or should be. Children rapidly acquire a working vocabulary, but their understanding of the concepts behind the labels is not very rich. My two-year old grandson recently saw a hypodermic syringe and correctly associated it with "the doctor." His understanding of the rationale for and uses of hypodermic syringes, however is, mercifully, quite limited.

As another example of the development of a concept, take the word *lariat*. The concept of a lariat is much richer than the mere fact that I can recognize a rope looped in a particular manner as a lariat. Specialized rope is marketed to cowboys to use in rodeo roping competitions. The rope is stiff so the loop stays open when the rope is thrown. A special type of knot is tied in the rope to form the loop which enables roping of livestock. On the other hand, similarly shaped structures are found in the splicing of RNA produced from genes coding for proteins so this is called the lariat model. All told the current Wikipedia entry for *lariat* lists nine very different uses of this term.[8] Learning the name for something is common to small children and to adults in new situations (especially in foreign travel). Knowing the name for an unfamiliar object is not at all the same thing as understanding the nature and purpose of the object.

Mortimer Adler calls this vocabulary orientation "The vice of 'verbalism' [which] can be defined as the bad habit of using words without regard for the thoughts [concepts] they should convey. . . . It is playing with words. . . . They [readers] possess . . . a verbal memory that they can recite emptily. . . . [It] results in slavery to words rather than mastery of them."[9] Adler suggests that the antidote is to expect readers (and, I would add, learners in general) to summarize what they read (or hear) in their own words and to be prepared to point to parallels in their own experience.[10] We'll be doing some of that later in this chapter.

Most college curricula are heavy on vocabulary. One study some years ago estimated that a first-year course in chemistry involved more new

---

8. Anonymous, "Lariat."
9. Adler and Van Doren, *How to Read a Book*, 128.
10. Ibid., 126–27.

vocabulary than the first year of a foreign language. The "mastery" of the vocabulary of a discipline gives an aura of learning and academic rigor that quickly fades. *The vocabulary orientation assumes that the ideas the words represent come along for free.* Such is not the case. Ideas are developed on purpose through mental sweat, not by accident. If memorized vocabulary will suffice to meet the demands of classroom assessment (and that's the case in most classrooms), then memorized vocabulary is what most students will aim at. Some faculty accept this as the best that can be done with undergraduates. They have a view of learning that says reasoning about the ideas of the discipline can come only *after* students have memorized the vocabulary and the fact base of the discipline (what I called information in the working layer of the logic of a discipline). Eventually reasoning with ideas will happen in higher-level courses, but not typically in the first two years, and in some disciplines, not until graduate school.

Common sense says otherwise. Common sense tells us (1) It is boring and unmotivating to be stuck at the vocabulary and fact level with no rationale in sight ("Why do I need to learn this?"). (2) It is an incredible waste of time to spend one or more semesters stuck with "inert information"[11] when I could be using the ideas of the discipline to solve problems of real consequence. (3) Learning at any level above rote memorization requires *meaning*. If we don't invoke meaning, many students develop their own faulty systems of "knowledge" shot through with misconceptions. This breeds overconfidence or "activated ignorance."[12] (4) Future encounters with the same "content" will be met with indifference, because we already "covered that" in a previous course. These future encounters will also have to try to unseat deeply rooted misconceptions. In corroboration Joseph Novak references a study showing that "information learned by rote *inhibits* subsequent learning of additional similar information."[13]

Part of the problem in higher education is the muddy vocabulary that the educational community uses. Rote memory is not knowledge in any meaningful sense, yet it was labeled as knowledge in Bloom's taxonomy (authored by a committee chaired by Benjamin Bloom). Incredibly this group labeled the first two levels in the taxonomy as "knowledge" followed by "comprehension"![14] How a group of educators can maintain it is possible to "know" something you don't yet "comprehend" is a sad commentary on the state of education. Mercifully these errors were addressed in a revised

---

11. Paul and Elder, *Critical Thinking: What Every Person Needs*, 64-65.
12. Ibid., 65-66.
13. Suppes and Ginsberg, "Fundamental Property of All-or-None Models" 139-61.
14. Bloom, *Taxonomy of Educational Objectives*.

taxonomy authored forty-four years later.[15] The first two levels in the revised taxonomy are now "remember" followed by "understand." However, this perpetuates the artificial separation of memory from understanding. Lasting memory is a by-product of understanding and can't be produced in any other way. There will be lots more to say about this relationship later in this book.

Another area of confusion canonized by sloppy word use is the triumvirate of content, information, and material. All of these implicitly assume knowledge is a commodity, a thing that exists "out there" that I need to get "in here"—pointing to student's heads. These three terms are effectively interchangeable synonyms and deal with the low level of fact as opposed to the higher level of concepts or ideas. Facts are not something intelligent people spend time debating. Facts just are. Granted that facts are the products of other people's thinking in the past, in the present they simply serve to inform and correct thinking. Occasionally something drops out of the fact base because it has been disproven, but that's not where the primary action is in learning. Practically speaking, the fact base is nearly static—certainly over the course of a semester. That's why trying to "master" *content* as a direct objective almost always results in memorization. Memorization is how the "stuff" of the discipline gets moved into a new generation of heads according to the transfer model of learning.

Lasting learning doesn't invoke the impossible dream of transfer. (Who wouldn't prefer downloads from the instructor's brain followed by uploads by the students' brains to the mental sweat that is actually required?) Real learning requires the *re-creation* of the logic of the discipline (learning to think like a historian, criminologist, biologist, etc., by the student with her own mind.) Thinking is done using concepts. Concepts are abstractions. They are ideas created within the mind of the learner in response to objects and events (which are types of facts). Learners think using ideas. It is a *non sequitur* to think using facts. If a student's ideas are sound, they will harmonize with the fact base and make the facts memorable. Facts can validate or invalidate student thinking, but they are external referents to the actual thinking. Nevertheless, I recognize that the father of concept mapping, Joseph D. Novak, says, "[M]y premise is that concepts are *primarily* what we think with."[16]

---

15. Anderson, *Taxonomy for Learning, Teaching, and Assessing*.
16. Novak, *Learning, Creating, and Using Knowledge*, 70 (emphasis mine).

Conceptualization

Novak's classic 1984 definition of a concept is "a regularity in events or objects designated by some label."[17] Looking for regularities in events or objects requires looking for patterns in which seemingly disparate particulars share one or more common attributes. There are too many particulars in life to handle as individual instances, so the human mind tries to create a much smaller number of categories and labels those categories with words. At the outset of conscious life, this process is primarily inductive. Inductive logic is the dominant mode of concept formation from birth (or possibly before) until about three years old.[18] In that period perhaps the most prodigious intellectual task that the individual will ever engage in is largely completed. We recognize this attainment through the formation of a working vocabulary that allows the child to communicate, but many of the words are much richer than labels; they are actually the names of concepts.

During the first three years or so of life many primary concept categories are formed along with attached labels appropriate for the individual's native language. This is done through a combination of repetitively encountering actual physical objects and events and then analyzing the sentences that older humans utter about those objects and events. Sometimes the parent, sibling, friend, or babysitter will purposely direct his verbalization at the child (picture a proud father regularly saying "Da Da" while pointing to himself), or the conversation can be directed at others and the baby simply overhears the conversation. There's a lot going on in that little mind!

It is important to recognize that each individual *invents* these abstractions in response to encounters with the physical world. The world doesn't come with labels on it that we learn to read, though it feels a bit like that because we mostly use the same labels for the same things.

Concepts are unusual in that they seem to be real, but they're not. David Ausubel was a cognitive psychologist who spent his life studying cognition and how it develops. Ausubel said,

> As abstractions, concepts obviously represent only *one* of many possible ways of defining a class and enjoy no actual existence in the physical world. Psychologically speaking, however, concepts *are* real in the sense that: (1) they can be acquired, perceived,

---

17. Novak and Gowin, *Learning How to Learn*, 4. Novak recently clarified as follows: "I would add 'perceived' before regularity or pattern, since our perceptions are influenced by many things and much of this is idiosyncratic; hence concept meanings about the same thing can vary pretty widely." Personal e-mail from Joseph D. Novak, March 2, 2014.

18. Ausubel, Novak, and Hanesian, *Educational Psychology*, 92–93.

understood, and manipulated *as if* they enjoyed an independent existence of their own; and (2) they are perceived and understood, both denotatively and in terms of their syntactic functions, in much the same way both within a given culture and from one culture to another.[19]

Before your earliest memory you were forming concepts—so you've practiced it a lot. At the same time, you can never remember a time when you experienced life any other way. Your concepts are your reality and you build on them. The process by which you created these primary concepts predates your earliest memories. You don't recognize that you are a conceptualizer. If you don't even know that you do it, how can you harness the process and make it better?

That's a hard question, and I'll try to suggest some helpful approaches in a moment. Before I do, I need to point out that most people *mainly* practice another type of conceptualization. Conceptualization in people over three years of age is chiefly by *concept assimilation* rather than through inductive *concept formation*. It's not impossible for people three and up to invent concepts; it's just not common.[20]

To assimilate a concept is to take in a concept and to find a place to incorporate it in your mental structures. We assimilate food when we take it into our bodies and incorporate it. For example, we eat cow proteins in meat or milk, and the building blocks of those proteins are used to make our own proteins. What was outside of us is now very much us. Similarly, to assimilate a concept is to make it a part of you, a part of your conceptual framework.

If concepts have no actual physical existence, how can we take them in? Remember that concepts are quasi-real but we treat them as though they are real. For primary concepts, there is an actual corresponding group of physical objects or events that the concept references. Secondary concepts involve significantly higher levels of abstraction that don't directly reference physical objects or events (such as love, intelligence, strength). Ausubel recognizes three ways in which concepts are acquired by assimilation,[21] and I'll develop those at length.

From about age three through age seven, learners are still working to acquire primary concepts that directly relate to tangible physical objects and events. Through direct experience with bodies of water ranging from a sipping cup to a bathtub to a wading pool to a residential pool through lakes

19. Ibid., 91.
20. Ibid., 92-94.
21. Ibid., 87-94.

and the ocean, the child recognizes what water is. The concept of water is progressively enriched as it becomes associated with drinking from a glass to quench thirst, with soap and warm water in the act of bathing, and with recreation and refreshment in swimming. These primary concepts become tied together in meaningful ways in simple conceptual frameworks in conjunction with secondary concepts that relate to the primary categories. Secondary concepts are moving away from concreteness to varying levels of abstraction. So young children learn not to drink their bath water and, perhaps, that ocean water doesn't taste good no matter how refreshing it may be to the rest of the body. Children hypothesize and explore the properties of water including splashing and making waves in the tub, much to the consternation of parents and grandparents. All of this results in a progressive refinement of their conceptual frameworks as they gain maturity and experience.

After the early elementary school years and until junior high school, learners acquire concepts (mainly secondary concepts) through an orderly interaction with "concrete-empirical props."[22] These are educationally orchestrated encounters with multiple exemplars of a category. A trip to the zoo with the intent of developing the concepts of reptiles, birds, and mammals would fit in this category. Likely this would involve the teacher or guide interacting orally with the students as they encounter the various animal examples of these categories. This could take the form of pointing out patterns and telling the students the common elements in the pattern or of asking questions designed to get the students to recognize (discover) the patterns for themselves.

From junior high school on, students are able to conceptualize without the need for props. This opens up the possibility of abstract logical concept formation where tangible physical exemplars may not exist. Disembodied ideas such as racism, greed, exploitation, altruism, monetary systems, philosophy, scientific method, and so forth are now within reach.

The educational system tends not to function very well during these years of transition to adult thinking. It is well known in science, for instance, that junior high (or late elementary school) is where most students lose their native curiosity and stop asking questions. This is likely due to teachers and curricula failing to recognize the possibilities for entertaining more meaningful and satisfying questions and losing their audience by "treating them like babies." Questions are crucial in concept assimilation, but assertions, not questions, rule the world of secondary (and higher) education. As a consequence, the acquisition of concepts comes off the tracks.

22. Ibid., 87.

What students get are labels (vocabulary). In small children vocabulary is developed as a *consequence* of concept formation. In older children and in most adults, vocabulary provides a thin veneer that counterfeits knowledge because it is *divorced from conceptualization*. From the student perspective there is virtually nothing underlying much of the vocabulary that we employ in the classroom. Biology, in particular, is taught as a vocabulary-oriented discipline characterized by massive amounts of memorization. I am sure you can fill in the horror stories for your discipline. The bottom line is that students during these years come to view education as an ordeal to be endured. The motivated ones almost all become converted into strategic learners who desire to beat the system and earn good grades, not because they want to learn but because of what good grades will get them. I'll get back in later chapters to what can be done, especially on the college level, to turn this sorry state of affairs around.

Discovering and Assimilating Concepts

Efficient conceptualization derails for most people in junior high school. That is probably not true of you within your academic discipline, but what about in other areas of your life? In the interest of illuminating the process of conceptualization in adults, let's try a simple concrete example as an entry point into the process.

I installed my first ceiling fan about twenty years ago. It was a fan with a light kit and I'm happy to report that it worked—for a while. After a time, the fan continued to work, but the light was erratic. In thinking about the installation process and the little I knew about electricity, I concluded that one of the wires that I twisted together using wire nuts had come loose in the enclosure above the fan. Painful as it would be, I needed to disassemble and dismount the fan to check on this. I found the offending bundle of wires and one of them was co-mingling with the rest, but not tightly twisted with them. When I remedied this problem, the light worked as expected—all of the time.

What happened in my thinking process that led me to conclude there was a loose wire? A very basic understanding of electricity recognizes that electricity "flows" over wires that are connected to each other. If you plug a cord into a wall outlet, the prongs on the plug touch metal surfaces inside the receptacle that divert some of the flow of current in the wall into the device, such as a floor lamp, through its power cord. If the lamp fails to shine, the bulb may have burned out, or someone may have unplugged it. Unplugging the device physically separates the wires in the device from the wires (and the current) flowing through the receptacle in the wall. It is not much of a jump to realize that a wire for the light in my fan was physically separated from the source of current in the ceiling. There was no plug, but there was a device (a wire nut) that was supposed to keep all of the relevant wires in tight physical contact with one another. The concept that is behind all of this is called "continuity."

Continuity is a fairly high level concept in electricity that explains how many devices work, and why they sometimes fail to work. If you have an electric oven and the heating element has stopped producing heat, the most common reason is that the element has "burned out." To be "burned out" simply means that current can no longer flow through the heating element because there is a physical gap in the element. An electrician or appliance repair specialist would check for continuity within the element. A similar problem often occurs when an electric water heater element needs to be replaced and a burned out incandescent bulb likewise lacks continuity (in the latter case you can actually see the gap in the tungsten filament).

Continuity in these examples was interrupted unintentionally and the device was broken as a result. Continuity can also be broken (and restored) intentionally through switches. These include power switches and circuit breakers. When you flip the switch to turn on a light, you provide a path for current to flow to the light bulb. The path had a physical gap in it when the switch was in the off position, but continuity was produced by flipping the switch to "on." A circuit breaker is designed to break the circuit when the load on the circuit exceeds a certain value. We say the breaker was "tripped" by the excessive load. We can always reset the breaker to restore continuity (after we remedy the excessive load).

If I had not created the concept of "continuity," all I would have would be the physical realities like plugs, power cords, switches, circuit breakers, and wire nuts. I would recognize that these all have something to do with electricity, but I would not be in a good position to solve electrical problems. These are all physical objects, so I can formulate primary concepts about them; but it is difficult to see what they all have in common without the important abstract secondary concept of continuity. To get to the higher-order abstraction requires careful analysis and logical thought. Compare the following two figures to see the difference in cognitive frameworks of people in these two different states:

DEVELOPING AND CLARIFYING YOUR IDEAS 73

Naive/Concrete:

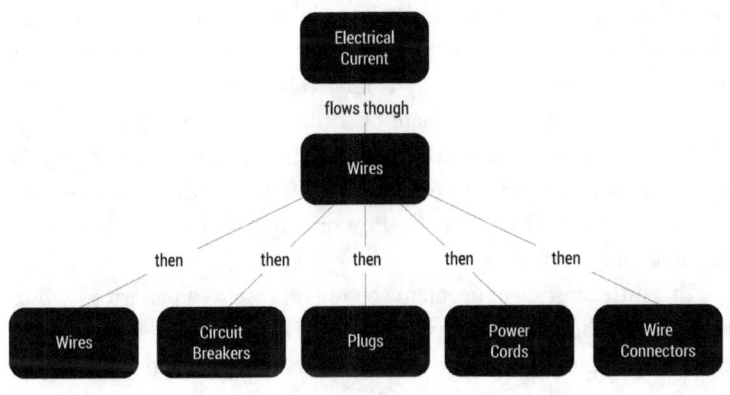

Abstract:

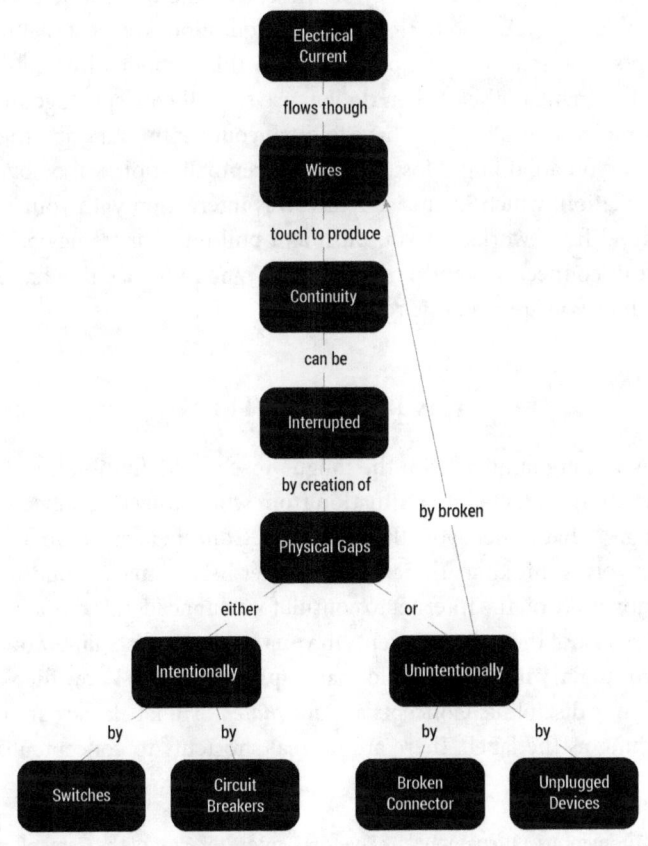

Notice that as a result of inventing the concept of continuity, we now have "how" and "why" elements in our thinking ("to produce" and "by creation of" are causative). Continuity is the basis for problem solving, and I'll say more about that in the next chapter. Notice that in the abstract diagram of cognitive structure, continuity is relatively high in the hierarchy. David Ausubel calls this a superordinate or a subsuming concept.[23] It is a more inclusive concept than those that come farther down the hierarchy. Some people call the more inclusive concept the parent and the more specific subsumed concepts children. The creation or acquisition of such concepts is a major goal of expert thinking.

This little episode of problem solving represents a pattern by which we can start the wheels of conceptualization. Think about a specific question that your discipline addresses and use it to catalyze your thinking. Jump right into the middle of it. The question you address is often a problem that can be explained using the assumptions, information (facts), and concepts of your discipline. (If you're rusty on these, it would be good to review the previous chapter.) As you try to answer this question, see what mental tools (concepts) you reflexively employ and then think about why you use one tool rather than another. When do you use several concepts together or in series to solve a problem? You have to catch yourself thinking and then analyze what you are doing. Most of your conceptualization will be by means of assimilation, which intrinsically involves interaction with your existing conceptual frameworks. As you push and pull on your framework, you'll find weak connections and missing parts. When you see this happening, you'll know you are making progress.

Has It Come to That?

Perhaps you are familiar with the tongue-in-cheek definition that "Teaching is leading students into a situation from which they can only escape by thinking."[24] That's where you, the reader, are. Concept acquisition or assimilation involves thinking. There are no master lists or maps found on some little known site on the Internet to consult for your academic domain. Think about it: a list of the major concepts in your academic discipline would look like a vocabulary list. How would that help? You already know the vocabulary of your discipline. Concepts are *designated* by a label; they are not the same thing as the label. There are no real shortcuts to conceptualization,

---

23. Ibid., 58.

24. Anonymous. Often quoted by Spencer Benton, director of the Center for Teaching Excellence at the University of Maryland.

only exercise routines that will create mental sweat (aka frustration) and a fatigued mind. This is hard work; perhaps some of the hardest you have done in a long time—maybe since the magnificent outburst that allowed you to acquire language in the first place. If you did it intuitively then, you can certainly do it thoughtfully now!

When I ask faculty in the summer programs I direct to produce the conceptual framework of their discipline, I typically get a very long pause. Eventually someone thinks about their textbook or an outline of their course and they try to push that structure into a conceptual framework. Conceptual frameworks are not merely another name for the vocabulary of your discipline. They are not the chapters or the units or the boldface terms from your textbook. They are not the items on study guides you may produce for your students. When faculty behave this way, they are trying to hold onto content and just relabel it as concepts. Most content is factual. What you are trying to move toward is a way of thinking. What kind of thinking *produced* the fact base for your discipline? What does this thinking look like in action? How are you going to teach students to think this way?

Conceptual frameworks, at least in their rudimentary form, are in your head. The truth is that these frameworks are opaque to most experts, and yours probably are to you. Experts use some of their mental constructs (ideas or concepts) all the time, but they are in a hidden layer of the mind that is never inspected. The most powerful tools in your mental workshop are likely unused, because they are unrecognized. You need to gain full control over your own disciplinary thinking before you can teach your students how to do it.

A More Excellent Way

A more methodical process to uncovering and developing your conceptual framework is related to what I suggested earlier. As before, *start with a compelling question that your discipline can answer well*. It may be a question that has already been fully answered or one that is currently a hot topic and really gets your creative juices flowing. Do a bit of reading from your text or experts that you trust to see how they engage the question. Talk to a colleague who shares your expertise about the question you are considering. Then follow these steps:[25]

---

25. The core ideas for this process are derived from rules 4-7 for becoming an analytical reader as listed on p. 163 (and articulated elsewhere) in Adler and Van Doren.

1. Scan. Look for key words that are used in the argumentation. Don't allow yourself to get bogged down in technical jargon. Look for words that represent ideas, especially abstract ideas. Keep the list short. Ten is a good upper limit.

2. Try to explain what is meant by each of these key words *in your own words*. Don't look up a definition (at least initially). A definition is not exactly the same thing as the meaning. A definition attempts to get at the meaning; the meaning tries to get at the idea itself. Recognize that you're trying to get to the idea behind the label.

3. Remember that the underlying concept is a mental abstraction that recognizes *patterns* in objects or events. What is the pattern? There is a regularity in regard to what? State this succinctly in your own words for each of the key terms.

4. With the key terms clear in your mind, go back to your sources and look for the most powerful, convincing logical propositions utilizing these terms (concepts really) that have some relationship to the question you are trying to answer. Propositions in the simplest sense are "two or more concepts connected with other words to form a meaningful statement"[26] Powerful propositions are assertions that marshal evidence and/or logic to persuade. They often invoke cause and effect relationships. You can quote propositions as you find them (or hear your colleague voice them) or you can write out summary propositions that your sources remind you of. These propositions, taken together, should constitute an explanation or an answer to the initial question (problem), but don't try to organize them that way yet.

5. State each of the propositions succinctly in your own words. Do not use technical jargon. You should be able to clearly explain each word in your propositional statements.

6. You should be able to state parallel ideas or analogies from your own experience for each of the propositions.

7. You should be able to clearly articulate, in your own words, the logic behind propositions that employ logic directly.

8. Put your propositions in a logical sequence that answers the question. Try to keep the total number of propositions at or below ten. If the logic isn't immediately apparent from seeing the propositions in this order, perhaps you need to change the order and/or the wording of one or more of your propositions. It is also possible that you have left

---

26. Novak, *Theory Underlying Concept Maps*.

DEVELOPING AND CLARIFYING YOUR IDEAS

out a step in the chain of logic and need to create a new proposition. In that event, go back to step 4 and take your new proposition through steps 4-7.

I'll deal with the role of logic in more detail later in this chapter. For the present it is enough to recognize that conceptualization employs logic (typically in the form of inferences) in the process of assimilation.

Since I've given you a suggested path, this would be a good place to take time out from this chapter to try this "exercise routine" on one of the major questions that drives a course that you teach. If you do this, be warned of the side effects of vigorous mental exercise, but I don't think you need to consult your personal physician for permission!

If you're back from exercise, welcome! I'm sure you have some questions, and I hope at least some of those will be answered through an example that we're going to work through together. I'd like to develop with you the conceptual network of a chef in the remainder of this chapter. I have carefully chosen the word, *chef* as compared to *cook*, to emphasize the thinking of an expert. I freely confess to aspiring to think like a chef from my regular intake of cooking shows, but alas, I am still just a cook. It should be noted that my ideal chef is pretty analytical, *a la* Alton Brown.

To get started on this journey into the thinking of a chef, I previously developed the logic of a chef and it is referenced in Appendix 1. If you haven't looked at it, I'd invite you to do so to get some context for what we're going to do here. In this chapter I'll be working with you to develop the conceptual framework of a chef. This was only present in rudimentary form in the logic of a chef document as a short list of concepts.

The relevant question that we'll use to start this exercise in analytical reasoning is "*How can this dish be improved?*" I think it is one of the basic questions that separate someone who just follows recipes from a true chef.

The sources I referenced in looking for key terms were (1) numerous cooking show episodes of various syndicated programs, especially *Cook's Country from America's Test Kitchen* and *Julia Child: Cooking with Master Chefs*; (2) discussions with a friend who is a chef; and (3) Alton Brown's book, *I'm Just Here for the Food: Food + Heat = Cooking*

Step 1. In scanning my sources I came up with this list of ten key words or phrases:

Recipe

Cook

Flavor

Seasoning

Quality Ingredients

Time and Temperature

Chemical Reactions

Planning

Creativity

Rationale

There's not much out of the ordinary on this list except, perhaps, chemical reactions and maybe rationale. It is important to recognize that this is not merely a list of cooking vocabulary—terms relevant to cooking.

Step 2. The ideas behind the labels. What does each concept *mean*? No dictionary definitions allowed.

Recipe: A document to guide ingredient acquisition and preplanning of work flow.

Cook: To elevate the temperature of individual or combined ingredients using an appropriate source of heat.

Flavor: Complex combinations of tastes and smells that the body can detect.

Seasoning: Ingredients added to the recipe in small quantities solely for their influence on the flavor of the dish.

Quality Ingredients: Components of the dish that are obtained in an optimal or near optimal state of ripeness, freshness, and purity.

Time and Temperature: Measurable attributes of the cooking process.

Chemical Reactions: Chemical compounds in food that react with each other in complex ways to produce new chemical compounds.

Planning: Mentally walking through the recipe to make certain each step is anticipated and prepared for.

Creativity: The process of purposefully innovating within the recipe in light of a broader understanding of the rationale of the recipe and of cooking in general.

Rationale: The logic of the recipe. This includes a recognition of *why* the ingredients and the cooking methods were chosen.

Step 3. Recognizing the patterns that make each of these a concept. A pattern is a regularity in regard to one or more attributes of a collection.

Recipe: All recipes vary in regard to ingredients, techniques, and timing.

Cook: Cooking procedures vary in the manner in which heat is applied.

Flavor: Chemical compounds the body can detect and categorize either as one of five basic tastes on the tongue and/or hundreds of specific odors sensed by the nose.

Seasoning: Ingredients that are all flavor intense, but which vary in regard to the particular combination of tastes and odors they contribute.

Quality Ingredients: Components obtained from vendors or farmers with an expected profile of attributes of color, texture, moisture content, flavor, and freedom from microbial and chemical contamination.

Time and Temperature: Various temperatures above room (ambient) temperature that cook the food at various rates. Time ranging from seconds to hours (and possibly days) is required to achieve the desired end result.

Chemical Reactions: Vary in regard to the type of chemical substances involved, their relative tendency to react with other substances present, and the kinds of products produced.

Planning: Varies in regard to the mental intensity required ranging from a simple mental run-through to detailed notes required to capture complex multitasking.

Creativity: Varies from simple additions or substitutions of ingredients within the recipe to using novel cooking methods not included in the recipe.

Rationale: There are various schools of thought about cooking so there are alternative logics that can be embraced in crafting a dish.

Step 4. Recognize in your sources or create with your own mind powerful propositions from *combinations of the concepts* under consideration. All propositions should relate to the question under consideration, *"How can this dish be improved?"* Collecting quotes is a perfectly acceptable way to go about this. You will refine them later. A bigger list of propositions is helpful. You can always prune the list later. So that I can reference individual items in the list below during the pruning process, I've numbered the propositions below.

1. "The most underused tool in the kitchen is the brain. . . . We don't think about recipes as much as we perform them."[27]

2. "Taking control of ingredients is the first step in taking ownership of food."[28]

---

27. Brown, *I'm Just Here for the Food*, 10.
28. Ibid., 11.

3. "In order to brown, the food in question must contain high levels of either carbohydrates, which brown via caramelization, or proteins, which brown thanks to the chemical chaos that is the Maillard reaction."[29]

4. "When certain carbohydrates meet up with certain amino acids in the presence of high heat, dozens if not hundreds of new compounds are created. Some create flavor, others create color."[30]

5. "Why This Recipe Works . . . For flavor, we seared the chicken breasts first and then poached them in the sauce before broiling."[31]

6. "Why This Recipe Works . . . We prevented this sauce from separating and clumping by using evaporated milk and American cheese—the stabilizers in these ingredients kept the sauce from breaking."[32]

7. "One of the secrets, and pleasures, of cooking is to learn to correct something if it goes awry; and one of the lessons is to grin and bear it if it cannot be fixed."[33]

8. "The more you know, the more you can create. There's no end to imagination in the kitchen."[34]

9. All of the ingredients in the dish are composed of chemicals (usually in mixtures of various types of molecules).

10. The chemical compounds react with each other in complex ways to produce new chemical compounds.

11. Gustatory sensations are produced by chemical components of the food.

12. The cooking temperature and how long the food is subjected to that temperature determine the progress of chemical reactions that change texture and develop flavor components.

Step 5. Work on stating the core propositions succinctly in *your own words*. Prune your list from step 4 to those that are most relevant to answering the question in front of you. Right now the question is "*How can this dish*

---

29. Ibid., 28.
30. Ibid.
31. Editors of Cook's Country, *Complete Cook's Country TV Show Cookbook*, 8.
32. Ibid., 6.
33. Child, "Cooking."
34. Ibid.

DEVELOPING AND CLARIFYING YOUR IDEAS

be improved?" You will likely find that multiple items from step 4 can be combined into a single proposition that cuts to the essence shared by all.

Statements 1 and 7 both indicate that it is appropriate to think about the recipe and make adjustments. A summary proposition might be "A chef analyzes recipes and monitors outcomes."

Statement 8 particularly accents a linkage between thinking and creativity in cooking.

Let's restate this as "The knowledge of a chef is the basis for creativity in cooking."

You could ask, "What kind of knowledge is important for a chef?" Statements 3 and 4 both indicate the strategic role of chemistry in cooking. Statements 9–12 in some sense account for statements 3 and 4, so they seem to represent the underlying ideas more clearly.

Here's a simplification of statements 9–12, leaving the original numbering intact:

9. All of the ingredients in the dish are composed of chemicals.
10. The chemical compounds in food react with each other to produce new compounds.
11. Flavor is a group of sensations resulting from our detection of chemical compounds as we eat them.
12. Chemical reactions are controlled by choosing cooking conditions to produce desirable outcomes.

Statement 5 seems to be an example of both 11 and 12 working out, so no new proposition is needed.

What's left? Statements 2 and 6 haven't been addressed. Both refer to choosing ingredients purposefully. Let's combine them to form this proposition, "A chef specifies ingredients in light of her understanding of cooking and flavor."

Step 6. In this step you are trying to probe your understanding and give additional insight and clarity to your thinking by trying to find parallels/analogies in your experience. Let's leave the propositions in their current order and give them letter designations.

A. *A chef analyzes recipes and monitors outcomes.*

A builder studies blueprints and compares the emerging construction to what the blueprints specified.

B. *The knowledge of a chef is the basis for creativity in cooking.*

As a client requests changes from the blueprints in a building under construction, the ability of the builder to improvise and accommodate the changes is directly related to the builder's mastery of the logic of building.

C. *All of the ingredients in the dish are composed of chemicals.*

All of the physical universe is made up of chemical elements.

D. *The chemical compounds in food react with each other to produce new compounds.*

Mixing cleaning products should be done only with extreme care because new substances may be produced by means of chemical reactions.

E. *Flavor is a group of sensations resulting from our detection of chemical compounds as we eat them.*

Odors (e.g., rose scent) are typically complex combinations of chemical compounds that our noses can detect.

F. *Chemical reactions are controlled by cooking conditions to produce desirable outcomes.*

Soldering of wires in an electrical circuit is produced through controlled application of heat that melts solder but doesn't overheat the circuit components.

G. *A chef specifies ingredients in light of her understanding of cooking and flavor.*

An electrical engineer species circuit components in light of his understanding of the properties of the individual components and their properties when wired together in the circuit.

Step 7. In this step you are trying to articulate the logic inherent in your propositions.

A. *A chef analyzes recipes and monitors outcomes.*

A recognition of attributes a chef possesses that allow her to reach a desired outcome.

B. *The knowledge of a chef is the basis for ~~creativity~~ innovation in cooking.*

Creativity, to be useful, must be variation on a theme of what works (knowledge). In that light, *innovation* would be a better word. Creativity is not just random acts but is based on (indicating a cause-effect relationship) an understanding of the logic of cooking.

C. *All of the ingredients in the dish are composed of chemicals.*

The previous parallel statement that "all of the physical universe is made up of chemical elements" must include the ingredients in the dish since they are part of the physical universe. Food ingredients are a subset of all the physical universe. Many food ingredients were once living plants or animals and, thus, living things are also made of chemicals.

D. *The chemical compounds in food react with each other to produce new compounds.*

Products result from reactions between starting compounds. The final dish has additional chemical components that were not present in the starting ingredients.

E. *Flavor is a group of sensations resulting from our detection of chemical compounds as we eat them.*

There are several logical implications. One is that food consists of chemical compounds (much to some people's chagrin). Another is that flavor is a matter of detection. It turns out that not all people are equally sensitive to certain flavor-related compounds. Food literally tastes different to some people because of these differences.

F. *Chemical reactions are controlled by cooking conditions to produce desirable outcomes.*

The possibility of chemical reactions and the rate at which those that are possible occur is controllable through the cooking conditions. This is a statement of causality.

G. *A chef specifies ingredients in light of her understanding of cooking and flavor.*

"In light of" is causal in nature. By implication more understanding of cooking and flavor opens new possibilities of ingredients. Foodies delight in exploring these inventive possibilities.

Step 8. A logical sequence of propositions that answers the question, "*How can this dish be improved?*"

Here is at least one logical order based on the seven propositions. If you came up with a different one, try to explain it. (The letter designations from step 7 have been retained.)

B. *The knowledge of a chef is the basis for innovation in cooking.*

G. *A chef specifies ingredients in light of her understanding of cooking and flavor.*

C. *All of the ingredients in the dish are composed of chemicals.*

D. *The chemical compounds in food react with each other to produce new compounds.*

F. *Chemical reactions are controlled by cooking conditions to produce desirable outcomes.*

E. *Flavor is a group of sensations resulting from our detection of chemical compounds as we eat them.*

A. *A chef analyzes recipes and monitors outcomes.*

Here's my explanation for this sequence. When considering the *improvement* of a dish, we're asking the chef to suggest *modifications* to the recipe. (Only a very limited amount of improvement is available if you just repeat the same recipe adhering to the directions more closely [unless you slipped up in a major way]).

Improvements will ultimately be based on the knowledge of the chef. (B)

Knowledge about possible substitutions for, or modifications of, ingredients is a good place to start. (G)

It is essential for the chef to come to grips with the fact that most of the process of producing a tasty dish is food chemistry.

(C) helps move us into the chemical perspective.

(D) helps us recognize that chemical reactions will produce new chemical substances.

(E) could come next, because the new compounds include flavor components. I prefer to center on controlling the chemical reactions that produce the new compounds, so I would put (F) immediately after (D) to indicate the causative nature of the cooking conditions. (E) flavor is a result of the control or lack of control of the cooking conditions (including selecting a more appropriate cooking method based on the chef's knowledge). We end up with the characteristics of a chef (A) that can produce improvement in the dish as she monitors the outcomes and considers alternatives.

Logical Thinking

We started by talking about the process of conceptualization; concept formation and concept assimilation are the two ways to acquire a concept. Acquisition of a concept is not like signing for a package that's been delivered. Remember, in a very real sense everyone constructs his own concepts. Young children formulate concepts from the ground up using logic. They use inductive logic in recognizing patterns within the physical world of objects and events. In contrast, most of our conceptualization for the last few pages has been concept assimilation—re-creating the concepts in our own minds as we wrestle with the ideas and come to see their usefulness in explaining the phenomena we are examining.

If we retrace our steps, you note that we used the arguments of experts who were engaged in answering the questions appropriate to their discipline to extract key words in their argumentation. We then isolated those key words and used several different methods to get underneath the label to find the core idea (concept) that the word was intended to stand in the place of. With this meaning in hand, the rest of the process of assimilation involved the explicit use of logic. There is no conceptualization without logic. Concept assimilation especially utilizes logical inference. An inference is something that is not explicitly stated but which logically follows from what has been stated. It is just within logical reach. Inferences are the stuff of deductive logic, which reasons from more general ideas to more specific instances of those ideas.

Richard Paul isolates inferences as one of the eight elements of the logic of a discipline, right up there on the level of Point of View and Implications and Consequences.[35] I find it more satisfying to view inferences as located within the working layer and operating to enable conceptualization. Indeed Paul himself says, "We understand 'conceptualization' to be a process by which the mind infers a thing to be of a certain kind, to properly belong to some given class of things."[36] I don't think inferences are separable from conceptualization. I think conceptual frameworks imply the process of inferential logic as their creative mechanism.

35. Paul, *Critical Thinking: What Every Person Needs*, 29-30.
36. Ibid., 23.

It is crucial to recognize that conceptual frameworks don't arbitrarily enlarge just by having concepts stick to them. Concept assimilation involves a process of logical justification by which the concept is constructed using logical inference to fit it into the right spot in the conceptual framework. As soon as we got to the level of propositions in the eight-step process above, we were using inferential logic. This kind of logic involves statements of the form "If ___, then ___." For example, I said, "*The knowledge of a chef is the basis for innovation in cooking.*" Very simply put this looks like "If *knowledge*, then *innovation*." That's a little abrupt, but you get the idea—innovation is based on—dependent on—a base of knowledge. Look back over step 7 in my development of the logic of a chef and you'll see this over and over. In fact six of our seven propositions explicitly use inferential logic. The single exception, "*A chef analyzes recipes and monitors outcomes*," is the logical outworking of all of the other propositions as we saw in step 8. There were multiplied reasons I declared these to be attributes of a chef.

In terms of learning, the dependence of conceptualization on logic means that the relationships between concepts is not random. You put the framework together using logic, and you can use logic to reconstruct the framework if you need to. You don't have to rely on memorization to access concepts and their relationships!

It is probably obvious to you that by engaging one-at-a-time with the big questions your discipline can answer, you can use this eight-step procedure to construct the logic of your discipline. Faculty in my summer programs often prefer the intermediate step of constructing the logic of one course they teach and the big questions that it answers. In time they gain the confidence to construct the overall logic of their discipline.

Systematizing Concepts

I hope you agree that you've moved a long way in this chapter toward becoming mentally organized, and I hope you feel as though you now have the basic tools to conceptualize your academic discipline. Remember that you're trying to unpack the logic of your discipline and much of the logical action of thinking is in the making and remodeling of your sophisticated conceptual frameworks. This is what you appeal to when you solve problems. This is the lion's share of expertise. This is what you need to instill in your students as you teach them to "think like a _____."

There is one final tool that will clinch and deepen your mental organization. It involves a further condensation of your propositions and a two dimensional organization of these as a network or map. What you're going to make is called a concept map. Much of the hard work has been done through the preparatory eight-step process above. What you want to produce is a compact portable method of sharing the insights gained through the eight-step process.

Concept mapping was invented by Joseph Novak and his research group at Cornell in response to David Ausubel's cognitive assimilation theory of learning. For practical purposes the outside world was introduced to concept mapping in 1984 with the publication of *Learning How to Learn* by Joseph D. Novak and D. Bob Gowin (Cambridge University Press).[37]

In moving concepts to a map, the propositions must become considerably more compact. Compact propositions should not be simplistic, watered-down assertions. What you need is to find the core message and state it strongly in just a few words. That is much easier to do at this stage than it would be if you had tried to go straight to the concept map. (That said, eventually you may be comfortable going straight to mapping without the eight-step developmental process).

What you're looking at in the map below is a distillation of the concepts that we developed above, but the logical relationships are not presented in the linear fashion we saw there. We're now looking from a broader perspective at a simplified view of the conceptual structure of a chef's thinking. We want a map that will allow us to answer more than just the single question that we focused on above. A good map should allow us to answer any of the questions that are legitimately in the domain of a chef. This map will need to be developed further to allow it to have that much functionality.

---

37. Moon, *Applied Concept Mapping*, 4-5. Provides a brief history of the development of concept mapping on pages 4 and 5.

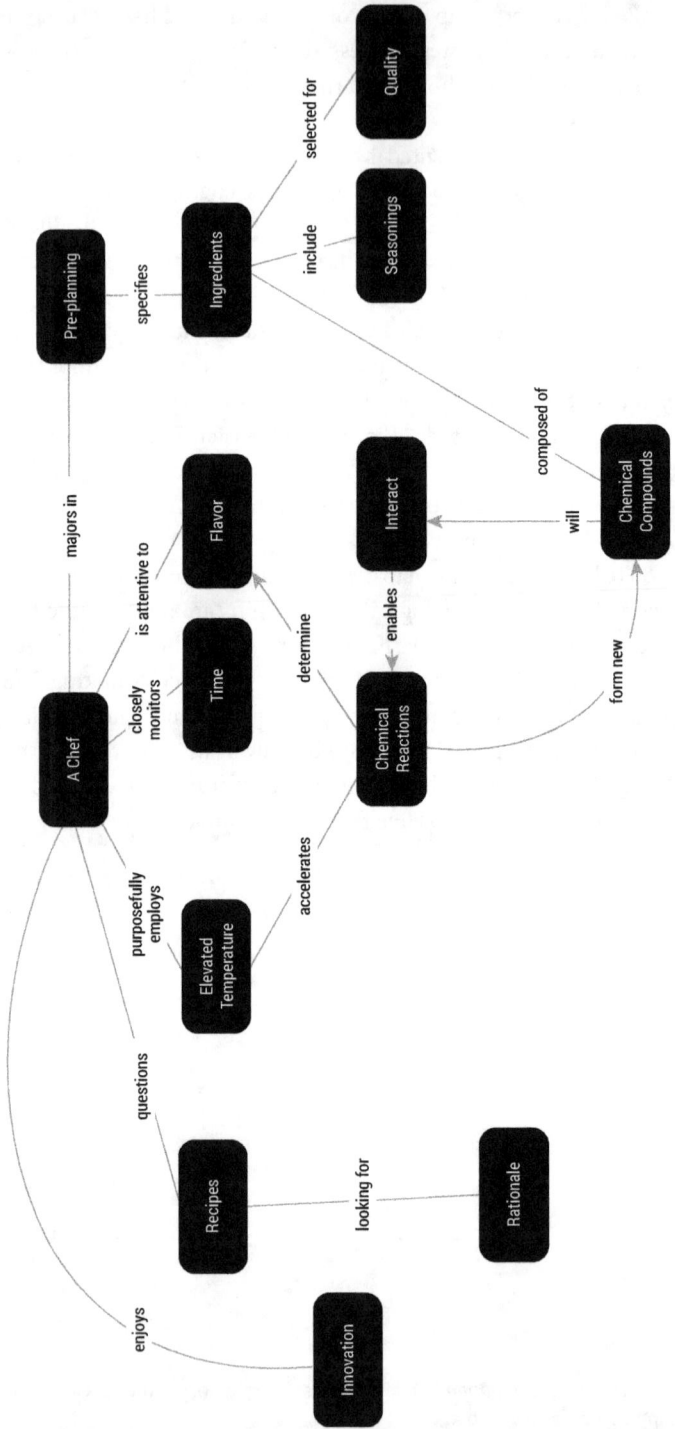

Let's see what this map captures that we have already learned about a chef's thinking.

Step 8	Concept Map
A. A chef analyzes recipes and monitors outcomes.	A chef questions recipes—looking for rationale.
B. The knowledge of a chef is the basis for innovation in cooking.	None directly stated.
C. All of the ingredients in the dish are composed of chemicals.	Ingredients [are] composed of chemical compounds.
D. The chemical compounds in food react with each other to produce new compounds.	Chemical compounds will interact; interact[ion] enables chemical reactions; chemical reactions form new chemical compounds.
E. Flavor is a group of sensations resulting from our detection of chemical compounds as we eat them.	Flavor is in the map, but this proposition is not directly stated.
F. Chemical reactions are controlled by cooking conditions to produce desirable outcomes.	Elevated temperature accelerates chemical reactions; chemical reactions determine flavor.
G. A chef specifies ingredients in light of her understanding of cooking and flavor.	A chef majors in preplanning; preplanning specifies ingredients.

The map sometimes uses multiple propositions to capture the complexity of the sentences we arranged in step 8. In a few cases this map doesn't address the proposition, or at least, not directly. Let's improve the map by adding a few concepts (shown in black).

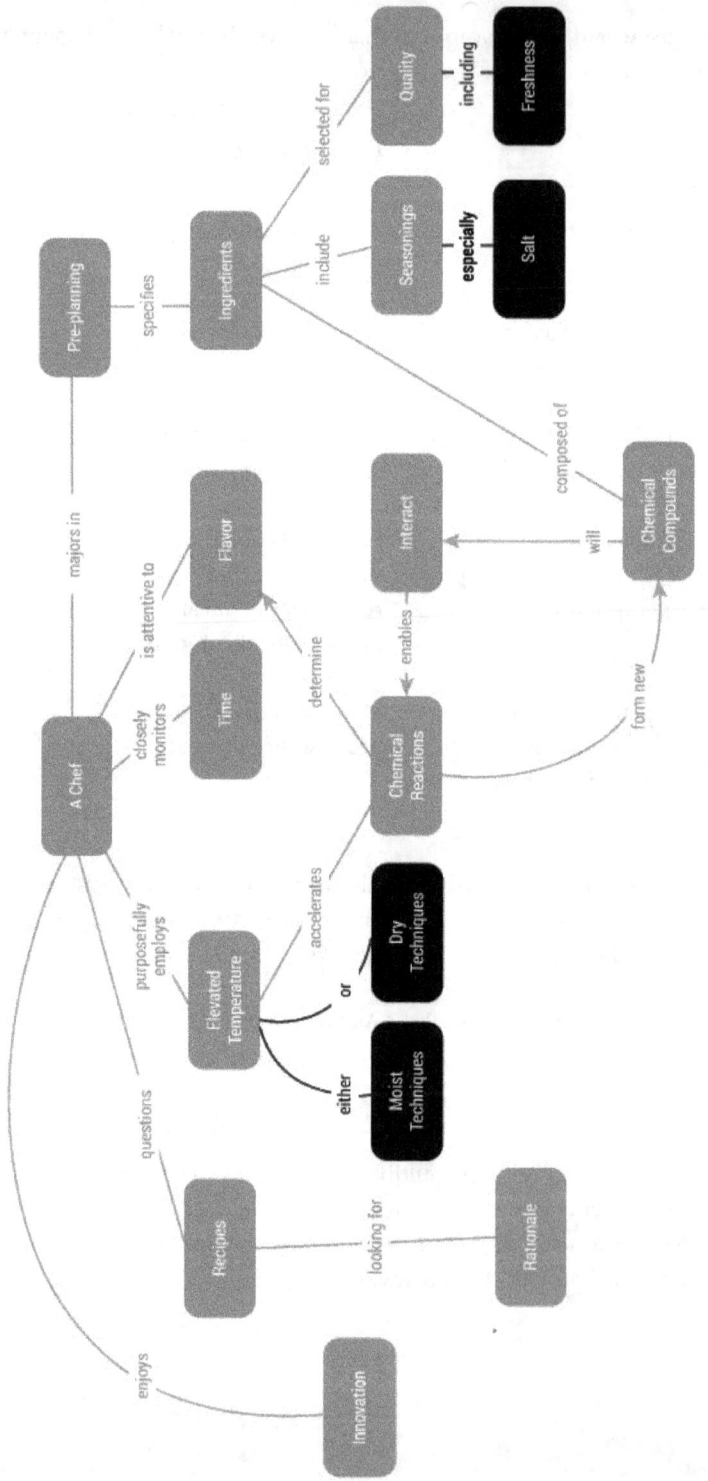

These are relatively minor changes. The versatility and clarity of the map is improved by introducing the concepts of freshness and salt. These are also hooks for the possible later development of the map. (Can you imagine a chef who isn't concerned about these two things!) The map has also been improved by recognizing that cooking is not just about heat but about how the heat is used. There are large numbers of different techniques that fall into two main categories depending on whether water is involved. Boiling is an obvious example of a moist technique, while grilling is an example of a dry technique. A chef is very aware of the strengths and weaknesses of the various techniques, and these might be added in a future (very complicated) map. No one wants dried-out food or soggy food!

Let's try to keep things simple, while recognizing that we haven't yet addressed all of our previous propositions adequately. The final phase in the development of this map will be to add a few additional links that can express better the complexity of the cognitive relationships. (The words on the new links are in black so that you can track the changes). Did you notice that arrows are only used when the linked ideas are not read from top to bottom? These propositions are called cross-links.

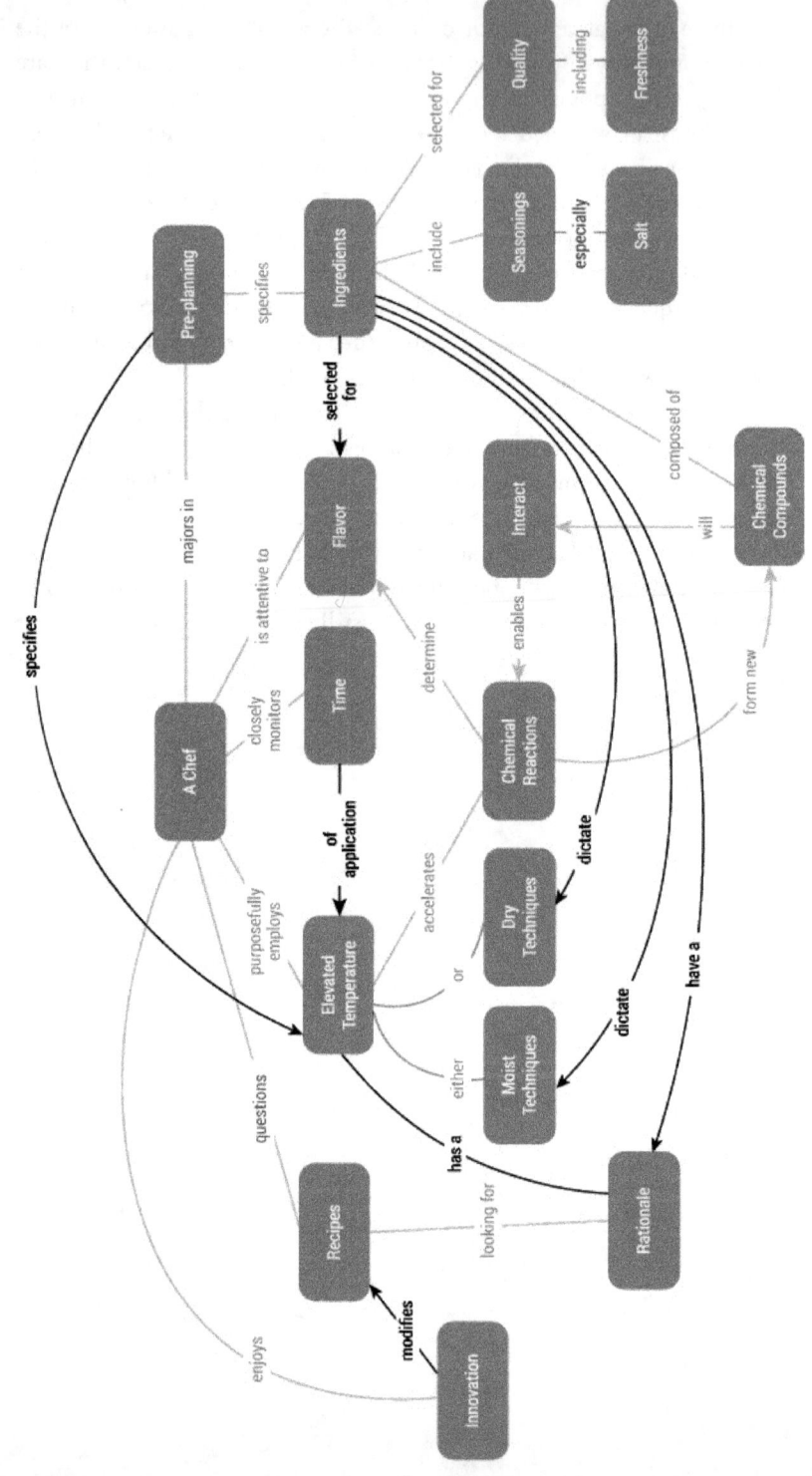

This is a pretty busy map! Notice that we've developed further the concept of cooking by recognizing that cooking is about time and temperature. The map now indicates that the chef closely monitors the cooking time (no doubt in part to keep undesirable flavors from developing, i.e., to keep from burning the food!). There is also now a cross-link flying over the top that indicates the preplanning recognizes the need to choose a cooking method, including time and temperature. A good chef thinks about how long he has to prepare the food and when dinner is going to be served. We're enriching the map's portrayal of the knowledge base of the chef. This was proposition (B).

Realistically this whole map is dedicated to unpacking the thinking (the knowledge base) of a chef. There are now new links with arrows at the bottom of the map to drive home the reality that there is an interplay between the ingredients the chef is using and the cooking techniques that are realistic choices. The strong word *dictate* indicates that some ingredients rule out some cooking techniques. Finally, additional links at the bottom emphasize that there is, in the mind of the chef, a *rationale* that underlies his choice of ingredients and cooking methods. This map is now a reasonable representation of the thinking of a chef. Salt and freshness haven't been developed further, but they easily could be. The main original proposition that still could use development involves flavor (E). Perhaps you can find a way to capture this idea in the map.

It is important to realize that multiple good concept maps of the same domain of thought are possible. Maps are arguable, not right or wrong (although misconceptions that need to be corrected can surface in a concept map). Perhaps considering my map leads you to think that you could make a better map. I'm sure that's possible. In fact my experience is that reexamination of an old map that I've made almost inevitably results in a revision. Revising is a healthy sign that I'm thinking and probably thinking with greater clarity than I had when I created the original map.

Isn't There Another Way?

Perhaps you've seen other mapping methods such as flow charts and mind maps. Flow charts are useful to indicate sequence in a process or a line of thinking, but the reason for the sequence is not typically stated. Flow charts are also quite limited in the amount of branching and cross-linking that is possible. Mind maps are definitely not sequential. Mind maps start with a main idea which radiates in many different directions with links to other ideas in an almost purely associational manner. The link between any two ideas does not state the nature of the relationship between the two ideas. That means that the propositional character of the relationship remains unspecified.

It is my view that nothing else comes close to concept mapping as a representational and developmental tool for thinking. Human thinking is incredibly sophisticated, as our incomplete map of the thinking of a chef demonstrates. One concept links with many others, including concepts on the other side of the map. Mature thinking is not linear but hyperlinked. On the other hand, the tendency many of us have to jump from one idea to another can destroy a "line of thought." When we are thinking in a purely associational manner, it is easy to veer off topic and to wonder, "How did we end up talking about this?" or for others in the conversation to scratch their heads in puzzlement as if to say, "and your point is?"

Concept mapping allows your thinking to be made explicit for purposes of discussion. It represents your thinking so that others can evaluate it and so that you can improve your thinking. The very process of concept mapping challenges your thinking to be clearer and more explicit by (1) insisting that your propositions be stated directly and as strongly as possible (as you never leave a link unlabeled), (2) requiring you to organize your ideas hierarchically from the most general (inclusive) concepts to the most specific concepts, and (3) inviting you to recognize unexplored propositional relationships through opportunities for cross-linking.

What Makes a Good Map?

A concept map is good because it exposes your thinking so that others can interact with it and help it to get better. A good map encourages others to enter into your thinking. A good map is in line with the spirit of critical thinking that says, "There is a logic to this, and I can figure it out." You don't want your map to discourage anyone. You don't want it to be unnecessarily hard to follow. You don't want your map to be ambiguous so that your conversation partners aren't sure what you are trying to say.

In the interest of encouraging the development of analytical thinking, let me offer nine "rules" of concept mapping:

1. Show a particular concept in only one place. (It is in only one place in your brain although it may be linked with many other concepts).

2. Label *all* links and craft the *strongest* propositions possible without overreaching. (Lack of link labels indicates you are not sure what to say because you are not sure what you think.)

3. Write *short* and easily readable propositions.
4. Concepts are almost always nouns (or are used as nouns).
5. Link labels are typically verbs (or adverbs).
6. Link labels should not overlap.
7. Recognize cross-links showing significant relationships between map segments.
8. Reserve the use of arrows for cross-links.
9. Put the link labels for the cross-links close to the origin, not close to the arrowhead.

Maps are communication tools. Perhaps you're thinking about how to use concept maps, not just to clarify and develop your own thinking, but to develop rich, well-organized conceptual frameworks of your discipline in your students. I'm heading that direction in several later chapters, but the next thing you need to do is to interact with the gold that lurks in your concept maps. The next chapter is about mining that gold, the principles in your conceptual frameworks.

Chapter 5

Explanatory Power

> This book is the result of my own desire to "get" the basics; to really understand.... I know there are those who would say "who cares? As long as I know how, why bother with the why?" I can only offer that for me, until I deal with the why, I don't really know the how.[1]
>
> ALTON BROWN

Focusing on concepts automatically sharpens and deepens learning because the brain thinks in terms of concepts, not facts. But you've learned through the mapping process that not all concepts are equally important. Some concepts are subsumers or superordinate (as named by David Ausubel[2]), and that attribute makes them more valuable to learners. Superordinate concepts contain subsumed concepts in seed form. Superordinate concepts are sometimes called "core concepts." Through a rich network of connections, a single core concept can be related to a dozen or more additional concepts.

The relationship of concepts to one another is propositional. Two concepts and the linkage between them constitute a proposition: an assertion created by the learner. The assertion may be a mere opinion that conflicts with the evidence, or it may reflect profound understanding, or it can be something between those two extremes. Even when propositions are factually correct, they are not all equally powerful. The gold I referred to at the end of the last chapter constitutes a group of particularly powerful propositions that you need to create in your conceptual framework. This chapter

---

1. Brown, *I'm Just Here for the Food*, 7.
2. Ausubel, Novak, and Hanesian, *Educational Psychology*, 67-68.

is designed to help you create and master these propositions, which I call principles.

Let's contrast two propositions from the last chapter. The first is "A chef analyzes recipes and monitors outcomes." This asserts two behaviors as characteristic of a chef. It is not entirely clear what the analysis of a recipe would involve, but at least the chef is giving the recipe a close reading. With regard to monitoring outcomes, you might assume this happens when the chef acts on the directives of the recipe to ensure a satisfactory result. Reformulating this proposition to include it in the concept map in the last chapter resulted in a strong focus on just one of these behaviors: "A chef questions recipes looking for [their] rationale." *Rationale* is a very powerful term indicating an appeal to reason: "Why does this recipe work, or why doesn't it?"

Focus on Understanding

Many cooks are simply focused on "how," but Alton Brown focuses on "why." The distinction is not merely pedantic dissection. "How to" guides can be followed by pure imitation. There is no sense of acquiring mastery—of becoming more expert. Your thinking is not being changed by slavishly following a recipe. Your thinking changes to the degree you *understand*. You might say that you understand when you grasp what *stands under* what you're doing or the ideas you're working to reconcile. Deep understanding focuses on what is foundational.

Let's look at an illustration of this truth. The mature concept map I created in the previous chapter contains these related propositions: (1) A chef majors in preplanning. (2) Part of preplanning is to specify ingredients. (3) The specification of ingredients has a rationale.

Rationale—there's that word again. There are *structured* reasons behind the ingredients that a chef specifies. For a chef who is concerned with local sourcing, what is in season is a pivotal question. Suppose the chef has to deviate from the recipe because a strategic ingredient that is specified is not available locally in an optimal state. Deborah Madison takes us through the thought process:

> When we look closely at the plants we eat and begin to discern their similarities, that intelligence comes with us into the kitchen and articulates our cooking in a new way. Suddenly our raw materials make sense. We can see how we might substitute related vegetables when cooking . . . [this knowledge] can free us as cooks, make us unafraid to use some amaranth that's going

full guns in the garden in place of spinach, which has bolted and dried up. They are, after all, related.[3]

Amaranth (aka Chinese spinach) is a member of a subfamily colloquially named (after the shape of the leaves) "goosefoots." Other goosefoot members include beets and Swiss chard. Notice that Deborah Madison speaks of the awareness of shared characteristics because of relatedness as "intelligence." Vegetable ingredient substitutions now make sense.

In the big-picture context, we might say that we have just learned a bit of culinary wisdom. We know part of the "why" for ingredient substitution. Wisdom has been defined as "pursuing . . . the best ends by the best means."[4] Wisdom is inextricably linked with understanding. Understanding is evidenced by being able to satisfactorily answer "why" questions. Most current education doesn't require understanding. Mere recall will do. In Information Age classrooms we are enamored with the new; we are inundated with information and sometimes with mere data. The acronym DIKW has been created in recognition of the progression: Data—Information—Knowledge—Wisdom.

T.S. Eliot in a stanza from *Choruses from the Rock* is sometimes credited with inventing the basic idea behind DIKW:

> Where is the Life we have lost in living?
>
> Where is the wisdom we have lost in knowledge?
>
> Where is the knowledge we have lost in information?[5]

There have been various modifications of DIKW. One that is particularly germane to our discussion is pictured below:[6]

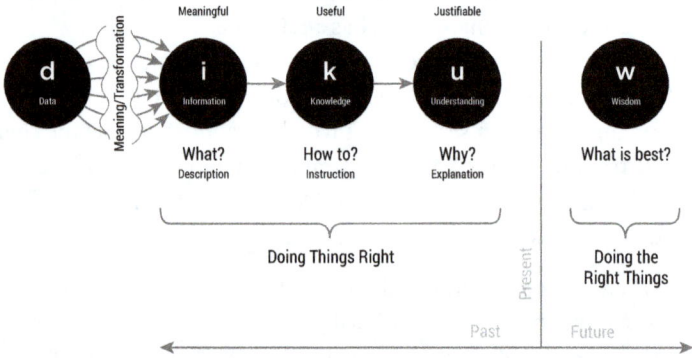

3. Madison, *Vegetable Literacy*, 1.
4. Hutcheson, *Inquiry into the Original of our Ideas*.
5. Eliot, *Choruses from the Rock*.
6. Omegapowers, "DIKW."

Notice that there is a progression as you move from left to right. Data is acquired and processed or transformed by various means (this is how the barrier to information is crossed). Information feeds into knowledge and knowledge should lead to understanding. Understanding acquired in the past (and the present) should ideally lead to making wise decisions in the future, when we are faced with issues of priorities and new problems to solve.

I view learning as tripartite. The elements of learning are facts, concepts, and principles. Facts are the nuts and bolts of an academic discipline; they are the *information* characteristic of the discipline. Information is the product of previous intellectual effort by practitioners of the discipline. Information is the evidence base that must be accommodated by the next level, knowledge. Notice that the information level is called "what" in the diagram on the previous page. Information just is; it is a what.

Knowledge is the level of conceptualization. Conceptualization imposes order on information and experience by abstract category creation. We call these categories concepts. The mind assimilates concepts (after early childhood) and requires logical justification to properly incorporate a new concept into preexisting conceptual frameworks. The diagram categorizes this stage as "how to." A person with well-organized conceptual frameworks can properly relate ideas to one another and take generally appropriate actions. This is where most practical areas of study stall. Students in those disciplines learn "how to" but not "why." Cooking is a prime example.

Understanding requires learners to answer "why" questions. If these questions cannot be satisfactorily answered, adequate understanding has not yet been achieved. Notice that understanding is linked in the diagram to the ability to provide an explanation. The ability to explain means that a question can be answered satisfactorily. As we noted in chapter 3, explanation is one of the outputs of expert thinking (the other being the ability to recognize implications/consequences). My goal in this book is to empower you to help your students think in expertlike ways. You must enable your students to understand with sufficient depth that they can answer authentic discipline-based questions with an appropriate depth of explanation. These are higher-order thinking goals that cannot be achieved by lower-order approaches.

The idea of higher-order and lower-order learning is derived from a consideration of Bloom's Taxonomy. In the previous chapter I criticized the original taxonomy for its naming of the lowest level of learning as knowledge, followed in the next level by comprehension! The taxonomy was revised in 2000 and the revised taxonomy of cognitive processing addresses the knowledge misconception:

Remember—>Understand—>Apply—>Analyze—>Evaluate—>Create[7]

In spite of the arrows, I personally do not view Bloom's revised taxonomy as a progression to higher and higher levels of thinking with the ability to create standing on an exalted pinnacle. This view has been used to legitimize "creativity" as an ultimate that is unaccountable to thought processes. I view understanding as a gateway. It is the *essence* of higher-order learning and depth of understanding is demonstrated in various ways: the ability to apply, analyze, evaluate, and create (in no particular order). The ability to solve authentic problems in a discipline typically involves analysis and evaluation to delineate the problem and possible solutions. It involves an application of relevant concepts and principles. The solution involves the creation of something new because the problem is not a trivial iteration of something the students have already seen.

Sharpening Your Vision

A newborn infant can't see things very clearly. The reason is fascinating. Newborns have too many neurons handling vision. Fuzziness is created by having several different neurons handling overlapping points in the visual field. The natural solution in the first few months of life is for a built-in mechanism to prune the neural network to remove redundant neurons so that there is a precise correspondence between the number and position of neurons and the number and position of points in the visual field (like pixels on a computer screen). I propose that we have a similar problem in the world of learning. We have too many cognitive terms that we use interchangeably as though they mean the same thing. The result is fuzziness of communication and, not infrequently, miscommunication.

Here's my short list of cognitive words that are used imprecisely by the educational community and by others: adage, axiom, big idea, concept, dictum, doctrine, fact, hypothesis, information, law, maxim, model, philosophy, postulate, precept, principle, proverb, rationale, rule, tenet, theme, theorem, theory.

Good words, all of them. All of them potentially useful words where there are subtle differences of meaning that need to be communicated with precision. *The problem is that many of them are being used as synonyms when they are not.* This causes confusion and sometimes outright miscommunication.

---

7. Krathwohl, "A Revision of Bloom's Taxonomy," 215.

To encourage clear thinking about this welter of terms, my colleagues Bill Lovegrove and Brian Vogt have developed a tool they call the Big Idea Sorter. This tool was developed to help faculty in our summer programs evaluate big ideas that could potentially be strategic in organizing their course. What kind of ideas are they? The sorter is really a kind of flow chart, and Bill is an engineer who frequently uses flow charts in his engineering life. It would be good for you to push the pause button here and study the sorter.

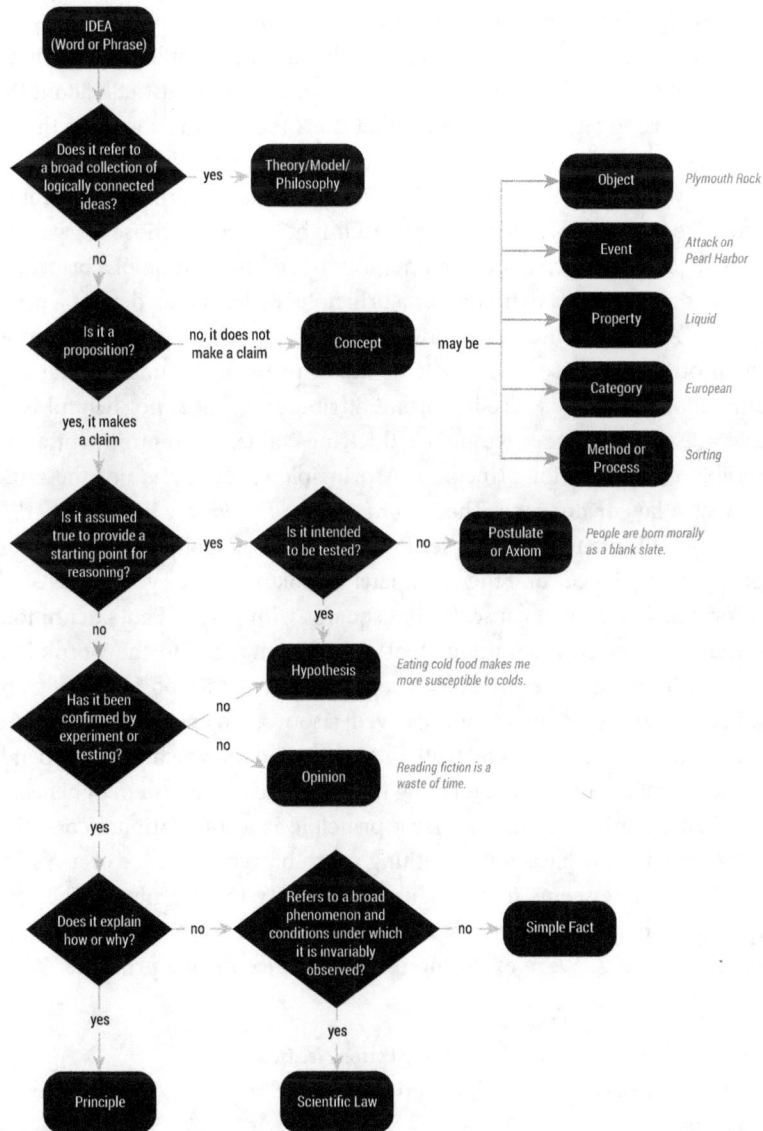

You've probably noticed that not all of the terms in my list made the cut for the Big Idea Sorter. What is in the sorter is there because of faculty need demonstrated over several summers. A bigger sorter would have been more imposing and harder to use.

A Reclamation Project

My goal in this chapter is to reclaim the concept of a principle. The concept of a principle seems to be a non sequitur based strictly on the Big Idea Sorter. Concepts are at the top left and principles are at the bottom of the sorter. Doesn't that mean they aren't the same thing? Didn't we just talk about the danger of using terms as synonyms that don't really mean the same thing? "If you're not confused, you're not paying attention."[8] In the interest of clarity, I want to highlight the distinguishing marks of a principle. I want to recognize instances where a better word might have been chosen. I want to argue for a more precise and parsimonious use of the concept of a principle.

Let's start with a definition of a principle. Richard Paul defines a principle as "A fundamental truth, law, doctrine, value, or commitment, upon which others are based."[9] He tells us that a principle is fundamental and foundational and those are important attributes. What is not helpful is to have a list that includes truth, law, doctrine, value, or commitment as all possible candidates for principles. A principle especially is not the same thing as a law or doctrine. The *Oxford English Dictionary* lists twenty different definitions for a principle. *Principle* was originally a "fundamental concept in a science," and then a bit later it took on a more general sense of an "origin, source, first cause."[10] That squares with part of Paul's definition. In the OED the two definitions that are relevant, both to the word's history and to the use of a principle in cognition, are definition 1a, "That from which something originates or is derived; a source, an origin; the root"; and definition 3a, "A fundamental truth or proposition on which others depend; a general statement or tenet forming the (or a) basis of a system of belief."[11]

What we have so far is that a principle is a foundational cognitive concept that is the basis for something much bigger (a science or a system of belief). There seems to be linguistic authority for this much. The *concept* of a principle is a bit tricky. A concept, we have learned, is a pattern in events or objects. We're exploring the *idea* (concept) of a principle. We're

---

8. Peters, *Thriving on Chaos*.
9. Paul, *Critical Thinking: What Every Person Needs*, 662.
10. *Oxford English Dictionary*, s.v. "principle," noun.
11. Ibid.

not yet examining statements to see if they *are* principles according to the restricted usage I'm proposing. About ten years ago, I simplistically thought that principles would turn out to be über concepts. I envisioned in a map a particularly potent concept that would have links that went everywhere to a whole host of other concepts. The "bristles" surrounding the concept in a map would be a tip-off that I was looking at a principle in the map. That turns out not to be a reliable indicator of a principle for many reasons. The main reason is that, unlike concepts, principles are intrinsically propositional in nature. David Ausubel is helpful when he says, "Principles differ from concepts in that they involve meaningful relational combinations of concepts that are propositional in nature. In other words, a principle, by definition, is a composite idea."[12]

A principle is a fundamental proposition that puts two or more concepts into a relationship that is the basis for something much bigger than the concepts themselves. Likewise, individual principles often figure into a group that collectively forms the skeleton of a science or system of belief. If "system of belief" sounds hopelessly theoretical, it needn't. Mortimer Adler in a discussion of books that are practical as compared to those that are theoretical makes this observation: "A practical book may contain more than rules. It may try to state the principles that underlie the rules and make them intelligible."[13] This is a helpful clarification. Rules have a *basis* in reason, and principles form that basis. Pedagogically it would be most useful to appeal to principles rather than a simple memory of the rules or even the repeated application of the rules in solving problems. When a rule makes sense because it is based on a clearly articulated principle, we can easily remember it and use it appropriately based on that logic.

A pragmatic approach to education centers on listing the rules by which a process is accomplished, but rules often have an arbitrary character that makes them difficult to master and remember. Take for instance GAAP, Generally Accepted Accounting Principles. These are "the common set of accounting principles, standards and procedures that companies use to compile their financial statements. GAAP are a combination of authoritative standards (set by policy boards) and simply the commonly accepted ways of recording and reporting accounting information."[14] Further at the same site we are told, "Companies are expected to follow GAAP rules when reporting their financial data via financial statements."[15] Are they GAAP

12. Ausubel, Novak, and Hanesian, *Educational Psychology*, 96.
13. Adler and Van Doren, *How to Read a Book*, 194.
14. Anonymous, "Definition of Generally Accepted Accounting Principles—GAAP."
15. Anonymous, "Investopedia Explains GAAP."

principles or are they rules? Principles explain the basis for rules, but rules are mere assertions of the way experts say things should be done. I expect there are some principles behind GAAP, but GAAP is a declaration of a consensus on a procedure, not an explanation of the rationale behind it. This is lower-order thinking masquerading as higher-order thinking.

Laws are very important, especially to scientists. A noted science educator reflects on Newton's second law of motion: "Principles tell us *how* events or objects work or how they are structured. In physics, for example, we have the principle: force equals mass times acceleration (F = ma)."[16] I would agree that principles tell us how things work. When we know how things work, we can explain. To know how things work is to *understand* at a very foundational level. I think *law* is the right word here. F = ma is mathematical shorthand for Newton's second *law* of motion. It is descriptive of a relationship among three concepts (force, mass, and acceleration), but it states a "what," rather than a "how" or a "why." It is very useful in making predictions, and it is difficult to imagine physics or engineering without it; but I don't think it is helpful to call it a principle.

Newton's second law is a classic example of a law. *Law* has a well-established meaning. I think it is important to reserve the word *principle* for propositions that are explanatory in character. You will note this distinction in the Big Idea Sorter. Laws describe what we may expect under appropriate conditions, but they don't really *explain* how or why. Another example is the Second Law of Thermodynamics, which states that entropy (disorder) in isolated systems always increases. This can be empirically verified, but not explained. It just is. Using *law* and *principle* as interchangeable synonyms robs us of a distinctive term to use in pinpointing propositions that are truly explanatory.

Physicists and engineers generally love mathematics. My father was an aerospace engineer, and his favorite academic course was differential equations. Dad practiced engineering back in the early part of the U.S. space program (ending his design career when Apollo landed on the moon), and he used a slide rule for most of his calculations. I was very happy when slide rules passed into oblivion and were replaced by calculators and computers because I didn't have to understand math at the same level to punch numbers into a computing device. Physicists and engineers tend to talk in mathematics (like F = ma or worse, much worse). It turns out that, for some of them, mathematics is a *substitute* for true understanding. Their equations allow them to do the calculations and to share the basis for, and the results of, their calculations with others of their ilk. Ask them to talk in conceptual

---

16. Novak, *Learning, Creating, and Using Knowledge*, 26-27.

or principle-based terms leaving aside the mathematics, and you'll get a cold stare that implies the profundity of your ignorance in even making such a request.

Is it true that the equations are the explanation? Here's one engineer's take:

> So, just how much does a guy have to know to still call himself an engineer? My conclusion is that engineering is qualitative, not quantitative. Engineering is a mindset and training to know there are losses in electrical conductors, stresses in support members, and electrically induced energy in magnetically coupled conductors . . . [but] knowing how to calculate it is an exercise for those who remember all the equations.[17]

Engineering professor David Goldberg of the University of Illinois (Urbana-Champaign) agrees and succinctly says, "excellent quantitative understanding needs to be *built on* better foundations of the qualitative."[18]

A clear example of the disconnect between the "what" and the "how" and "why" behind the "what" is the Copenhagen interpretation of quantum mechanics. It recognizes a disconnect between objective reality as experienced by humans and the predictions of the equations. The tension between the two generated the famous statement, "Shut up and calculate!" which has been variously attributed.[19] One of the ideas associated with this interpretation is Heisenberg's Uncertainty Principle, which maintains that one cannot simultaneously determine with precision the momentum and the position of an atomic particle. The Uncertainty Principle is anything but a principle since it states what *can't* be known and does not explain *why* it can't be known. Another ersatz principle from the Copenhagen interpretation is the principle of duality, the idea that matter exhibits both the properties of a wave and of a particle (depending on the experiment) even though these are incompatible with each other.[20] The idea of duality is an egregious misappropriation of the cognitive certitude that is part of the essence of a principle.

Another frequent categorical error occurs when theories are equated with principles. Theories are broad collections of logically connected ideas. Theories should contain principles, but theories are much more expansive and are often stated in ways that don't address "how" or "why." A student who is ready for an explanation, but who gets a theory instead, will be

---

17. Ciarcia, "What Makes an Engineer?" 96.
18. Goldberg, "Bury the Cold War Curriculum," 68 (emphasis mine).
19. Anonymous, "Copenhagen Interpretation."
20. Ibid.

disappointed and confused. Take Keynesian Economic Theory as an example. "Keynesian economics is a theory of total spending in the economy . . . and its effects on output and inflation."[21] That's a sentence begging to be memorized because it doesn't aim at understanding. It will have to be unpacked considerably before a "how" or "why" is evident. The author goes on to list "six principal tenets" of Keynesianism.[22] All of these tenets (at least he didn't call them principles) are *assertions* that Keynesians make. The logical rationale is not unpacked in this article, though, presumably, there are logical reasons to be a Keynesian.

Before I leave the idea sorter, let me touch a few more pressure points. Educators and students often confuse other categories in DIKW with principles. Facts are deployed without justification or explanation. Facts form the information component that is the "stuff" students have to "master" (talk about a misnomer) during their education. Another point of confusion has to do with concepts. Concepts are a significant step up from facts, as I have already noted. But by themselves concepts are simply abstractions created in recognition of perceived pattern regularities. Conceptualization is challenged using evidence (information) and especially using logic. One of the enemies of logical thinking is opinion. Opinions are generally not based on evidence and are often impervious to reason—and everyone seems to have one. This was famously captured by Tom and Ray Magliozzi (Click and Clack) in their address to the graduating class at MIT in 1999. "We're going to help you to become not smarter. Smarter is no good. That's the wrong direction. . . . You must repeat the mantra. And the mantra, which happens to be emblazoned on our flag, . . . says: *non impediti ratione cogitationis.* Which, of course, means: Unencumbered by the thought process."[23]

Principles Rehabilitated—Much Ado About the Main Thing

Principles are the most important aspect of real learning. They are gold. I'm arguing for the idea of a principle because it is vital to learning with understanding. The idea of a principle is being lost in the current fog of misusing the word. I haven't tried to invent a new term simply because *principle* is the right term based on its etymology and its historical usage. I'm arguing that we need to recover the term *principle* and the idea it represents, namely, teaching for understanding. When a student really understands,

21. Blinder, "Keynesian Economics."
22. Ibid.
23. Dabek, "'Car Talk' Brothers Address Graduates," 9.

everything changes. Remembering related information is easier. Articulating pattern regularities for associated concepts is simpler. Asking the right questions in order to properly negotiate the concepts into existing conceptual frameworks can become almost intuitive. Solving authentic problems leads to real satisfaction with learning. All because the student "gets it"—she understands!

Everything I have talked about in the book so far has been driving toward this focus on principles. The big picture is that you want your students to "think like a _____"—to demonstrate expertlike thinking within your academic domain. To get your students to think that way, you need to articulate for yourself the logic of your discipline, using the tools found in chapter 3. Also in chapter 3 you learned that the logic of a discipline has three layers. The core layer recognizes your motivation, your point of view, and the questions that your discipline tries to answer. The working layer consists of assumptions, information, and conceptual frameworks. Conceptual framework formation and remodeling is a continuing work in progress, and all of chapter 4 is about how to think conceptually. The current chapter is the logical culmination of the thinking process because it moves conceptual thinking toward asking and answering the "how" and "why" questions that will allow the output layer of your student's thinking to be expertlike. Appropriate "how" and "why" answers demonstrate understanding. Understanding, in turn, allows the solving of problems and the answering of questions pertinent to your domain of knowledge. Answering questions through explanation coupled with facility in solving problems shows a command of the implications and consequences of thinking in terms of principles. The diagram below shows the progression in these ideas.

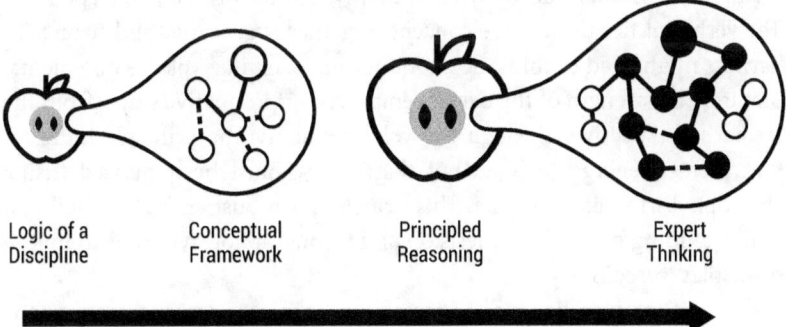

Logic of a Discipline   Conceptual Framework   Principled Reasoning   Expert Thnking

Rather than simply offer another definition, I think that the best strategy is to characterize what I mean by a principle. (I'm indebted to my colleague Brian Vogt for helping me to establish this approach over ten years ago.) A principle, as I'm using the term, has all of the following attributes:

(1) it is propositional, (2) it is broadly applicable, (3) it is explanatory, and (4) it is predictive.

As a simple example, consider the phrase "fire requires a source of oxygen." Is this a principle? It is certainly propositional because it asserts something (makes a claim). Without question it is broadly applicable because it applies to combustion in general. Is it explanatory? Absolutely. This principle explains why you can smother a fire using water or dirt. Furthermore, it is inherently predictive because one who has mastered its meaning can use it to predict in many different situations how to start and stop fires.

Many ideas sound like principles when they are actually only conceptual propositions. The statement "ferns are green" makes a claim, is broadly applicable (implied: all ferns are green), and has some predictive power (as yet undiscovered species of ferns are probably green), but it doesn't explain anything. Why are ferns green? Why does it matter that ferns are green? How do ferns become green? These and many other legitimate questions are not answered. It is helpful on some level to relate the concept of a fern to the "green" concept, but simply saying that ferns are a subset of the set of all green things is not very profound. These are primary concepts as formulated in the mind of a very young child.

Young children also ask questions. They often are not content with simple claims. They might ask, "Why are ferns green?" To reply that "ferns are green because they contain chlorophyll" is a step up in precision, and it may be all an early elementary school child needs to know. There is a principle underlying "greenness" that is powerful, however. The principle might read: "Chlorophyll harnesses the energy in light." This is a much more useful proposition. With this in mind, the primary concept green ties to the secondary concepts chlorophyll and energy, and the primary concept, light. The verb that ties these three concepts together is evocative and strong. To harness might lead to thinking about putting oxen in a yoke as one mental picture. The strength of the oxen is employed in productive ways (from the farmer's perspective) through the yoke. Similarly, the principle indicates that there is energy in light, but that energy must be harnessed (using chlorophyll) to benefit plants. This principle is robust enough to build an understanding of photosynthesis on and through photosynthesis to link to principles in ecology.

Because principles are so powerful in learning, I want to preserve the concept of a principle by using *principle* in a very specific and restricted way. A noted science educator starts in a promising manner. He says "Principles. These describe *how* things work or how they appear to be structured."[24] Re-

---

24. Novak, *Learning, Creating, and Using Knowledge*, 97.

membering the four attributes I listed earlier, it appears that he is homing in on the ability to explain as the hallmark of a principle. I basically agree that the ability to answer a "how" (or "why") question is the essence of a principle—it is explanation. The educator then goes on to list principles articulated by his young granddaughter as she worked in the garden with her grandmother and asked questions. His granddaughter "manifested several operating principles: (1) weeds look different from flowers (i.e., weeds were grass-like in our garden of marigolds and zinnias); (2) plants use dirt to grow; (3) when dirt goes into plants, the soil has fewer nutrients."[25]

Candidate principle number 1 is an example of primary conceptualization. It is much like "ferns are green," except that it is less focused. It amounts to saying, weeds don't look like the flowers in the garden. Fair enough. This is a pragmatically useful observation for sorting things into categories. This is what we do when we conceptualize. The difference in appearance of weeds and flowers is ultimately a difference in "how they appear to be structured." But that doesn't add anything of consequence to our understanding. A principle is very different. Principles *explain*. How does this observation explain? What does it mean to explain? This is the heart of a principle, so we need to be really clear on this. I'll develop the concept of explanation just a little later in this chapter.

Candidate principle number 2 sounds promising. It relates plants, dirt, and growth through the verb *use*. *Use* is a simple replacement for the concept of assimilation and is an age-appropriate way of saying that plant growth takes place *because of* dirt. This sounds like an explanation and it meets the other criteria for a principle as well. I'm comfortable with calling this a principle (stated at the level of a young child). In the big picture of plant biology, it must be said, however, that dirt is a *very* minor contributor to plant growth. *Most* growth occurs because of photosynthesis. Allowing principle 2 to have much influence in the thought life of a young child can lead to a common deep-seated misconception. This misconception is strong even in graduates of Harvard and MIT. It keeps them from embracing the reality that the vast majority of the mass of a plant comes from CO_2 taken from the air as a part of photosynthesis. Minerals from dirt make a minuscule contribution.[26]

Candidate principle number 3 seems to take as a given (through the word *when*) that dirt has to go into plants in order to cause plant growth. It actually shows the predictive power of the proposition in number 2 and further reinforces that it is a principle, albeit a very small one. This is a

25. Ibid.
26. Anonymous, "Lessons from Thin Air."

refinement of the granddaughter's thinking on what it means to "use" something. I think it is a corollary principle that deals with a "how" question related to principle 2. How do plants use dirt to grow? Answer: The dirt has to go *into* the plants. A consequence of this is subtractive: the soil as a result has fewer nutrients.

I believe the ability of principles to explain is unique. Just as we found that scientists and engineers sometimes unhelpfully view laws as explanations, so it is with theories. One scientist refers to theories "as *explanations* for why and how things appear the way they do."[27] Theories provide a framework to hold multiple ideas together in logical relationship, but I don't think that theories themselves explain. The theory of gravitation, for instance, says that objects attract each other with a force that is related to their masses and the distance between the objects. Gravity is the *name* we typically give to the force (commonly the "pull" of the earth on other objects). We do not know what the *nature* of that force is, so there is, as yet, no gravitational principle. Explanations reside at the level of principles. Theories are broad collections of logically connected ideas as shown previously in the Big Idea Sorter.

Principles—The Power of the Package

A principle is the most important part of real learning because thinking in terms of principles can produce understanding. It is important, therefore, to be as clear as possible about what constitutes a principle. Mishandling the concept of a principle is rampant, as I have illustrated above.

Two of the four attributes of a principle are shared with other educational terms—that principles are propositional and that they are broadly applicable. A *proposition* is an assertion that states the nature of the relationship between two concepts. Some propositions are particularly powerful and helpful. A second attribute of a principle is that it is *broadly applicable.* This is important because the extended range of applicability elevates the potential importance of such ideas compared to more narrowly focused provincial alternatives. It is helpful to gain a thirty-thousand-foot aerial view of a discipline, looking at just what you can see from that altitude. *Molecular Biology of the Cell,*[28] referenced earlier in this book as a formative influence on my thinking, explains in the first chapter of the 5th edition what the authors call "universals." The term speaks to the universality of application of these ideas (they are characteristic of all cells in all organisms). These universals are also propositions. Many of them also have two more

---

27. Novak, . *Learning, Creating, and Using Knowledge*, 97.
28. Alberts, *Molecular Biology of the Cell*, 5th ed. chapter 1.

characteristics that make them principles in my sense of the word. These distinguishing characteristics are developed in the paragraphs that follow.

The two attributes that are unique to a principle are worth considering in some depth. The first of these is that a principle is *explanatory*. I've found in working with faculty that this is the hardest attribute to understand, but it is also arguably the most potent. The OED has multiple definitions of *explain,* including "To make plain or intelligible; to clear of obscurity or difficulty."[29] Even more helpful in the specific context of a principle is this OED definition, "To make clear the cause, origin, or reason of; to account for."[30] To explain means that you have answered a "how" or "why" question pertinent to your discipline. (That's what expert thinking does). You've clearly pointed out a cause-effect mechanism, or what governs the phenomenon. If this sounds too strong for your domain of knowledge, think in terms of "accounted for." You've satisfied the questioner within the limits of your discipline. Explanation looks different for different disciplines.

As a case in point, let's consider Hitler's rise to power in Germany. Here is the focal question: "What accounts for Hitler's rise to power in post-WWI Germany?" On the surface this looks like something only a historian or sociologist would be able to contribute to, but there are various stakeholders with different kinds of explanations as illustrated in the table below.

Expertise	*Explanation*
Historian	Germans felt that they were betrayed by their leaders at the end of WWI through surrender to the Allies and signing the Treaty of Versailles.
Sociologist	A fragmented German society with various extremist groups and political parties vying for control and willing to use violence to achieve control in the aftermath of WWI set the stage for an upheaval.
Economist	Rampant inflation and high unemployment in the days of the democratic Weimar Republic following WWI created economic stress that made Germans hungry for leadership.

---

29. *Oxford English Dictionary,* s.v. "explain."
30. Ibid.

Expertise	*Explanation*
Geneticist	Hitler's view that a significant subset of the German people were "Aryan" and were a "master race" appealed to the masses who were trying to recover from the shame of WWI defeat. This perspective made Hitler a popular figure.
Communicator	Hitler galvanized the dispirited masses through "electrifying" oratory.
Writer	Hitler captured the imagination of Germans through his book *Mein Kampf*, which sketched out a future vision for Germany.
Psychologist	Hitler's upbringing with a domineering and brutal father and an adoring mother produced a man with a huge ego who used violence to remove obstacles to his will.

Notice how each expert marshals evidence selectively and answers the same question in very different ways. Each explanation is part of the complete answer, which is ultimately unattainable because of the number of contributing elements. Each explanation at least attempts to *account for* Hitler's rise to power and some utilize *cause-effect* language (although no single cause is adequate). All of the answers are plausible and logical within a given domain of knowledge. Because the explanations "make sense," they are not hard to remember.

The explanations given in this table are propositional in that they assert something as the basis for Hitler's rise to power. To be effectively communicated as principles they would need to be stated in a more general and compact fashion. They need to be refined to pithy propositions. For instance a writer might broaden the explanation in the table above to "An individual book can change the course of a nation by articulating a compelling national vision." The writer would illustrate this principle through books such as the Old Testament of the Bible, *The Communist Manifesto*, and *Mein Kampf*. In other words, Weimar Germany and the years immediately following it is not the only time in history that a single book has been so influential (an appeal to evidence, i.e., information). Multiplied examples testify that the proposition is broadly applicable.

A writer could go further to predict that there will be such books written in the future. When are the conditions right for such a book, and what are the common attributes by which we would recognize such books? The second distinguishing characteristic of a principle, then, is that it is *predictive*. This aspect of a principle is extremely valuable as experts make their contributions to the future of companies, cultures, and civilizations. Why do we listen to engineers to try to avoid bridge collapses? Why do we listen to public health experts in regard to the likelihood of a flu epidemic next winter? For that matter, why do we look at weather forecasts that daily test the predictive acumen of meteorologists? In every instance, we believe that the expert's command of a group of principles produces some likelihood of accurate prediction. In the near term such predictions are *implications* of the principles. In the long range the principles tell us what the *consequences* will be for acting (or failing to act) in a certain way.

Principle Construction

We value expertise because experts incisively cut to the heart of a problem and identify cause and effect. They appropriately apply the principles of their discipline in devising solutions. Since you are trying to develop expertlike thinking in your students, you need to teach them how to formulate principles on purpose rather than hoping they will develop that level of insight by serendipity. If you are going to teach your students how to "principialize,"[31] you're going to have to get this process out in the open so that you too do it on purpose. Fortunately "principialization" is directly related to conceptualization. You innately know how to conceptualize and, hopefully, the previous chapter helped you to get better at thinking about the process. *Principialization primarily involves being much more intentional in your formulation of propositions.*

Conceptualization involves the formulation and assimilation of concepts. Assimilating concepts requires that you negotiate them into your existing conceptual framework. You find a place where a concept (pattern regularity) fits based on logical justification. Generally it fits in a specific

---

31. I coined this term, but it is not arbitrary. Principia (prin KIP ee uh) are collections of principles. Two historical examples are *Philosophiae Naturalist Principia Mathematica*, a three-volume set authored by Sir Isaac Newton in 1687, and *Principia Mathematica* (also three books) by Alfred North Whitehead and Bertrand Russell (1910).

place because it answers a specific question. There is a view within the science of cognition that mental indexing is the result of asking (and answering) the right question.[32] Principle construction thrives in an atmosphere that generates questions. What question(s) does this proposition (that I'm constructing) answer? This ought to be right up there with "What is the logically defensible way to link this concept into my existing framework?" Rather than settling for a spot that works, strive to find the best place to put the concept. Part of what makes a spot the best is that it answers a significant question when placed there. An important part of answering a question is the wording of the proposition. Time spent here with carefully chosen words is invaluable. Try to push the wording to make the proposition as powerful as possible. See if you can justify a strong cause-effect wording. Don't overreach, but don't be timid either.

Because our mental structures are not easily inspected, concept maps were developed as a tool to expose our thinking to ourselves and others so that our thinking can be improved. Initially most principialization will be generated on the basis of deeply pondering a good concept map that you have made. Later on you will probably develop the ability to articulate principles without using a concept map as an aid. Aggressiveness in looking for new cross-links in your map and selecting the strongest propositional links possible is the right strategy to begin with.

The propositions you identify and modify on your map as principles should be denoted with a thicker line to set them off visually as particularly important. This strategy restricts you because the map restricts you. Each proposition is typically between two and only two concepts. The same concept might be robustly linked to many other concepts, but each link makes only one propositional statement. As you pursue this strategy on your map, you may notice a number of principles that tie to a single concept. When you observe this, it is time to think about articulating a single principle that ties three or more concepts together in one propositional statement. Currently there are no good ways to enter such principles into a two-dimensional map, so you will probably just want to write out a sentence that captures the proposition you've inductively formulated. Once you have it written down, try it out to see how well it works, reformulating as necessary.

That's enough theory for now. We need a few concrete examples of principles to chew on.

Remembering that principles are typically formulated as answers to questions, let's think about this question: "Why do I need to apply a coat of primer before I apply the finish coat of paint?" Notice that I'm answering

---

32. Bain, *What the Best College Teachers Do*, 31.

a "why" question, and that usually means the answer is going to involve some type of cause-effect relationship. Thinking within the logic of a professional painter yields a couple of principles: (1) Paint adherence is based on chemical compatibility with the old surface. (2) Priming a surface creates a uniformly chemically compatible intermediary.

Let's run each of these potential principles through our principles checklist:

Principle Attribute	*Paint Principle 1* *Paint adherence is based on chemical compatibility with the old surface.*
Propositional	It makes an assertion.
Broadly Applicable	It applies to any paint and any surface.
Explanatory	Adherence is *based on* [appeals to a root cause] the concept of chemical compatibility.
Predictive	Negatively that chemical incompatibility between the old surface and the new paint (without primer application) will compromise adherence. E.g., application of latex-based paint over oil-based paint will not work because they are fundamentally incompatible.

Principle Attribute	**Paint Principle 2** *Priming a surface creates a uniformly chemically compatible intermediary.*
Propositional	It makes an assertion.
Broadly Applicable	It applies to any primer.
Explanatory	Primer creates a chemically compatible intermediary that works with both the old surface and the new paint. This concept of an intermediary that arbitrates whatever differences may exist between the old and new is a key idea.
Predictive	Most primers function equally well over a variety of types of old paint (e.g., latex-based or oil-based) and surface conditions (minor soil, most stains).

These principles (and others) will be valuable for a painter to know in trying to solve problems created by amateur painters, such as peeling or flaking paint. Painters encounter these situations regularly and are expected to solve these problems and to be able to explain their actions to clients.

Here's another question we'll use to go fishing for a principle, "How was the oil from the BP Deepwater Horizon disaster in the Gulf of Mexico largely dissipated within just a few months?" There are many aspects to this question, including the unprecedented scale of the use of chemical dispersants; but ultimately this comes down to a question of how to remove (and not just disperse) the oil. The principle comes from microbiology (the study of microscopic life forms—microbes). The principle that undergirds the area of bioremediation (using microbes to fix chemical contamination of the environment) is "All naturally occurring organic compounds are used as food by some microbe or community of microbes."

Let's check this out against the criteria for a principle.

Principle Attribute	**Bioremediation Principle** *All naturally occurring organic compounds are used as food by some microbe or community of microbes.*
Propositional	It makes an assertion.
Broadly Applicable	It applies to every naturally occurring organic compound (including the complex mixture in crude oil).
Explanatory	Microbes exist which naturally exhibit metabolic processes that can break down the naturally occurring organic compounds in crude oil to harmless waste products.
Predictive	In the vicinity of oil deposits (which often naturally leak into surrounding soil and water) we would expect there to be a population of organisms capable of degrading the organic compounds that make up crude oil.

This principle of bioremediation tells us that, for naturally occurring organic compounds (a very diverse collection), the process of decomposition is mediated by microbes. This is a cause-effect relationship. Microbes exist that thrive on crude oil components and produce harmless waste products. The population of these microbes will increase explosively if the concentration of chemical compounds they can use as food increases significantly in the environment. A related principle that extends this idea is "Chemical compounds that humans engineer will be biodegradable (capable of being metabolized by microbes) if they are sufficiently similar to naturally occurring organic compounds." Evaluate this second principle in light of what you have learned from studying the first bioremediation principle. Can you articulate how this principle explains? Can you make a prediction based on this principle?

Principles possess explanatory power. Their ability to explain and to answer a diverse group of "how" and "why" questions (with a common core) is called extensibility. Like a good power tool that is right for the job, principles can help you solve a diverse group of problems. But it is also important to formulate multiple principles and not be content with the first few that are the result of your initial analytical probing. You want a good collection of these cognitive "tools"; otherwise you may succumb to the old adage "If the only tool in your tool box is a hammer, then every problem looks like a nail."

Here's one final example to tap into the rich divergence of principles that undergird serious thinking in any area of human thought. Let's explore microbiology a bit more and then work with one more principle. First, some background. Microbes are found in huge numbers all over our planet. They are actually the dominant life form on earth, both in terms of numbers and mass. You don't think about this because you can't see microbes without a microscope.

A more concrete reality is that there are two to three times more microbes in and on our bodies than our own cells. (They weigh only a total of several pounds per person because they are tiny.) We have just considered a principle of bioremediation that relies on microbes. Now let's look at the problem of infectious disease. Antibiotics are frequently (much too frequently!) prescribed for treating relatively minor infections like middle-ear or sinus infections. Most people have had the experience of taking a prescribed antibiotic only to find that it really didn't fix the problem. Eventually they get better without a second antibiotic. No harm done, right? Wrong!

Let's base our answer to the question of failed prescribing on a principle that allows us to think properly about this and not just offer an opinion. One relevant principle is this: "Antibiotics always select for resistant microbes." This is pretty compact and initially may not sound like a principle. Let's check.

Principle Attribute	*Antibiotic Use Principle* *Antibiotics always select for resistant microbes.*
Propositional	It makes an assertion.
Broadly Applicable	It applies to every use of antibiotics (including agricultural use).

Principle Attribute	*Antibiotic Use Principle* **Antibiotics always select for resistant microbes.**
Explanatory	The key phrase is "select for." To select is to advantage some and not others. Here the antibiotic kills many microbes (including natural inhabitants that keep us healthy) and spares others. Those that survive the use of an antibiotic are by the nature of the case resistant to the antibiotic (that's why they survived).
Predictive	Increased use of antibiotics increases the proportion of resistant microbes carried by people and the environment.

This principled reasoning process leads us to conclude that there is *always* risk associated with antibiotic prescribing. The hope should be that the prescriber is very sure that an antibiotic is necessary and that the right antibiotic that will really cure this infection has been prescribed. The "just in case" kind of prescribing with a short list of "go to" antibiotics that some physicians engage in makes it (1) more likely that resistant microbes in your body will gain the upper hand and increase their "market share," (2) more likely that that particular antibiotic won't work for you in the future, and (3) more likely that when you pass your illness on to other people you will pass on resistant organisms.

The reality is that most infectious illness in humans comes from other humans. If those humans have been taking antibiotics, it follows that those same antibiotics are less likely to work for you. Other people's choices do affect yours. This "social contract" view of antibiotic prescribing is something we as a society need to discuss, but most people are still looking out for number one.

As you might imagine, there are many other principles that impinge on this discussion. Microbiology matters. It explains lots of things that I care about. Your expertise should have a similar central role in the questions you are passionate about. As a teacher, you should go one better; you should gain new expertise in areas outside your formal training. You should love the process of learning and be a voracious assimilator of ideas, and, especially, the propositions embodied in powerful principles.

I know the antibiotic use principle is provocative. On some level all of the principles in this chapter should be provocative because real learning *should* matter. It should engage us and our students in answering questions of significance about matters that we care about. I hope I got you thinking, whether you agree with my conclusions or not. If you don't agree, make certain that it is on the basis of principled reasoning and evidence!

How can you structure your course so that principled reasoning is the order of the day, each and every day? That's where we're going in the next chapter.

Chapter 6

This Is the Way: Designing the Optimal Learning Path

Knowing a subject is profoundly different from knowing how that subject is best learned.[1]

CARL WIEMAN

The previous three chapters have, I hope, made a strong case that lasting learning is based on understanding and that understanding is arrived at through a process of logical thought. Those chapters were written especially for you, the expert. They aimed at helping you to clarify your thinking so that you will be positioned to help your students.

However, it would be simplistic to think that your hard-won clarity about your academic domain can now be directly transferred to your students. As we have seen, the "teaching by telling" model is deeply ingrained in us, since we repetitively and nearly exclusively experienced this way of teaching through our formative and college years. It is our default setting whenever we think about teaching. It will take sustained conscious effort to resist its pull. Neither can we rely on the course textbook to do the job for us. The reality is that a textbook is a reference; it is a standardized source of information for which the students are accountable. Textbooks are primarily compendia of facts, not places where teaching goes on. Textbooks do not develop "the logic of the discipline." No doubt the author(s) understood the logic or they wouldn't be qualified to write the book, but the textbook is delivering content even if it says it is a conceptual approach.

The reality is that you are largely on your own if you are going to produce a course based on developing logical analytical thinking in your

---

1. Wieman, "'Curse of Knowledge,'" 8.

students. You probably need a textbook, but you are the pedagogue, not the textbook. The syllabus in my freshman General Biology course makes the distinction clear for my students: "The primary purposes of class time shall be to stimulate thought, promote discussion, and clarify definitions and the relationship of facts, concepts, and principles, rather than to present systematic factual subject matter in the form given in the text. . . . Class time will be used to do what no textbook can do: to *interactively* reason through the concepts of biology."[2]

I do require students to do assigned readings in the textbook, and they are expected to read analytically trying to dissect the thought process of the author(s). They don't start the semester in my class knowing how to read this way, so I need to teach them how to read. My students come to a class period expected to bring the understanding they have developed as well as the questions that have surfaced through their reading. Class time is spent developing conceptual and principial thinking through my interaction with the students. A class period is driven by deliberation on one or two big ideas or principles. Textbook reading at this level helps students prepare for the class discussion, but class discussion goes farther than the reading and involves engagement in thinking through the logic and the tentacles of big ideas or principles.

Archaeology and Purposeful Pedagogy

Generally when a building is constructed, there is a little digging that takes place at the construction site. Dirt is moved around to tame the topology of the site, and some excavation is done to allow for the pouring of concrete to serve as an underground foundation for the building. The structural integrity of the building is dependent on the quality of the foundation. This is not a place to skimp or to cut corners.

Occasionally when a building site is being prepared, construction is halted because something with archaeological significance has been unearthed. At that point archaeologists might be brought in to dig in a more restrained and deliberate way. Have you ever wondered why archaeology and the verb "dig" are so tightly coupled? The reason is that the passage of time naturally leads to an accumulation of dirt, especially so at places where human activity is not resisting the accumulation. This might be the case for an abandoned building in the country that is eventually absorbed so that there is no longer any trace of its existence on the surface.[3] I've

2. W. Michael Gray, "Bio 100: General Biology I Course Syllabus."
3 Anonymous, "Archaeology."

been surprised to learn while on vacation that there are major cities where the current street level of parts of downtown is built on top of an older city twelve to thirty feet below. In Atlanta[4] and Seattle[5] tours of parts of the old city are available.

I think there is a parallel between the science of archaeology and what you need to do in developing the pedagogy of your course. The passage of time in academia has caused modern courses to be built without regard for what is logically underneath them. It turns out there is quite a lot under most modern courses if one takes the time for "exploring the foundations, justification, implications, and value of [each important] fact, principle, skill, or concept"[6] on which the course is based. This is from Richard Paul's definition of higher-order learning, which, as he goes on to say, is *"Learning so as to deeply understand."*[7] Deep understanding is durable and extensible to solving real world problems. It's what we have been aiming for in the previous chapters. You and your students need to go on a dig together daily. You need to continue to excavate and explore together until your students arrive at deep understanding.

The concept of exploration alternately sounds like an adventure or a headache depending on whether you're the student or the teacher. Almost everyone likes an adventure, but explorations need to be planned; and planning can be a headache for teachers.

Perhaps the idea of preplanning your course sounds dangerously naive—something like lesson plans teachers in elementary and secondary schools are expected to produce. As a first year high school teacher firmly planted in a textbook-coverage model, I found that the plans I wrote out were exuberantly optimistic and that invariably a large chunk of what I had mapped out remained untaught at the end of the week. This leftover content was then transferred *en bloc* to the following week's lesson plan, a few days of new plans "crafted" (an overstatement for my first year), and the pattern would repeat throughout the semester. I quickly came to view the need to turn in weekly lesson plans as educational busy work for teachers—an imposition that was not helpful to me or to my students.

On the other hand, failing to preplan your course also sounds dangerously naive. As an anonymous sage has observed, "If you don't have a plan, your students will." There is a difference between planning as a straitjacket and planning as prudence.

---

4 Anonymous, "Underground Atlanta."
5 Anonymous, ""Seattle Underground."
6. Paul, *Critical Thinking: What Every Person Needs*, 649.
7. Ibid.

It is definitely true that learning cannot be engineered. I cannot *guarantee* an outcome in any of the courses I teach. Paul Ramsden tells us where to aim and what our expectations should be: "Teaching is comprehended as a process of working cooperatively with learners to help them change their understanding. It is making student learning possible."[8] That's it. You want to work with students to make learning possible. You don't want them to be unduly frustrated with the process. To the contrary, you want learning to be exciting, an adventure, insofar as that is possible. You want students also to experience the growth that occurs through hard intellectual effort. You want students at the end of the term to look back from higher vistas than they could have imagined when they began. You want them to view with satisfaction the obstacles overcome and the intellectual mountains climbed. You want them to think expectantly of higher peaks yet with an enthusiasm for learning that will propel them into next semester or into their careers.

Guided Exploration

Exploration focuses on the process as much as on the destination. It may take a long time and a lot of effort to get to the journey's end, but there should be joy on the journey. Every day in class, every assignment thoughtfully read, every project seriously engaged should produce satisfaction. Satisfaction comes through struggle and through personal growth; it comes through accomplishment. Accomplishment is the result of intentionality on the part of the guide who nudges and sometimes redirects. This is in contrast to unguided exploration where no one is serving as a guide and no one knows for sure how to get to the intended destination. No one enjoys being lost in the wilderness, least of all those who have paid a guide (teacher) who gets lost with them.

Exploration needs to be planned, but the essence of exploration is that it is not entirely predictable. This lack of predictability may seem to frustrate your efforts at planning. It is surely easier to plan when you control every aspect of the situation, but control is usually just an illusion. It is certainly an illusion to think that you control the learning process—that you can predictably alter someone else's mind. You can craft eloquent lectures and deliver them flawlessly with great passion, yet your students can sleep through it all or check out mentally with their eyes open and riveted on you.

I suggest that there are two major kinds of exploration and that both can be stimulating adventures. There is first of all pioneering exploration. My exemplar of this is Sir Ernest Shackleton, who set out with a group of

---

8. Ramsden, *Learning to Teach*, 110.

men to cross the continent of Antarctica in 1914. This story was immortalized in the book *Endurance: Shackleton's Incredible Voyage*.[9] At that time no one had crossed the Antarctic, so obviously there was no guide. The second type of exploration is guided. Guided exploration varies. The guide can be a seasoned veteran directing a rafting trip down the Colorado River through Grand Canyon. The guide in this case knows what to expect along the route and can point out things along the way. No two trips are ever exactly the same, but they are very similar because the rest of the group is largely passive and follows directions. A guided exploration variant is to backpack down a trail to the bottom of Grand Canyon and camp overnight next to the Colorado River. I did this hike with my family about a decade ago. We did the hike together, and none of us had ever hiked the canyon before. Our guide in this case was information from the National Park Service both from their website and from an informative DVD they sent once our backpacking permit was granted.

Pioneering exploration involves intense study and preplanning, but there are bound to be huge surprises along the way. The lives of Shackleton's crew depended on his preparation for the trip including the ship and its provisions. In those days the maps of Antarctica that Shackleton had access to were only approximations. When their ship was crushed by ice, their lives depended on the decision-making of their leader, Ernest Shackleton. The closest parallel to this in academia is original research conducted by a Principal Investigator and his graduate students. New graduate students are sometimes surprised to find out that their boss doesn't know for sure what results an investigation will yield! Whatever the results, the boss and his students will have to work together to figure out what they mean. They will have to work together to integrate their findings with the accepted models, or they will have to try to define new models and work to unseat the old ones because they don't work.

Many teachers would select the Grand Canyon rafting adventure as the parallel experience to teaching. The guide has been down the river dozens of times, and he knows mostly what his group will do. To be sure, the guide will put his crew to work using their oars when appropriate, but mostly the current will move them down the river. There are few surprises over the normal trip other than minor medical problems such as blisters, muscle soreness, or sprains. Planning here looks mostly like provisions and equipment plus planning the route and obtaining proper permits. If this is

---

9. Lansing, *Endurance*. The story was also immortalized in the film *Shackleton's Great Adventure*.

your view, you'll expect this chapter to be fairly cut and dried. The preplanning will be a variant of what you are already used to in planning a course.

I would maintain that the backpacking trip of Grand Canyon is a better approximation of the role of the teacher. I helped to plan the trip, but I was also very much a learner and a participant. I learned from websites and the Park Service DVD that people die hiking the canyon every year—mostly because of poor preparation and overconfidence. I learned what I could expect from the weather; what facilities were available (almost none on the trail), how much water, Gatorade, and food to carry and consume; the kind of hiking shoes to use; how to keep our feet from developing blisters; the kind of fitness that was required to make it down to the bottom of the canyon and back up to the top! The trip was not old hat, not just because I hadn't hiked the full trail previously, but also because I was exerting myself every bit as much as the rest of the family. This would be true no matter how many times I had previously hiked the canyon. An effective teacher in a natural critical learning environment is working as hard as (or harder than) anyone else in the room. His planning provides the resources that will be needed for the semester and for the class period, but his planning is not a straitjacket. He is exploring along with his students. He is helping them to avoid pitfalls and intellectual blisters, to slow down if someone is falling behind, to adjust their backpacks, to redistribute weight through cooperative learning, to stop and ponder and take a drink or get some nutrients through a short informational burst (mini-lecture) and then it's back on the trail. He is always learning from his students and their differing perspectives and processing. There is always more exploring to do!

Defining the Optimum

Teaching for deep understanding within a way of thinking requires more of your students, and it requires a lot more of you in planning and implementation than teaching by telling. On what basis can we say that teaching a way of thinking is the optimum educational experience? Is it actually a pretty close call?

An optimum is as good as it gets. The optimum educational experience is the best experience of achieving learning compared to alternative approaches. I suggest that the criteria we use to judge what is optimum be those listed in the table below.

Please fill in the table (using a separate sheet of paper).

On a scale of 1-10 with 10 representing the best possible score, compare teaching by transmission (teaching by telling, the traditional model) with teaching a way of thinking through a learner-centered approach as advocated in this book. Your rating should reflect the comparative benefit for an average student. Please try to restrict yourself to one criterion at a time, although it is artificial to do so.

Criterion	Telling	A Way of Thinking
Content Coverage		
Efficient Use of Class Time		
Efficiency of Learning		
Depth of Understanding		
Durability of Knowledge		
Student Ownership		
Problem Solving		

Do not go on until you have completed your ratings.

I'll put my thoughts in the footnotes. Don't peek! I don't want my thoughts or data to influence your ratings.[10]

---

10. When I've used this rating form with university faculty, the telling model is rated higher with regard to content coverage (how much you can get through in a class period or in a semester) and with regard to efficiency in the use of time. Teaching a way of thinking focuses explicitly on the remaining criteria and is rated significantly higher than telling for all of the rest. Teaching thinking is the more efficient method of producing real learning. Such learning lasts (is durable) because it is owned by the individual student, and it is valuable because its depth allows students to apply their understanding to solving real-world problems. In the final analysis the coverage advantage for telling dissolves because so little is remembered or is applicable to solving problems. This means that telling is really not a time-efficient method in spite of the feeling teachers get when they are in coverage mode. The actual number ratings are of less significance in this form than the clear message that teaching thinking is superior to teaching by telling.

I know that the best traditional teachers can be polished in their delivery and passionate about their area of expertise. Students can even enjoy and be inspired by being in their classrooms. I'm not questioning any of that.

Coaching Is the Essence of Teaching

It is entirely appropriate and commendable for a teacher to have a passion to communicate her academic passion. The weakest link when the goal for the student is understanding is the frailty of communication. Communicating mere content as is done in most classrooms can be done with some effectiveness (though it doesn't endure) so long as the assessment rewards mere recall of the content (good as it may be). Teaching students how to *think* in a domain-specific manner is quite another matter. Thinking cannot simply be transferred. In the final analysis the student will have to do the thinking. No doubt you have to be thinking too so that you can help his thinking to get better. You are hiking Grand Canyon together, but you are not carrying your student. The student has to hike too.

A useful tried metaphor for teaching is to consider yourself to be a coach.[11] Poor coaching can cause the game to be lost, but probably more often the game is lost by the players who haven't internalized or aren't executing the coach's game plan. This kind of thing causes enormous stress for college football coaches every fall. The alumni expect their team to win, but the smartest coach in the world is dependent on the *performance* of eighteen to twenty-two year olds. Seldom will an impassioned half-time locker room speech by the coach turn around a 0-21 deficit because smart play is more about correct player thinking than it is about his emotional intensity.

Teaching for understanding is a process, not an act that is discharged by delivering an articulate and impassioned lecture during a given class period. As the teacher, I have to keep working and I have to cooperate with the learners. I have to take into account the kind of learners I have and work within their strengths and weaknesses. I have to diagnose and prescribe. I have to give them a path for changing their *own* thinking. They have thought they have understood some things, and in certain respects they have *mis*understood. I have to help them recognize when they have misunderstood, and I have to help them recognize a different and better way of thinking that they eventually embrace and internalize to the point that their conceptual frameworks change to more closely resemble those of an expert. As a result, their correct understanding of concepts allows them

---

11. Dunn, "Winning Teacher," 1–2.

to solve appropriate problems. Understanding becomes the benchmark of my (and their) success.

This is a quantum leap in expectation. Instead of being an academic figure who can lecture with some coherence, you're expected to be a coach with the requisite diagnostic skills and developmental focus. Eric Mazur of Harvard is someone who has undergone this transition personally, and he says faculty need to move from "teaching" to "helping students learn."[12] The cooperative nature of your new role demands that you learn more about your students to help diagnose the nature of their comprehension difficulties. You have to be right there with them as they struggle. As if that weren't enough, you need to help them develop as thinkers. Exactly what do the developmental processes look like that will enable intellectual growth? These are the questions we'll concern ourselves with in this chapter as we look at designing our courses to optimize student understanding.

Diagnosis Precedes Design

I teach at an open admission university. We take all comers with a high school diploma or its equivalent (e.g., GED). Perhaps you teach in a university with some level of selective admission. Regardless of your situation, you must teach the students you actually have, not a hypothetical group of students. For those of us who have been teaching for a long time, it is tempting to pine for the days when students were better prepared, more focused on learning, had a stronger work ethic, or whatever. Rather than looking at today's students as "the dumbest generation,"[13] you need to simply recognize who you have in your classroom. This is not to say that your aspirations for the student have slid to all-time lows. The reality is that the complexity of our society and the challenges that face us are at all-time highs. We need to try to prepare the students we *do* have for the challenges they *will* face. The gap between these two realities is growing. That is not cause for despair but motivation to seek radical (but proven) solutions. This is no time for business as usual in education; we must find and implement the optimal path for learning. I believe the optimal path involves a focus on changing thinking and leads to deep understanding and personal ownership of the learning by the student. Understanding is power.

World Cup soccer is dominating the sports news as I write this chapter, so I'll use soccer coaching as a simple accessible analogy to what you need to consider as you design your course for optimal student learning.

12. Lambert, "Twilight of the Lecture," 23-27.
13. Bauerlein, *Dumbest Generation*.

Obviously soccer coaching begins with the reality of the kind of players the coach has to work with. Development of the players can't proceed very well without taking into account the strengths and weaknesses of the roster for the season. Drills and strategy are not developed in a vacuum by the coaching staff; diagnosis must precede the design of strategy.

Before you design your course, you typically look at the prerequisites for your course. Whether the prerequisites are previous courses or minimum ACT/SAT scores, they tell you something about who you will be teaching. If you teach a first-year course, you'll have to stay abreast of what kind of students you are getting from high schools; what does an A or a B in a foundational high school course mean? This is similar to the recruiting process in college soccer where recruits are sized up in play while they are still in high school and possibly later in a tryout with the coaching staff. You don't conduct academic tryouts, but on some level your school does in the admission and credit transfer evaluation process. With your knowledge of student background in hand, your course must be designed to meet them where they are, or you will lose the opportunity to engage them in learning. (If you ever learned how to drive a stick-shift car, you know that you have to start in first gear or you'll stall the engine.)

Diagnosis Informs Design

Soccer recruits who show up for training camp aren't expected to play a full game immediately. They may have worked out during the summer on their own, but they don't yet have the stamina to play the game at full tilt. The level of player conditioning is evident early on to the coaching staff, and their response is to design an appropriate conditioning process to get players ready for game day and the season.

Soccer recruits don't arrive at training camp fully known as soccer players no matter how effective the scouting and recruiting process was. There is no substitute for on-site assessment. As the coaching staff puts them through drills and in scrimmage situations, strengths and weaknesses surface. This is still part of the diagnostic process. As surprises about the recruits surface, there is still time for the staff to do something about them. Perhaps they'll move a player to a new position she is better suited for. Perhaps additional practice exercises are indicated for some of the recruits. The beauty of all this is that the season hasn't started yet. A breakdown in a practice or a loss in a scrimmage game or a preseason game is a wakeup call and may indicate that the team needs a lot more coaching before the first game of the season. These kinds of adverse events are where coaches earn their paychecks. Good coaches respond to diagnosis with design (not despair!). The design is a response to what the diagnosis reveals. The design is intentional. The coach has a range of design options, and he purposely chooses one or more of the options in direct response to the diagnostic information.

How can this soccer wisdom be applied to the academic realm? Don't expect your students to arrive at the beginning of your course in the peak of intellectual condition. There is an eagerness in many students at the beginning of the semester, but don't confuse willingness to learn with readiness to learn. Your students need some conditioning drills, some skill assessment, and a preseason mentality (ungraded or low-risk exercises). Your students need to be sold on your approach to the course and the benefits that it promises them. That should be the main thing about the first day of class (not your syllabus, which they can read). They need to be prepared for being intellectually out of breath and be persuaded that you know how to get them into shape and get them accomplishing at a level high enough to reach the goals you promise on day one.

Perhaps the soccer coaching metaphor can be pushed a bit farther. Good soccer coaches work year-round and not just during soccer season. During the offseason coaches ponder lessons learned from the past season and look for additional coaching insight through coaching publications, conferences, and networking. All of these actions fundamentally relate to the process of diagnosis. Diagnosis in the offseason is a calm and deliberate affair compared to the rest of the year. Design options can be evaluated deliberately without the pressure of games and teams. Coaches can be persuaded during the off-season to do something radical that they would never attempt during the season without a lot of lead-time for development.

That's where this book comes in. I'm making a case for a radical redesign of your course, and I hope you'll seriously entertain that idea the next time you are in the off-season. That's entirely appropriate and wise. Be thoughtful and deliberate. Radical redesign should not be conducted rashly. I especially encourage you to be much more intentional about diagnosing your students as you look toward next season. Look seriously at your course evaluations, paying particular attention to any comments. Perhaps there is some truth there. Perhaps you need something equivalent to a conditioning program, a skills development program, or something else that you haven't previously thought was your responsibility. This coaching metaphor says you are not successful unless your players (students) are successful. Coaching focuses on the reality of the team you've got rather than a dream team you wish you had. Coaching is individualized; it helps individuals reach their full potential. Look at your "team." Do any of the following look like your class? Students don't read analytically; they don't know how to extract the main point from a line of argument; they can't take notes properly; they don't know how to study for your kind of test; they can't evaluate their own thinking and performance accurately; and so on. Has it occurred to you (while you're in the off-season) that you need to help in these areas or others? These things don't magically get taken care of by referring students to the Academic Resource Center on your campus. I'll give you some guidance about these things in the next chapter.

Another application of soccer coaching pertains to the concept of a preseason. Perhaps you should design one into your course. I know that most of your colleagues will be playing "the first game" on the first or second day of their courses, but perhaps your students would be well served by a short preseason? In the preseason you assess and diagnose like crazy. You need to know where each player stands in readiness for the season. The intent of your diagnosis is to change the current reality. Your players need to know what to work on before they get into the season where every game counts (graded assignments). What developmental options can you offer your players? (You would choose among the options you designed in the offseason.)

Diagnosis and adjustments aren't over once the soccer season starts. Performance under game conditions either validates the design or calls it into question. It is usually not wise to abandon your game plan during the game, but the game might highlight the weakness of your strategy—at least a weakness in light of what that particular opponent is using. Perhaps as the opponents get stronger, different strategies are appropriate, or at least a difference in emphasis would improve the outcome. Adjustment at the point of demonstrated need is often called tactics. Strategy and tactics are important components of soccer and of the way you and your students respond to various intellectual challenges as the semester progresses. A good coach (a good teacher) has an appropriate level of flexibility as he approaches a difficult team (or intellectual task); he doesn't stick rigidly to a strategy that isn't working.

The Importance of the Fundamentals

Every successful coach stresses with his players the importance of developing sound fundamentals. Soccer coaching is no different. The National Soccer Coaches Association of America lists six fundamental skills that soccer players need to develop proficiency in: dribbling, receiving, passing, shooting, heading, and tackling.[14] These skills are primarily physical. The

---

14. Anonymous, "Soccer Fundamentals."

mental aspect for players is to know when to execute a particular skill. For coaches the fundamental reality is that "Soccer is a series of 1 v. 1 duels all over the field. . . . the team that wins the majority of these duels is likely to win the game."[15] The other major coaching fundamental is to help players learn to move to the proper place on the field given the position they play on the team and what the other team is doing.[16]

This is a significant simplification of the game of soccer, but it is not a misrepresentation or oversimplification. I believe that learning can profitably be simplified in a parallel manner. There are eight components of the thinking process that we considered earlier. You can think of these as intellectual skills, and they apply to every domain of thought. That means that the mastery of these intellectual skills is fundamental to learning. Your course should be a place where students adopt a particular *point of view* with a precise *motivation* and the goal of answering certain *questions* (the core of logic). The core controls the other dimensions of the thinking process. Most thinking goes on in the working layer, which consists of *assumptions*, *information* (facts) and a developing *conceptual framework*. Thinking becomes manifest in the output layer where questions are answered (*explanation*) and *implications* and *consequences* are explored. Details of this approach to thinking, the logic of a discipline, are found in chapter 3. It is your job as an academic coach to help your students learn to think within the logic of your discipline. Your discipline is particularly distinguished by the questions it attempts to answer and the concepts it characteristically employs in its explanations. The core concepts of your discipline are typically used to formulate principles. Concepts and principles were developed in chapters 4 and 5 respectively.

Academics are prone to lose their focus on the fundamentals. As I indicated particularly in chapter 2, academics are prone to focus on information rather than the thinking process that led to the information. Your job is to teach a way of thinking, and your students will be successful when they demonstrate facility with that kind of thinking. Your course must be designed intentionally to develop facility with the thinking of your academic domain. Don't allow content to be the tail that wags the dog. Content will take care of itself if your students learn to think deeply. Factual recall is a byproduct of understanding. Understanding is achieved only by intentionally focusing on its development through the process of logical thought.

The fundamentals of your course are the specific manifestations of the eight intellectual skills as they are used in your domain of thought. Since

15. Anonymous, "Soccer Tactics."
16. Anonymous, "Soccer Teaching Model."

thinking is driven by ideas and since the most powerful ideas are principles, your course should be principle-driven. You need to develop course principles based on the approach detailed in chapters 4 and 5. You can't plan your course properly unless you've identified the underlying principles. Principles are the propositions that are used in answering the intriguing questions that your discipline can engage. Consider taking a break from this chapter until you have identified at least a few principles that will drive your course. Having identified some principles will make what follows much less theoretical.

Design Backward

I've just argued that your course should be principle-driven. The fundamentals of your course are the principles, so start with the principles and design around them experiences that will engage students in principle-based reasoning. Other educators argue that courses should be designed around "desired results" and tell teachers to "consider up front how they will determine if students have attained the desired understandings."[17] Assessibility becomes key in this view. On the other hand, realistically if a student doesn't care about your course, it is unlikely that she will put forth the mental effort required to develop her thinking in your domain (or even stoop to memorize content in a content-driven course). Is relevance and student motivation therefore the starting point for course design? What should be the priority in course design? Who is right?

There is a happy answer to this question of priority. All of these are right. Before you turn me off as hopelessly illogical, let me explain that all of these points of view can be harmonized and that is how they are all, in a partial sense, correct. Ken Bain explains that "the best teachers plan their courses backward, deciding what students should be able to do by the end of the semester[;] they map a series of intellectual developments through the course with the goal of encouraging students to learn on their own, engaging them in deep thinking."[18] That certainly sounds like the "desired results" approach, especially with the emphasis on students' ability to "do" something (assessibility). Ah, but who determines the desired results? Is it some academic or government agency? Is it the student? How about the professor? Can you decide what you want the student to be able to do? Indeed you can, and if you're still with me on the centrality of principles, the student should be able to demonstrate understanding (by explanation or ap-

---

17. Wiggins and McTighe, *Understanding by Design*, 18.
18. Bain, *What the Best College Teachers Do*, 114.

plication) using the principles that the course is driven by. "OK, you say, but that still may be perceived as arbitrary by the student, and then she won't work on the course." That's possible, but consider this: "[The best college teachers] ask students to solve intellectual, artistic, practical, and abstract problems that *the students find intriguing, beautiful, and important.*"[19] Bain says elsewhere in his book that "students encounter the skills, habits, attitudes, and information they are trying to learn embedded in questions and tasks they find fascinating—authentic tasks that arouse curiosity and become intrinsically interesting."[20]

The one piece that Bain leaves out is the focus on principles that I am advocating as the primary tool for clear thinking. Questions that students finding intriguing should be the means by which you draw them into principle-based thinking. It is up to you to find questions that can inspire students and to which your academic domain with its principle base can provide satisfying answers. A group of such questions should be the backbone of your course. Actually there should be a question on the table that drives every class period of the semester in your course.

Constructing a Learning Environment

Here is a suggested process focusing on questions to catalyze your high-level course planning:

1. Start your course planning with a list of essential compelling questions that will be answered over the semester. Half a dozen big questions are plenty at this point. Questions always lead to more questions, but don't concern yourself right now with those additional questions that may drive a class period or two.

2. How is your discipline uniquely positioned through its point of view to answer these questions?

3. Arrange the questions based on the principle(s) that provide(s) the rationale for answering each question. (You'll need a list of course principles developed on the basis of chapter 5).

4. Determine a logical order in which to consider the questions and develop the relevant explanatory principles. You'll find that this is not a linear process. (A concept map of your course can be very helpful here. See chapter 4 for details.)

---

19. Ibid., 95 (emphasis mine).
20. Ibid., 99.

Remembering that you can't simply transfer to your students the thinking that you come up with through this question-driven course planning exercise, how will you place them in a situation from which they can escape only by thinking? Don Finkel in his provocative book, *Teaching with Your Mouth Shut*, talks about teaching as fundamentally organizing student inquiry.[21] Initially the teacher sets the task, but it is the student who does the inquiring. If the task is worthy, the student is fully committed as he asks questions and puts his skills to work.

In 1967 my aerospace engineer dad changed careers, drastically, to go into cross-cultural ministry. In preparation for living under primitive conditions my family (except for me) went through survival training. Survival is a pretty potent and motivating word! The training was about six months in duration. It began with a short didactic introduction to the basics of survival in the jungle, and then the family was led on a hike of several days' duration into the Guatemalan jungles, far away from civilization. Their first task was to construct housing that would shelter the family for months. Once the "house" was built, they had to construct a mud "stove" on which food would be prepared. Food was mostly whatever the jungle had to offer supplemented by a shipment of flour, sugar, salt, and a few other staples that arrived by river several weeks into their stay. After several months and some additional training, my father was led another day or two into the jungle and "abandoned" for three days with only the clothes on his back. He subsisted on whatever he could find. He got water from licking droplets off of the bottom of leaves in the early morning. He ate slugs that he found crawling on vegetation and ate plants that were deemed safe. Such was his final exam, immersed as he was in a critical learning environment. As you can imagine, the learning that occurred in this context was deep and durable!

Don Finkel talks in similar terms about a teacher-created environment:

> Problems . . . teach by their very structure. They don't Tell directly. Rather they encourage the making of discoveries. They create an intellectual environment with a shape—an environment with constraints, demands, orientations, limits, opportunities, and invitations—and they set the students free in it. They don't do the necessary thinking for the students and announce the results. They require the students to think for themselves, to find their own results, and then to test them in new circumstances. In this way, they lead to learning that lasts.[22]

---

21. Finkel, *Teaching with Your Mouth Shut*, 59.
22. Ibid., 93.

The teacher determines the problem or the question, but the students are the ones who pursue the inquiry and who learn as a result.

The central purpose of the inquiry is to change student thinking. In designing the learning, the teacher recognizes that the student will try to use her existing conceptual framework as long as possible. Some of her concepts will be enriched through the inquiry, and some of them will be shown to be misconceptions. Student inquiry is designed by the teacher to confront common misconceptions and conventional wisdom by creating "cognitive dissonance." Misconceptions are notoriously difficult to unseat, but when the student is repetitively confronted with the insufficiency of her existing understanding, she becomes receptive to remodeling her conceptual framework with superior alternatives that surface.[23] Learning is conceptual change. If concepts don't change, learning hasn't taken place. Conceptualization is therefore central to how we learn. In a classic article Posner et al. make this connection explicit: "Intelligibility . . . requires constructing . . . a coherent representation of what a passage or theory is saying. . . . no theory can function psychologically at all unless it is internally represented by the individual."[24]

Conceptualization, although a personal construction project, can be made more efficient in a variety of ways. These include (1) having the students read materials that do not all take the same position on a question; (2) requiring the student to sort through the disagreement and defend one of the positions or verbalize an alternative position; (3) verbalization that will ideally be in the presence of other students (the whole class or a small group) and/or the teacher, whose presence will help the student to be more clear and concrete than she would be in her own mind in isolation; (4) teachers who can help the student to clarify her thinking through Socratic dialogue with the student; and (5) writing projects that can force a degree of clarity in her thinking that is difficult to match through oral verbalization. This is only a partial list, but it is an indication that conceptualization benefits from structure. You don't simply throw your student into a challenging environment and admonish her to "Think!" without any direction whatsoever. It should also be noted that thinking is refined through interaction with others, even one's peers who may not have it quite right either.

---

23. Posner, "Accommodation of a Scientific Conception," 214.
24. Ibid., 216.

A Compelling Narrative

The learning scenarios you create should all require students to participate in the very process that experts use to answer questions in your academic domain. Learning scenarios should be carefully crafted as a means to the end of learning, that is, changing student thinking. If all that students leave your course with is a recollection of the scenario itself ("We had to read Martin Luther King Jr.'s *Letter from the Birmingham Jail*, but I don't know why"), your scenario has failed. It may have failed because the student failed to reckon with the question that he was supposed to answer as he reflectively engaged in this reading assignment. Additionally, it may not have been clear to the student that this scenario was not isolated from the rest of the course. There should be a logic that holds the whole course together as a unity, and for some reason the student has failed to see the big picture. The synergy of interconnected scenarios can be a powerful thing, but only when the connections are seen by the average student.

The best way to connect your course and give it an organic unity is by crafting a narrative for the course. This shouldn't be too hard—after all you are trying to teach "a *way* of thinking" to your students. Narrative helps us to tie things together so that we can always find our place. If that sounds simplistic, consider the fact that each us has a narrative through which we interpret our entire lives and into which we integrate the varied experiences and realities we encounter. We call it our worldview.[25] Your worldview is a cognitive construct. It is the lens through which you view the world. You also need to construct a lens for your course. This is really just another way of saying that your course embodies a point of view. Your discipline positions you to look at the world in a certain way and to entertain a particular group of questions that you will think deeply about. What is the common denominator among those questions? This is the path to crafting a course narrative to which all of the learning scenarios are connected like chapters in a book.

How do you write these "chapters" of your course? There is no template except that all of the "chapters" need to require engagement with a question that students care about that serves the end of pulling them into conceptualization, explanation, and application. To make them maximally powerful, all of the "chapters" need to tell or to utilize a story.

---

25 Anonymous, "Worldview." "The framework of ideas and beliefs forming a global description through which an individual, group or culture watches and interprets the world and interacts with it."

The story could be a detailed case study into which you place your students. It could be an analogy that you ask your students to critique, or it could be something intermediate in length, a parable perhaps.

Certain kinds of literature make extensive use of the compact stories that we call parables. Don Finkel makes a case for using parables: "[T]hey make effective teaching devices. Their concreteness, specificity, and narrative organization capture our attention. Their profundity—that they seem to signify more than simply the story itself—engages our intellect. We want to figure out what the story is 'trying to tell us.'"[26] We are all familiar with the mesmerizing power of stories as communicated in *One Thousand and One Nights* told by Scheherazade, who keeps the king from executing her through a series of interconnected stories each with a "cliffhanger" ending. The king didn't execute her as he intended because he wanted to know how the story ended, and she never really got to the absolute end![27] Never getting to the end can be frustrating for students, so be certain that they can experience a sense of accomplishment by successfully getting to the end of each of your learning scenarios (chapters).

Proverbs, parables, short stories (longer than parables), essays, book chapters, novels and other kinds of literary works can all be used to great advantage in structuring a wide variety of learning scenarios. "For the kind of learning that centers on numbers or the physical world rather than human relationships, there exists something very like the parable, and that is the puzzle, paradox, or perplexing problem. . . . It is, like a story, concrete and engaging. . . . it clearly has an answer, and it is sufficiently intriguing to make us curious about the answer. . . . it does not yield its treasure easily."[28] As a scientist, solving perplexing problems is my M.O. In some of my courses, my students solve problems together as the heart of most class periods. In the process they conceptualize and they recognize the fruitfulness of their maturing mental constructs in solving yet more riddles that they have learned to care deeply about.

We seem to be hard-wired to be hooked by stories. If novelists can induce you to take their stories with you on vacation to the beach, don't you think our students can be motivated to drink from the fountain of knowledge through the power of stories? The *New York Times* best-selling authors Chip and Dan Heath argue that stories are an intrinsic part of successful communication of any idea. By successful communication they mean that the idea sticks. It is remembered and it is acted on. The Heath brothers

---

26. Finkel, *Teaching with Your Mouth Shut*, 13.
27. Various, "One Thousand and One Nights."
28. Finkel, *Teaching with Your Mouth Shut*. 16.

happen to be in the business world, but they recognize that their ideas work in the educational context as well.

The Heath brothers argue that effective communication requires the SUCCESs framework:

- Simple message
- Unexpected turn
- Concrete (details)
- Credible (plausible)
- Emotion (caring elicited)
- Story (backbone of the communication)[29]

It is not an overstatement to call stories the backbone of communication. "Stories can almost single-handedly defeat the Curse of Knowledge. In fact, they naturally embody most of the SUCCESs framework. Stories are almost always Concrete. Most of them have Emotional and Unexpected elements. The hardest part of using stories effectively is making sure that they're Simple—that they reflect your core message."[30] Notice too the echo of Don Finkel (quoted earlier in this chapter) in the Heath brothers SUCCESs bullet points. Finkel zeroes in on concreteness, specificity (related to credibility), narrative (the story line), profundity (combination of emotion that draws us in and an unexpected element); and, of course, parables are compact—their message is simply stated.

Holding Yourself Accountable

Embedding your learning scenarios in a narrative is a very powerful strategy for pulling your students into the learning environment you are creating. Remember that the point of engaging your students is to aid them in the hard work of conceptualization. Make certain that you make your goals for the learning scenario clear to yourself and clear to your students. You are aiming for deep learning in your students as they work within the logic of your discipline.

As you craft learning scenarios, it is important that you hold yourself accountable for clear instructional design. What do you intend for the student to gain through each learning scenario? What are your intentions for the course as a whole? Although you're still in the planning stages of the

---

29. Heath and Heath, *Made to Stick*, 14-18.
30. Ibid., 237.

course, you absolutely must think about what you expect the student to be able to do and how you plan to assess it. The most straightforward way to focus yourself is through writing carefully worded learning outcomes for your course. Most faculty have learning outcomes in their course syllabi because accrediting bodies expect them, not because the faculty member views them as otherwise important. Course learning outcomes (or objectives) are often dashed off without a lot of thought—saying things that sound good but which are incidental to the course. It's a rare faculty member who thinks long and hard about learning outcomes, but you must. Take the time to think deeply about the kind of thinking you expect the student to regularly engage in through your class learning scenarios. How do you plan to evaluate the quality and depth of their thinking? The superficial answer is to point to quizzes, tests, papers, projects, or something else as the assessment tool. That's a start, but I'm asking that you focus deeper. How will the student demonstrate that she is thinking effectively within the logic of your discipline on a test or in a paper she writes? I know that's an assessment question, but you must think of the end as you plan at the beginning. Everything in your course should be intentional, and all of it should be aligned with your course learning outcomes.

Since everything should be aligned with your course learning outcomes, writing the learning outcomes is enormously important. They need to be the result of significant deliberation and demonstrate exceptionally clear thinking that you're willing to hold yourself accountable to and have your students and others hold you accountable to. I view the entire course syllabus as a learning contract that spells out the responsibilities of the teacher and the learner, the teacher's philosophy of teaching and learning, course structure, and promised learning rewards for students who diligently apply themselves.[31] When you write learning outcomes, make sure you center on what the student will be able to do, rather than on what you will be doing. After all, these are learning outcomes, not teacher inputs. Since you intend to teach a way of thinking, you must assess the facility that students are gaining with thinking that way. Since your course should be principle-driven, make certain that your learning outcomes focus on the course principles. Since you should teach for understanding and not mere recall, that reality should come out loud and clear in your outcomes.

Outcomes are usually written in the form of "The student will be able to _____." The blank is filled with a phrase that captures what the student needs to demonstrate her ability to think about and the level that her

---

31. O'Brien, *Course Syllabus*. This is a helpful resource for recasting your syllabus or crafting a new one with the learner at the center of your communication.

thinking should be done on. An example in a sociology course might be "The student will be able to cogently critique the current U.S. immigration policy employing sociological principles." To be able to offer a cogent critique, the student needs to know what the current U.S. immigration policy is; she must understand and apply relevant sociological principles; finally, she must know the strengths and weaknesses of current policy as viewed from multiple perspectives (this is basic to sociology). Here the reference to principle is explicit in the learning outcome. More often principles are not referenced directly. If you were writing an appropriate outcome for this sociology course, there should be at least one sociological principle at its base. It should be a broad sociological principle (currently unelaborated on because principles need to be derived through the thinking of the student) that is embodied in the way an idea, example, or case is handled in the course. As you write course learning outcomes, pay particular attention to the verb you use in the learning outcome. In the example just given, "to critique" is a form of evaluation. If the verb were switched to "describe," the level of learning expected would be significantly reduced. In either case, the assessment needs to focus on the stated level of thinking.[32] Your course should be focused on understanding. Understanding is demonstrated in a variety of ways including the ability to analyze, to explain, to apply, to solve relevant problems, and to make appropriate inferences.

There are many helpful resources available for planning your course, helpful as long as you keep the synthesis that I'm advocating in mind. *Don't lose your principles!* This chapter ends with a brief annotated bibliography to sources that provide lists and even templates to guide your course planning.[33]

[32]. Ambrose, *How Learning Works*, 244-47. This is a short, accessible introduction to the basics of writing learning outcomes. A more extensive treatment is found in Norman E. Gronlund, *How to Write and Use Instructional Objectives*, 6th ed. (Upper Saddle River, NJ: Merrill, 2000). Chapter 5, "Writing Objectives for Higher-Level Thinking Skills," pp. 49-56, is particularly helpful.

[33]. To guide you through the mechanics of course design I recommend *Understanding by Design*, which is available in an expanded 2nd edition. It was written by Grant Wiggins and Jay McTighe. There is also a workbook available, *Understanding by Design Professional Development Workbook* by Jay McTighe and Grant Wiggins, and a website: http://ubdexchange.org. A second resource is Ken Bain's iconic book, *What the Best College Teachers Do*. Bain's book is written more on the conceptual level, but the ideas he explores are simultaneously simple and profound. Bain's book is illuminated by concrete examples from the courses of many of the best college teachers that he identified in a fifteen-year study. Bain provides a few detailed lists including thirteen points on preparing to teach (his chapter 3), characteristics of a natural critical learning environment (his pp. 99-109), and seven principles for conducting class (his chapter 5). A third recommendation is *Made to Stick* by Chip and Dan Heath. Surprisingly, this is a business book; but learning is all about making ideas endure, and the Heath brothers have much to offer as you plan for principles to drive your course. Pages 266-80 are a

If you want to follow the coaching metaphor further in thinking about your course, refer to this footnote.[34]

This chapter has encouraged you to create a natural critical learning environment and to populate it with compelling learning scenarios that have an organic narrative unity. In each scenario your students will be

---

section called "Teaching that Sticks," but all of the book is practical and helpful in developing the SUCCESs model of messaging. A fourth recommendation is *Teaching with Your Mouth Shut* by Don Finkel. Finkel taught literature, and his thoughtful book will be especially helpful for those in the humanities. The title rightly presages an argument for a radical reformulation of the role of the teacher. Finkel taught at Evergreen State College, where students have no majors and don't get grades, so some of what he says may not be practical in your school. Chapter 4 of his book, "Let Us Inquire Together," is helpful for basing a course on inquiry. Finkel's chapter 6, "Experiences That Teach: Creating Blueprints for Learning," is especially helpful in crafting learning scenarios. Finally, one of the best books on writing instructional learning outcomes and using them to align your course is *Teaching for Quality Learning at University*, by John Biggs and Catherine Tang. Chapter 5 on designing learning outcomes is a classic. Chapter 8 is helpful in making certain you focus your learning scenarios on higher order learning, and chapter 9 helps to make certain your learning outcomes are aligned with the assessment you will employ.

34. Make a table with two columns. The items below are taken from coaching and constitute the first column in your table. Feel free to reorder these items. The second column you will fill in with aspects of your course by which you intend to flesh out the concept in academic terms.

Recruiting
Conditioning process
Fitness
Stamina
Scrimmage
Collaborative nature of a team
Solid fundamentals
Feedback to players
Coach as facilitator—not a player
Thinking within the system
Understanding the game
Decision-making on the fly in the game
Defining success
Timeouts to regroup
Ability to improvise
Scouting of opponents
Strength of schedule (start with weaker opponents?)
Reaching potential
Respect for the coach
Playbook
Off-season
Preseason
Season
Postseason

actively involved in conceptualizing with the aim of answering the absorbing questions your course is based on. Your students will need to be able to demonstrate understanding of concepts and principles in ways that you've clearly defined. In the next chapter we'll look at the course you've planned, but this time from the standpoint of the student experiencing your course. What will you add and what will you subtract as you strive to optimize your course for the sake of student learning?

Chapter 7

Student Flourishing

Surface and deep approaches to learning are not personality traits, as is sometimes thought, but are most usefully thought of as reactions to the teaching environment.[1]

JOHN BIGGS AND CATHERINE TANG

The learning environment you craft for your students is not an obstacle course designed to trip them up; neither is it an arena in which you can show them how much smarter you are than they. You are seeking their highest good. You want them to do better than you have done. You want them to flourish—to thrive, to grow at the maximum rate possible. Flourishing is a lofty goal, perhaps a higher goal than your students have for themselves. Perhaps they are disenchanted with education and view college as more of the same, just a means to an occupational credential, nothing more. Perhaps they are apathetic and don't view personal change, much less institutional or societal change as even a possibility. Your love of the process of learning (and not just your academic domain) needs to beckon them to a world they are currently unable to imagine. Your course needs to be a path for your students into the world of great ideas and to personal transformation through energetic wrestling with those ideas.[2]

---

1. Biggs and Tang, *Teaching for Quality Learning,*, 29.
2. This academic ideal is well expressed by Ken Bain: "Imagine for a moment a different world, a place in which students find deep meaning in everything they learn. In that universe, learning changes who people are and how they view the world. It makes them into better problem solvers, more creative and compassionate individuals, more responsible and self-confident people. Students are able to think about the implications and applications of what they learn. Not afraid to make mistakes and full of questions and ideas, the citizens of this place easily and happily explore new areas with ease while possessing a deep humility about how complex their world can be. Learning

Learning is ultimately done by the learners. Teachers who focus on anything else are misguided. The role of the teacher is to create an instructional environment that maximizes the likelihood of learning. Since students are individuals whose learning is idiosyncratic (in part because of differing conceptual frameworks), different students will respond differently to and require different kinds of support and challenge within the learning environment that is your course. The students themselves are one of the features of the environment. You will need to get to know your students so that you can help them. More fundamentally, your students will need to get to know themselves so that they can help themselves.

Many authors in the field of education divide students on the basis of their preferred learning orientation as surface or deep learners. Surface learners view learning as an ordeal to be endured and to be completed as quickly as possible. They want to find the path of least resistance through a learning environment, usually through memorization. Depending on their ability to memorize, they may be capable of some impressive feats; but at the bottom, they are not really interested in learning. The process of conceptualization is a mysterious black box to surface learners, and they'd prefer to keep the lid on that box. Like runners making their way through an obstacle course, they are not interested in stopping to smell the roses.

Deep learners are intrinsically motivated to explore ideas and their connections with other ideas. Conceptualization is always underway in their minds. Compare and contrast is their daily habit. They learn for the sheer joy of learning, and they frequently lose track of time as they go beyond the assigned minimums in the learning environment. They love the power their understanding gives them to answer important questions, solve important problems, and make inferences about new, but related, ideas.

For most people this characterization is artificial. Most of us tend to be pragmatists, so we adopt learning strategies based on the learning task and how much it interests us and the reward it promises. You might be a deep learner in the area of history and avoid mathematics wherever possible. Math might elicit a surface approach from you because the world of numbers is an alien and hostile place you want to exit as quickly as possible. Memorize the equations, plug in the numbers, get the answer, and get out!

The truth is that we are not hard-wired with an approach to learning. We respond to a learning environment with an approach that seems appropriate given our motivation and the promised payoff. The more different learning scenarios we "successfully" complete with a surface strategy (getting a grade

---

remains an adventure. Someone may forget a few facts but still know how to find them when needed." Bain, *What the Best College Students Do*, 9.

that we are satisfied with), the more we reflexively employ a surface strategy when faced with new learning opportunities. The educational system has conditioned most of our students to start with a surface strategy unless such an approach absolutely will not work. Students get really creative in trying to get a surface approach to work, including memorizing massive amounts of information that would have been learned much more efficiently through a conceptual approach aimed at understanding core ideas.

What all of this means for course design is that you must create an environment *where surface strategies will not work*, and then you must be prepared to help your students work within a deep strategy that is alien to most of them. They are novices when it comes to deep learning. They will try to stay with a surface strategy far too long because it is what they know best. Some of them have to be truly desperate before they retire their surface strategy. Help them find ways to *try on a deep strategy* in a small chunk of your course and experience success. Next, help them understand what they did that was an implementation of a deep strategy and how to do it again in another chunk of the course. Success with a new approach comes slowly and incrementally. Help them remember why a surface strategy hasn't worked (and won't work) in your course. Encourage them to reflect on the power and durability of the deep learning they've employed and the personal sense of satisfaction they have gained.

The learning environment you've crafted is intended to develop student intellectual expertise—the ability to think in a particularly way—like an expert in your academic domain. That's the right goal, but it's light years away from where most of your students are, especially if they are first-year students. They need to become critical learners before they can become critical thinkers.[3] They have to learn to walk before they can run. Your course needs to wrench them from their familiar surface approaches to learning and show them instead "a more excellent way."

Learning How to Read

The more excellent way starts with learning how to read properly. Your students have been trained to view reading as a passive activity that involves the absorption of content. This isn't a recent development. In 1939 James Mursell of Columbia University wrote the following:

> It has been shown, for instance, that the average high-school student is amazingly inept at indicating the central thought of a

---

3. Chew, "Helping Students Get the Most Out of Studying," 215.

passage, or the levels of emphasis and subordination in an argument or exposition. To all intents and purposes he remains a sixth-grade reader till well along in college.[4]

Things had not improved by 1984 when Mortimer Adler wrote, "No . . . answers come without a close interpretation of the text, but such skill in reading seldom, if ever, exists in the twelve years of basic schooling."[5]

The beginning of critical learning is to get your students to become analytical readers who actively engage with the author in a kind of dialog. Such readers react as they read. They highlight, circle, or underline the key ideas. They write comments in the margins. They number points in a line of reasoning. They question rather than passively accept what the author says. They look for evidence, for contradiction, for connections, for hierarchy—in short, they do with a book what you want them to do in class and in learning scenarios you've constructed for them.[6]

The longer I teach, the more I'm persuaded that the inability to read analytically is the root of the inability to think analytically. For too long I assumed that my students were reading reflectively in this way, but classroom discussion revealed the awful truth that even those who had indeed read the assignment had failed to uncover the author's argument. They knew some facts; they could find some relevant quotations when I asked a question; but our discussion couldn't get off the ground because the assumed starting point based on the reading was much too ambitious. Realizing this, you can go one of two directions. You can throw up your hands and do the work for your students by spoon feeding them what they should have gotten from their own reading (further disincentivizing student reading) or you can teach them how to read for meaning. I opt for the latter.[7]

Part of the short version of Mortimer Adler's *How to Read a Book* that I communicate with my first year students is the following:

> The goal of analytical reading is nothing short of understanding what you are reading.

---

4. Mursell, "Failure of Schools." Professor Mursell of Columbia University's Teacher's College wrote this article in 1939.

5. Adler, *Paideia Program*, 50.

6 Adler and Van Doren, *How to Read a Book*. There is no finer book on learning to read this way.

7. W. Michael Gray, "Bio 100: General Biology I Study Guide" (supplement). This study guide contains a two-page condensation of *How to Read a Book* by Adler and Van Doren that applies the principles of analytical reading to the course, General Biology I.

Level One Analytical Reading (What)

1. What is the chapter about?

    Succinctly and carefully state what the chapter is about *in your own words*.

2. What are the key concepts?

    Scan the chapter looking for the key concepts (the major ideas). These may be listed at the beginning and/or end of the chapter. Do not confuse vocabulary (boldface terms) with the key concepts.

3. How are the key concepts arranged to formulate a logical argument?

    It might be helpful to outline the chapter to show this arrangement.

Level Two Analytical Reading (So What)

"To make knowledge practical we must convert it into rules of operation. We must pass from knowing *what is the case* to knowing *what to do about it* if we wish to get somewhere. This can be summarized in the distinction between knowing *that* and knowing *how*."[8]

1. Summarize *in your own words* the logical argument that the author is making.

2. What are the author's major propositions (assertions that may be true or false)?

3. What are the implications of the author's argument? Are you comfortable with the implications? If not, why not? Is your lack of comfort due to a difference of opinion with the author or are there deeper problems such as illogic or lack of evidence?

4. What are some specific situations where the author's propositions or overall argument apply? Can you think of analogies that help to illustrate?

---

8. Adler and Van Doren, *How to Read a Book,* 66.

The classic response of a college academician is to say that students who can't read analytically aren't "college material." This is akin to a physician wanting to see only healthy patients. A reading development course in your campus Academic Resource Center might be of some help for those who haven't mastered the mechanics of reading, but referring most of your students to outside experts is a mistake. Biggs and Tang point out research showing that students prosper when faculty embed *how to learn* strategies with *what to learn*. "If study skills are supported by the context in which they will be used, it becomes clear why those strategies are useful."[9] When both of these aspects of learning are integrated in your course, there is less opportunity for misunderstanding and more implementation of skills and dispositions. From the interpersonal side, students can tell that you are invested in helping them to succeed and that positive communication will pay dividends throughout the course.

Learning to Listen and to Take Notes

It is probably obvious that what I said above about analytical reading applies to analytical reasoning in general. Wherever the student is interacting with ideas, he should be seeking to understand them. To reach understanding, the student must ask questions; and in the process of asking questions, the student should zero in on both the *what* and the *so what.*

The classroom is the place where you have the most input into and control over the student experience. How do you intend to use the precious time when you and your students are in the same physical space? This is an ideal time for interaction through dialog; yet, sadly, most faculty use class as a place for didactic monologues not unlike an audio book. Students have been taught that their role is to be passive listeners to a faculty-crafted monologue. All but the most aggressive students stifle their questions so as not to interrupt the flow of the faculty monologue. Students who persist in asking questions in this environment are often perceived as a nuisance by the faculty member who is interrupted (and may not cover as much content as anticipated!) and by their fellow students who worry about whether what the faculty member said off-script will now be on the test.

Notice the passivity that traditionally defines the role of the student. He is passive as he absorbs authoritative content from the textbook and other source materials outside of class, and he is passive as he listens to a faculty expert deliver a didactic monolog. The ideas are already there in both the text and the lecture, and it is the job of the student to *absorb* the

---

9. Biggs and Tang, *Teaching for Quality Learning*, 150.

ideas. The author or the teacher will give him the *what* and whatever *so what* is important. As we've seen previously, this is not how we learn. Learning takes place exclusively through a process of active conceptualization on the part of the learner.

Conceptualization demands that the process of reading must be recast as a dialogue even though the author is not physically present. The reader asks questions and then has to search the text for clues about how the author would answer. The reader is interacting as energetically as possible with the thinking of the author. Much more so should class time be constructed to optimize the dialogue between student and expert (you). There are various ways to construct dialogical learning scenarios that we'll talk about later, but it is imperative that student questions are provoked and student thinking is interactively guided. Class time should be a model of what reflective analytical thinking looks like.

G. K. Chesterton said, "There's a lot of difference between listening and hearing."[10] Most students bring an adequate sense of hearing—an ability to hear and interpret sounds—to the classroom. Being an intelligent, involved listener is a skill that students (and every educated person) must acquire. A good listener is anything but passive. Such a listener is "all ears." Her body language expresses a desire to understand. She hears what you say, and she asks good questions all along the way to show that she is listening and to improve the quality of the communication so that she really understands what you said and why it is important. To listen well inevitably means that she will participate in the dialogue. Well-timed questions help her understand and help you the speaker by letting you know to what extent you have been understood.

It is hard to really listen because you're constantly juggling what the speaker is saying and what you are thinking about what she is saying. In the classroom we add a third ball to juggle—note taking. The result of this third ball is that you stop juggling. You stop actively participating in the dialogue, and you just try to write it all down. In the process you largely stop listening. Every time you write something down, you're not listening to what is being said while you're recording what was just said. Note taking then becomes a very poor substitute for an audio recording of a class period.

Students need to be taught how to listen for the questions that drive the discussion and the ideas that help to answer the questions. These are the things that need to be written down (along with unanswered questions that occurred to the note taker). In this way note taking can actually enhance the precision of student listening and the depth of his understanding. Rather

---

10. Chesterton, *Heretics*.

than being the clerk of court who records every word, the student is a reviewer who neatly summarizes the intellectual business that we, the class, transacted. If there are no notes, most students won't be able to reconstruct what happened in a class period. If there is no note taking, the student will likely lack intellectual focus and hear without really listening.

Note taking is challenging enough that beginning students need some help in learning how to do it well. Students who are thinking in terms of the transmission model will sometimes request a copy of your PowerPoint presentation (especially if it is full of bullet points—which I don't recommend because it scripts the class too closely and aborts discussion). Some students go so far as to ask for *your* notes. In the transmission model, possession of your notes is the ultimate. Both of these practices abort training your students to be analytical listeners. Other faculty, who want to help students have a good set of notes, produce "note takers" in the form of a printed outline of the content with blanks representing missing words or sentences. This is better than turning your notes over to the students, but it also conveys that you are operating from a script that they need to record.

To allow a genuine discussion to occur, your PowerPoint and any note-taking aids you provide should be minimal. You don't want students to be able to avoid engagement because you've done the hard work for them in recording the central questions and the answers to those questions. How much of a framework (if any) you need to provide depends on the level of the course and the way in which you intend to involve students in the process of conceptualization. An effective way to get a sense of how well students are assimilating a discussion is through the use of a one- or two-minute paper at the end of class in which you ask for two sentences: one that summarizes the central question and the other the essence of the answer. When you look these over after class, you'll get a sense of the effectiveness of note taking. In the act of writing these summaries, students will find out whether they "got the point." In the early days of a first year course you might share the best summaries the following class period. Students can also be encouraged to spend ten to fifteen minutes right after class (if possible) consolidating their notes—filling in gaps and adding clarification that will be needed if their notes are to be useful long-term. Doing this right after class is much more helpful than waiting for a day or two. Students might look at each other's notes to see what others are doing, but they should be discouraged from copying another student's notes verbatim. (Doing so puts them right back into passive mode, and easy access to notes will encourage them to check out mentally in class.)

Learning How to Write

Writing to produce a product that communicates with clarity is a worthy accompaniment to many kinds of learning scenarios. It provides a permanent record of the thoughts of the student that can be reviewed, critiqued, and thereby improved. The ability to write well is one of the marks of an educated person. Educationally there is a rub: writing to serve these purposes must be evaluated, and that evaluation is time consuming and subjective. As a consequence, in many academic areas writing has been dispensed with on the lower levels because of the sheer number of students. Partly as a result of the withering away of writing, Writing Across the Curriculum developed as an educational movement in the 1970s and continues to the present. It calls for writing to be done in all academic areas and not just in composition courses housed in English departments.[11] The process of writing forces a clarity of expression that enables efficient communication by avoiding vagueness. Francis Bacon, the first major English essayist, memorably observed the salutary effect of writing as producing "an exact man."[12]

It cannot be denied that the ability to communicate effectively in writing is one of the skills that employers want. Employers expect production, and written products are especially important. What I find even more intriguing, however, is the idea of using writing to *catalyze* learning.

Writing is actually a unique mode of learning. This was the contention of Janet Emig, who published an influential paper to that effect in 1977.[13] The very process of writing stimulates the formation of thoughts in words. Many words representing many different concepts separated by fine shades of meaning are available, and writing calls for intentional choices to be made. "Clear writing by definition is that writing that signals without ambiguity the nature of conceptual relationships."[14] We've already noted that the heart of learning is conceptual change. It is also true that the learner must do the conceptualization in her own brain, and that puts the *process* out of view of the teacher. Concept mapping is one of the few methods of getting thinking out in the open for purposes of examination—because it produces a product. Concept mapping is even more strategic to learning in that it can actually help the learner to conceptualize. Concept mapping is fundamentally a process of concept formation that also produces a product that can be reviewed and clarified.

---

11. Anonymous, "Writing Across Curriculum."
12. Bacon, "On Writing."
13. Emig, "Writing as Learning," 122-28.
14. Ibid., 126.

Like concept mapping, writing produces a product that communicates clear or fuzzy thinking or something in between. (It is the need to evaluate the degree of clarity that makes writing maddeningly frustrating to assess.) But writing, like concept mapping, is also a *process* that *produces* learning, and I'd like to focus on using writing that way.

As a writer, I've always been a square peg in a round hole. My major way of viewing life is through the lens of inquiry. I'm fueled by questions, and I love the unexpected twists and turns in the road that are inevitable as I explore a question. In contrast, my composition courses emphasized thesis statements and outlines. More than once I've written the outline for a paper *after* I completed the paper (and then only to fulfill a requirement). The paper developed through the process of inquiry rather than being shaped by my mandatory thesis statement. Sure, I had ideas (and sources) that I thought about exploring at the outset of the inquiry, and I wrote them down; but it was by no means obvious which of those ideas (and sources) would be pay dirt, nor did I know the logical order in which the ideas would best be developed.

I realized clearly in the process of writing this chapter that my composition courses emphasized writing as communication, while my writing process emphasized discovery. I viewed the writing process as an early step of "'thinking on paper,' not just a means to report the *results* of [my] thinking, but as a means to extend, develop, refine, and crystallize [my] thinking."[15] I used writing to *discover what my thesis was going to be*, while my composition courses assumed I would declare a thesis and then write to support that thesis. Once I discovered my thesis, I worked to find the best arguments and the best sequence of arguments to support that thesis. My writing was usually well received as a product, and none of my teachers knew about my approach to writing.

It now seems to me that since the logic of your course starts with questions and not answers, the discovery of answers through the process of inquiry can helpfully use the writing process. Rather than having students produce written products, encourage, even require them to "think on paper"—to use writing to *catalyze* their thinking and then to improve and develop the quality of their thinking though rethinking and revision. Discovery writing can be a powerful tool to *enable* conceptualization, which is the heart of learning.

Arguably there is more writing going on now than ever before in human history. It doesn't take paper and ink to support writing anymore. (I very seldom use them.) We text, tweet, write e-mails, blog, post on Facebook,

---

15. Finkel, *Teaching with Your Mouth Shut*, 79.

and so forth. It is now far too easy to produce a product that was not the result of analytical thought. We're admonished not to send an e-mail that we wrote while we were angry or agitated, and rightly so. The product can't usually be retrieved. The ease of writing today can be put to use in profitable ways when we explore writing as a process of catalyzing and clarifying thinking. Don Finkel speaks of a way to do this:

> Making students write to each other also provides a strong way to help students pursue inquiry within a course. Their essays become both means and ends: *means* for publishing their thinking, testing their ideas, reaching conclusions, and *ends* as published accounts of their conclusions, which can be read by their classmates. Once read by the class, the essays turn back into means again, because they function as provocations to the thinking of others.[16]

Finkel is talking here about a composition course he taught in the late 1990s, but his approach presages a strategic use of online discussions if you have a learning management system (LMS) available to you. In an issues-based class where I use this extensively, I require a student to compose a brief position paper (two to three paragraphs) that he then deposits into an electronic dropbox. This then opens a discussion in which his position paper is his opening salvo. He can't see the discussion that has been going on among other students until he commits to a position. This turns out to be crucial because reflexively no one wants to take a position until he sees what his peers think. This requirement for the student to take a position on a controversial issue (embedded in a case which has already taken them to primary source documents) is designed to *catalyze* clear thinking in that student. Knowing his peers are going to interact with his position (another requirement) is also a strong motivator to take ownership and to be persuaded in his own mind. Without this requirement (when students could view the discussion and lurk in the background), students tended to shop for a prepackaged position among the posts rather than thinking themselves to a position. (This shopping for a prepackaged position is also characteristic of most of us in the information age.)

Learning How to Study

Most college students have study habits that morphed thoughtlessly throughout the course of their secondary education and are purely pragmatic—they

16. Ibid., 82.

produced the desired grades. This focus on grades rather than learning is epidemic in education and represents the majority of your student population. This focus represents a subset of the surface learner disposition: the strategic learner. Surface learners as a group are not focused on understanding. They focus instead on attainment. To some surface learners just getting by is the level of attainment they seek. "Good enough" is their motto. To the strategic learner, what grade they get is ultimate. An A (or perhaps a B) is what they really care about. Learning is nice, but grades are ultimate. Such students don't waste emotion, energy, or intensity on ideas. What matters is their grade on an assignment or a test. Strategic learners fight for points, not for understanding.

A recent conversation with a strategic learner who was fighting for points on a quiz took an unexpected turn when I asked the student to talk to me in my office instead of in the front of the classroom at the end of class in a rushed public conversation. In the office I tried to take her through the logic that should have led her to eliminate the answer she had chosen on a quiz question, but I sensed she was only partly listening. Since she was in a non-majors science course that is structured around bioethical issues, I stopped talking about the quiz and reminded her of the potentially transformative nature of the course. She was a bright girl and I could tell that, beneath her quibbling about grades, she was intrigued that the course could help her to take intelligent well-informed positions on issues she cared about. She ended up agreeing to try to learn for the joy of personal transformation and to try to relegate the pursuit of an A to a secondary concern. At the end of the semester I received a note from her, which said in part: "your class and your patient talk with me at the beginning of the semester really humbled me and corrected my unconscious over-focus on grades. I really realized how perfectionism is really pride and I just learned to enjoy learning for the sake of learning . . . even if my grades aren't perfect! This class, more than any other so far in college, has profoundly changed the way I think. Thank you!" (By the way, she finished with a 95 percent A).

You need to communicate to your students the centrality of understanding in your philosophy of assessment. More than that, you must win them over to embracing understanding as the only worthy goal. If they remain strategic learners, understanding won't be the prize that it needs to be, and they will lack the motivation to do the hard things you'll be calling them to do. In fact, those hard things will encourage them to think hard things about you. In contrast, the joy of discovery and personal growth through deep learning will cause just the opposite—gratitude to you for opening their horizons. Sound far-fetched? I've seen it happen literally thousands of times.

Learning (especially deep learning) requires time. Students are incredibly naive in this regard. They mostly view themselves as a "quick study." They are surrounded by strategic learners who seem to get A's with minimal effort. There is a tacit admission that she's not college material if a student has to study long hours. Some studies show that today's college students spend more time using social media in a week than they spend studying. Thirty-seven percent of the students surveyed in one large study spent fewer than five hours per week studying. The average student studied about twelve hours weekly.[17] This compares to the rule of thumb in use for many decades: two hours of study outside class for every hour in class. For an average load of sixteen hours that amounts to thirty-two hours of study per week. Most students don't come close. Even by self-evaluation only about 11 percent of first year students surveyed in the National Survey of Student Engagement (NSSE) said they spend twenty-six or more hours per week studying.[18] These numbers are also in rough agreement with the Bureau of Labor Statistics, American Time Use Survey. For full-time college students the bureau calculates just 3.4 hours per weekday in academic pursuits. That's not even enough to get them to all of their classes![19]

Convincing a student to change her schedule because of the demands of your class is no mean feat! Your three-hour course expects her to carve out six hours of study time every week!? This reprioritization of her schedule will happen only if there is no other way. No other way for what? That depends. No other way she will pass your course. No other way she will get an A (or a B). Or no other way that she will be able to understand something she is really wants to understand? The last motivation seems almost laughable to hardened academics, yet this is exactly where we're headed in this book. This, in fact, is the entire premise around which Ken Bain wrote *What the Best College Students Do*. Bain puts it directly: "Straight A's in high school or college are great, but—and this is a big qualification—they say little about who you are, what you are likely to do in life, how creative you are likely to be, or how much you understand. . . . Sure, high marks have their rewards. . . . [B]ut if we had to choose between good grades or deep learning, I'd pick the latter every time."[20]

When we get down to the nitty gritty of how they study even with the limited time they tend to give it, we find students habituated in strategies that promote recall but not understanding, recognition but not application.

---

17. Arum and Roksa, *Academically Adrift*, 69.
18. McCormick, "It's About Time."
19. Anonymous, "Use of Time."
20. Bain, *What Best College Students Do*, 10.

These strategies are promoted by scores of books and web sites. Take this classic from WikiHow: "When you sit down to study, how do you transfer that massive amount of information from the books and notes in front of you to a reliable spot in your mind?"[21] Understanding is not even on the radar in the procedure that follows—it's all about memorization. Tactics that target memory are legion because, for most students in most courses, memory will get you where you want to go. Flash cards, outlines, acronyms/mnemonics, recopying notes, labeling diagrams, even anatomy coloring books—it's all about drill for recall. So another seismic shift will be to persuade your students to abandon most of the study methods that have gotten them to your course and try who knows what? Good luck with that. For most of them it will take a collision with reality in the form of the grade on their first assignment. For the hard-headed it may take most of the semester. This is where a collision through a low-stakes formative assessment may serve your purposes better. You don't want a high percentage of your students digging a deep hole early on that they try to recover from for the rest of the semester.

When assessment sends the message to your students that "learning is hard work, but not all hard work leads to learning,"[22] what will you have to offer them? You need to have an answer. You need to be prepared to offer new study tools. Be warned—these tools will suffer by comparison. They cannot be as straightforward as the tools of memorization that students know so well. Learning for understanding doesn't yield to a template-driven approach. Stephen Chew of Samford University has produced a series of five videos to direct students into this virgin wilderness, and I recommend them as the best that are out there.[23] Be advised that this is no simple fix. It is really a cultivation of a way of thinking that focuses attention on the central ideas, the principles as I would say.

Breaking this down into a rough list of tools that promote higher-order learning may be helpful.

1. You can really assist the student to derive principles (the central ideas) inductively and to make this process of principialization fundamental (principle-driven instruction) by repetitively placing him in the middle of a learning scenario that confronts him with a compelling question.

---

21. Anonymous, "How to Study."
22. Chew, "Helping Students Get the Most out of Studying," 218.
23. Chew, "How to Get the Most out of Studying." A video series available on YouTube.

2. These principles should constantly be turned over in the mind of the student who should be looking for connections to other concepts and principles. The connectedness of all understanding is vital to recognize, and it is light years away from the flash-card approach, which demotes concepts to mere terms and disconnects them to separate flash cards. Developing connectedness can be assisted through discovery writing exercises and concept mapping.

3. Providing problems to give a context in which the student has to apply each principle will be helpful in demonstrating the power of the principle. (You can start with a few solved problems, but discourage pattern imitation as a strategy and highlight the thinking process involved. Even with solved problems, ask thoughtful probing questions to push student thinking beyond the immediate problem context.) Ask students questions that force them to explore the implications and consequences of the principles.

4. Move students to a position where they are able to articulate their own probing questions (and answer them).

5. Encourage students to *explain their reasoning* to another student orally or in writing. This gives them feedback about the depth of their understanding. Note that this is not at all the same as reciting information that they get from some other source. They need to demonstrate personal ownership of the thinking that they espouse. To that end they should be prepared to answer probing questions from other students.

Tool number 5 is actually metacognition—thinking about their thinking. Good students get good at assessing the quality of their own thinking (depth of their understanding) and knowing thereby where learning is still needed and what kind of work will best address the deficiency. Students who have a surface approach to learning tend to be unduly optimistic about their understanding and are often blind-sided when they get test results back.

A week or two in advance of a test, when principles have surfaced and connections have been explored, a simple exercise may be helpful. Students can write down the major concepts (but not their definitions) without elaborating. The same sheet of paper (or computer document) can contain compact student versions of the major principles (propositional statements). When the list is complete, the student should close all other sources of information and use the document they have created as a catalyst for exploratory thinking. Can the student explain to herself what a given concept is and why it is important? Can she articulate and defend connections of that concept with other concepts on the list? Can she give examples or concrete analogies of the principles? Can she explore questions that she is now able to answer? Can she recognize the implications of the principles? How can the principle be used to solve problems? What kind of problems does it address? This exercise with a nearly blank document can initially diagnose an almost equally blank mind. If so, frustration will probably surface. I call frustration "mental sweat." In the physical realm we know that exercise that doesn't cause us to sweat doesn't do us much good. Likewise in the mental realm lack of frustration may indicate that I'm traveling well-worn grooves and not making intellectual progress.

The concreteness of the task of memorization is appealing to your students. Drill is a pretty straightforward process, and the ability to recall terms and definitions is easy to assess. In contrast, the development of thinking is much more abstract, and it is difficult to know when you have thought deeply enough. Help your students to recognize that recall should be a byproduct of understanding. I like to say "never memorize something that you can remember by understanding it." The thoughtful student recognizes that substituting memory for understanding is pointless. Counterfeit learning can't buy anything in the realm where understanding functions.

The process of repeated practice is part of learning for understanding, but it is not as simple as drill. Students will still need to repetitively practice thinking and exploring the depth of their understanding, not just flip through a stack of flash cards. Even with flash-card memorization, it has been amply demonstrated by educational research that distributed or spaced practice is much more efficient than cramming. This is also true of learning for understanding. However, when considering deep learning strategies, you need to recognize that the brain can maintain focus on a demanding task for only sixty to ninety minutes and then the student should do something else, preferably nonmental, for at least ten to fifteen minutes and then go back to a mental focus, but on a different subject. Another thing your students need to recognize is that repetitious practice is much less effective than practice interspersed with testing. Testing early and often during the study process (preferably low-stakes or no-stakes formative assessment) is a powerful tool in learning for mastery of ideas.[24]

It is important for students to recognize the need for a quiet place to study as an essential. This includes imposed quietness through isolation from personal electronic devices for the duration of the study time. No phones and, if they are on a computer, no e-mail, Facebook, or alerts of any kind. The Internet itself is full of distractions, so have the student turn off access unless the study task clearly requires it. Nothing should intrude on

---

24. Pyc, Agarwal, and Roediger, "Test-enhanced Learning."

the student's mental focus. The high level of thinking your students must learn to maintain cannot be accomplished when they are distracted. Multitasking is a myth.

What about study groups? Study groups generally are not as time-efficient as solo studying. For some students they are an opportunity to parasitize their more diligent peers. Conscientious students grow to resent group members who are only takers and never show significant advance preparation. Group study should be the culmination of solo study by all of the members. Each member should bring a few questions that he is having difficulty with. Each member should contribute to the discussion, and no member should be allowed to dominate the discussion. In my first-year biology course, I've profitably employed peer-mentoring groups led by two upper-class students. Regular attendance at such groups produces on average a letter-grade improvement above what would have been anticipated based on science ACT scores.[25] These upper-level mentors report significant personal mental growth as they interact with the questions first-year students bring to these sessions. This is not surprising since it is well known that "teaching is the highest form of understanding."[26] Peer mentors in my first year biology course operate Socratically and try not to merely provide right answers. The clarification of thinking that comes through a line of questioning is invaluable to my students who are neophytes in learning to think like a biologist. Their mentors become thinking role models with whom they can directly interact since group size is held to eight students.

One final consideration when thinking about studying is the extent to which you should scaffold study time. Certainly you've constructed learning scenarios that students need to immerse themselves in outside of class, and these are intended to be intellectually developmental.[27] However, your students should understand that doing their "homework" is not the same thing as studying. Studying is an initiative they take to integrate and consolidate what they are gaining from "homework" and class sessions to synthesize something bigger than the sum of these experiences. It is telling that in a 259-page book, *What the Best College Students Do*, Ken Bain devotes a scant

---

25. Batdorf, "Analysis of the effects of inquiry-based peer mentoring." John Biggs and Catherine Tang, 118, report similar results. Peer-assisted study sessions (PASS) were led by second- or third-year students. "At the University of Queensland, over many thousands of student [sic], regular attendees of PASS averaged a whole grade higher than students who did not attend."

26. Aristotle, "Teaching and Understanding."

27. "Effortful study" is creating challenges which are "just beyond [the] current competence" of students. This is a major part of developing expertise. See Philip E. Ross "The Expert Mind."

nine pages to the question of how to study.[28] Most of the book has to do with the disposition of the best students toward learning and why and how they embrace learning as a means of personal change. Learning is central to who the best students are. Learning is not reducible to a set of templates. You are rightfully concerned that student study time be profitable, but quench your desire to micromanage. Dorothy Sayers says you won't be doing your students any favors. "[Teachers] are doing for their pupils the work which the pupils themselves ought to do. For the sole true end of education is simply this: to teach men how to learn for themselves; and whatever instruction fails to do this is effort spent in vain."[29]

Since studying is often motivated by the desire to do well on a quiz or a test, it might seem that another way to promote student flourishing would be to help them to do well on these kinds of assessments. I don't object to that sentiment at all, but I won't devote a section of this chapter to that purpose for two reasons. The first and most important reason is that assessment should be aligned with the structure of your course; that is, testing is not a game of trying to stump your students. Students who are working in harmony with your learning objectives should regularly be practicing the kind of thinking that you will be assessing. In that sense, the test should not be full of surprises. The second reason is that I view testing as a continuation of the learning environment (rather than a time for inspecting the products produced in the environment), and I won't develop that view of assessment until chapter 9.

Consider Cognitive Load

About forty years ago I borrowed my father's four-wheel-drive truck to pick up a load of dirt to be used for filling in a low spot in my yard. Although on the outside it looked like a fairly normal red long-bed ¾-ton truck, this was not just any truck. My father had special-ordered many unusual features when this truck was built at the factory. It had an eight-speed manual transmission that, coupled with a very torquey motor and a low gear that seemingly would allow it to climb telephone poles, gave it a "go anywhere" aura. It also had special two-ton-rated axles front and rear.

I had to drive about fifteen miles to get free dirt, and I wasn't eager to make two trips, so I kept shoveling more dirt into the truck bed. The springs bottomed out, so I anticipated a jarring ride back to my home. I started the engine, put it in low gear, and let out the clutch. The truck sure-footedly

28. Bain, *What Best College Students Do*, 241–49.
29. Sayers, *Lost Tools of Learning*.

moved ahead as I moved from the dirt lot and back onto the highway. As I began to come up to speed, I was horrified to realize that I could just barely steer. The load in the back was so large that the front wheels were hardly touching the road!

I had not entertained the possibility of lifting the front wheels off the ground when I thought about the concept of load. In a similar fashion, don't assume your students have an unlimited ability to absorb the cognitive load you intend for them to shoulder. The concept of cognitive load was first articulated in the 1990s. Cognitive load focuses on working memory as the weak link in the process of thinking. The inputs into working memory are sensory, primarily sights and sounds. We have a large capacity to react to our environment through the visual and auditory channels (which correspond to different parts of the brain), but that leads to a severe bottleneck in working memory. Working memory is so limited that we can handle only about seven items (words, numbers, images) at once.[30] Learning involves cognitive processing (primarily conceptualization) that leads to long-term memory. In sharp contrast to working memory, our long-term memory is essentially unlimited in capacity.

Cognitive load is not a bad thing. Learning requires effort, and effort not infrequently is sufficient to produce mental sweat (aka frustration). What would be a bad thing is to *unwittingly* put your students under a load they are incapable of handling. Kalyuga in 2011 helpfully suggested that there are actually two components to cognitive load. There is an intrinsic load and an extraneous load.[31] The intrinsic load is inherent to the intellectual task. You want to make certain that the intrinsic load isn't more than your students can handle. This isn't psychological double-talk to keep students from the hard work of thinking. "As intrinsic load directly contributes to learning, it should possibly be maximized for motivating and guiding learners to higher-level skills."[32] We should maximize intrinsic load—intentionally. To keep their wheels from coming off the ground, we need to also consider extraneous load. Load that is not intrinsic to the learning task should be eliminated wherever possible. In the case of my truck load of dirt, the extraneous factor was the type of soil and the moisture content of soil. I had seen my father put a similar amount of dry top soil in the truck, but I loaded it with the same volume of dense moist clay!

Cognitive load is a reality that is due to the limitations of working memory. If you want to document this limitation for yourself, get out your

---

30. Miller, "Magical Number Seven," 81-97.
31. Kalyuga, "Cognitive load theory," 1-19.
32. Lee and Kalyuga, "Expertise Reversal Effect," 33.

credit card. Look at your credit card number. Chances are the number is broken down into groups of three or four numbers to aid in reading the number. You would have a hard time with a fifteen digit number containing no spaces. That's because of your working memory, which all your visual and auditory inputs feed into. Think about your social security number—there are three groups of numbers separated by hyphens like this: XXX-XX-XXXX. Phone numbers (including area codes) are hard to remember if we don't break them into chunks. So phone numbers are ideally represented as (YYY) YYY-YYYY. A simple example of an extraneous factor then would be not breaking up long strings of numbers. Such strings are hard to read and even harder to memorize.

Your students are working to process what you and your sources are giving them via their eyes and ears. When you consider the possibility of extraneous factors, I'm really asking, "Are you making this harder than it needs to be?" I like to tell stories (in case you hadn't noticed), and my wife often tells me after I've told a story that I put in too many details that were not really necessary to the point of the story. They at least elongated the story, and they may have distracted my listeners from the point I was trying to make. I enjoy the details, but they may not help my listeners. Similarly academic experts treasure complexity while novices crave simplicity. This is part of the curse of knowledge. It is very difficult to put yourself in the shoes of the novice learner, but that's what you are trying to do in harnessing your expertise for their benefit.

I'm not asking you to dumb down your course because of the cognitive load limitations of your students. It is not that they are dumb. They simply need to be given ideas in manageable bite-sized pieces. If you respect these cognitive realities, your students will go farther faster.

It is obvious that human thinking is not nearly as limited as it feels when we try to read a long string of numbers. If the working memory limitation is real, how do we overcome it? The answer is chunks. Your working memory is like the special checkout line at the grocery store—the cognitive line is not ten items or less; it is nine items or less (seven plus or minus two). It doesn't matter what those items are at the grocery store. They could be ten cans of soup, ten boxes of cereal, ten twelve-packs of soda pop, ten cases of paper towels—you get the picture. Your working memory doesn't care either. The largest chunks we manipulate in working memory are called schemata.

A schema is a logically connected chunk in our long-term memory. We produced it by conceptualization, and now we can reference it by the tag we have given it. For me DNA is a schema. Of course "DNA" stands for something (deoxyribonucleic acid), but to me it really stands for an entire model of information storage and processing in the cell. For someone with expertise in literature, "Shakespeare" references a schema (the works of Shakespeare and all that binds them together). "Keynesian economics," "Congress" and even "China" can be schemata. Schemata can be as large as models and systems of thought. They still count as one item to working memory.

When students are novices, they haven't yet developed the schemata that experts move through their working memories. Your job is to help them (through learning scenarios) to construct such schemata, and then your students should start using their schemata to cement them and to get cognitive value out of them. To harness your expertise, first break down your big chunk schema into chunks conducive to conceptualization. Once the relevant concepts have been formed, you should then construct scenarios in which students grapple with the concepts (no more than nine!) from which they'll construct their own schema. Thinking that transacts cognitive business using schemata is called schematic thinking. When students get to this point, they have gained a very powerful tool. We've called these networks of connected propositions conceptual frameworks. Conceptualization and schema formation are foundational to constructing conceptual frameworks. Since learning is mainly about constructing conceptual frameworks, teaching is mostly about creating the optimal environment in which this can happen.

Active Learning

"Active learning" is actually a redundant expression since learning involves conceptualization, and concepts are only formulated by active minds. Mortimer Adler recognized this when in 1984 he said, "[A]ll genuine learning arises from the activity of the learner's own mind. It may be assisted, guided, and stimulated by the activity of teachers. But no activity on the part of teachers can ever be a substitute and become the sole cause of a student's learning."[33]

Nonetheless, the phrase "active learning" is in common use. The problem is that it means different things to different people. To many it simply conveys activity. Students need to do things rather than passively listening to lectures or watching teachers do things. That's probably an advance, depending on what the things are that they are doing. If the designed purpose of an activity is aiding and abetting conceptualization, that would be active learning in my book. To reactive traditionalists active learning is just a buzzword that threatens their livelihood as lecturers. They sense a loss of control

---

33. Adler, *Paideia Program*, 47.

and efficiency in a classroom that doesn't run precisely according to a script. I'd be the first to recognize that learning is messy, but scripts straitjacket teachers and would-be learners and only ensure that real learning isn't going to happen.

Active learning strategies include Socratic discussion, collaborative learning (like "think-pair-share" exercises), peer instruction, debates, "just-in time" teaching, "flipped" classrooms, studio learning, group projects, laboratory learning, problem-based learning, case-based learning, and others. Some of these will be discussed in the next chapter. We're now getting to the meat of what your classroom sessions will look like and how you're going to construct learning scenarios that will help your students develop schematic principle-based thinking.

Even by a minimalist definition of active learning that included filling in worksheets during class and teachers whose students used personal response systems, STEM instruction was demonstrated to be significantly enhanced by active learning. A meta-analysis of 225 previous studies demonstrated an average of a 6-percent increase on exam scores when active learning approaches were used. Even more important for those who view the deep learning paradigm as elitist, failure rates for traditional lectured classes were 55 percent higher than the rates in active learning classrooms.[34] Anecdotal evidence across the board points clearly to improved learning when active learning strategies are employed regardless of the academic area or the ability level of the student. Given what we know about how people learn, that would be expected.

Learning Environment

I don't want to encourage a grab bag approach to employing active learning strategies in your classroom. Some of these strategies are more experimental than others. I'm going to assume you are going to change your course learning environment in stages and not be radical. So I'm first going to approach thinking about altering the learning environment through an approach that gained some traction in K-12 education during the 1980s and 1990s. It is called the Paideia Proposal and was championed by Mortimer Adler and a group of education luminaries (including Ernest L. Boyer, president of the Carnegie Foundation for the Advancement of Teaching) who called themselves the Paideia group.[35] There are many reasons the proposal has not

---

34. Freeman, "Active Learning Increases Student Performance."

35. Adler, *Paideia Proposal*. Adler, *Paideia Problems and Possibilities*. Adler, *Paideia Program*.

had a lasting impact on K-12 education, and this would not be the place to explore them all. (One reason is the level of control that states and local school districts exert over curriculum and the approaches their teachers are permitted to use. Typically college faculty enjoy considerably more freedom in making academic decisions.) The Paideia Proposal was sharply critical of teaching as telling and is aligned in significant ways with active learning philosophy. In fact, Paideia presages in significant ways the "flipped classroom," which has recently begun to gain a following in K-12 education.

The core of the Paideia Proposal was an emphasis on "teaching for understanding."[36] Adler's group recognized the need for students to be coached and made that role primary for teachers. The whole of the student experience was described in terms of "three columns." The three columns are reproduced below.[37]

	Instruction	Coaching	Seminars
Component	Acquisition of organized knowledge	Development of intellectual skills	Increased understanding of ideas and values
By means of	Didactic instruction	Coaching	Socratic questioning
Using	Textbooks	Exercises and supervised practice	Active participation in discussion of primary source materials
Proportion of Class Time*	10-20%	60-80%	5-30%

*Proportion varies depending on age level.

This matrix will serve as a useful organizing tool to think about the learning environment you've constructed for your class and how to optimize it.

36. Roberts and Billings, *Paideia Classroom*.
37. Ibid., 7.

Even at the high school level, the first column gets the least emphasis in the Paideia Proposal. That's because "teaching by telling" is a myth. Knowledge cannot be transferred directly from the teacher to the student. Even if it were possible, you are trying to teach your students to think in a particular way using the core explanatory principles of your discipline, not just to transmit content, material, or information to them.

If you prepare your students to read analytically and you scaffold such reading (early in the semester and progressively remove the scaffolds as they gain facility), there is absolutely no reason the textbook for your course should occupy the lion's share of your precious time together with your students. Students can be enabled to teach themselves through reading. Classroom time should then be based on what students should have learned on their own, and you can be emphatic with your students that they will be lost in class unless they do their own analytical reading outside of class. (It is incredibly boring to be taught didactically through a book that students can read for themselves.) At the college level, most of the didactic instruction disappears from the classroom. Didactic verbal instruction in the college classroom should be restricted to *occasional brief bursts* (perhaps ten minutes maximum duration) as needed. With the textbook off stage, you now have time for the other two columns, coaching and Socratic questioning!

The Paideia Proposal in some measure resembles the modern "flipped classroom." In its most common modern incarnation, the didactic class lectures are flipped to home where students watch prerecorded lectures (usually about the textbook). In exchange, class time is used for working on problems and exercises with assistance from the teacher, who helps individuals and gives brief explanations to the class to address common misunderstandings. (Or, better, calls on students to work at the board solving problems, diagramming sentences, drawing a timeline of historical events, outlining the geographical features of a country, etc.)

The most frequent objection to "teaching a way of thinking" is that there is no time for it because class is already brim full of "content" that needs to be covered. That's a specious objection that puts inappropriate emphasis on transmitting a body of content by lecturing. Because students don't learn by transmission of knowledge, but by active construction of knowledge (conceptualization), class time needs to be reserved for conceptualization. And because students are the ones who need to be *doing* the conceptualizing, it follows that the role of the teacher is to assist interactively so that conceptualization develops as efficiently as possible. That interactive help is called coaching.

Engagement

Coaching as introduced in the previous chapter is much more than ensuring that students do their homework (which is now the class work). Coaches in our classroom are not drilling for skills but engaging students in conceptualization. Coaches can do this because they have demonstrated expertise in playing the game of conceptualization and principialization. The operative term for such a class is not lecture, but *engagement*. The teacher keeps students engaged. I don't mean by this that the teacher cracks his whip and keeps the student's noses to the grindstone. There may be a bit of that on some difficult days, but class is organized around compelling questions (for which the students *want* to know the answer). In this classroom, however, the teacher will find ways to help the *students* wrestle with the question and think their way to an answer. This intellectual wrestling is the process that *students* are engaged in nearly all of every class period.

The role of the academic coach is twofold: (1) to provide experiences that will engage the students in "a way of thinking" and (2) to move students to reflect on the experiences so that their thinking is clarified and matured by means of the experiences.[38] This is all about students being engaged to the end that students will reflect and have their thinking enhanced. The teacher has failed if the students are entertained (even engrossed) but fail to conceptualize and principialize. The teacher has likewise failed if she simply delivers by means of the learning experience the products of her own reflective thought and does not require the students to independently *generate* similar (and even additional) concepts and propositions. Active learning is sometimes called generative learning for this very reason. Properly viewed, the purpose of active learning is not activity but creating a framework by means of which significant relevant ideas are generated.

Every time the student successfully conceptualizes and creates a new concept or principle, her thinking is enriched and empowered a little bit more. Her success needs to be leveraged in solving problems at frequent intervals to show her the power of her maturing conceptual framework. Progress otherwise may seem too slow to be worth the effort and mental sweat (frustration) she has been through. Just as someone on a long hike through the Rockies needs to stop to catch her breath and look around her to appreciate how far she has come and to see how far she yet has to go to get to the next milepost or mountain peak, your student needs perspective, encouragement, praise, and time to savor the victory before pressing on to the next challenge.

---

38. Finkel, *Teaching with Your Mouth Shut*, 154.

Good coaches are aware of the psychological and physical realities, and they don't push their players too hard for too long without rest and a water break. As an academic coach, recognize the cognitive load your students are under and develop a proper pacing to your course. Be generous but genuine in your praise. Learn and use student names; where possible come to class a few minutes early and stay a few minutes late and engage students in informal conversation. It is not too much to say that this is what love looks like in an academic setting. Students work harder for teachers who love them by showing them respect, courtesy, and support while holding them to high standards. Another benefit is that your students may well share with you comments that will encourage you about where you are on target as well as incisive perspective that can help you improve your course.

A significant aspect of engagement is wholehearted participation. Good coaching invites all-out participation. Athletes need to throw themselves completely into the game without fear of looking stupid or uncoordinated. The kinds of moves that surprise the opponent during a game are unanticipated or they would be guarded against. Take the risk out of participation in your class. Make certain that class discussion has the tone of a conversation, not an inquisition. Invite student participation verbally and through nonverbals. Involve everyone, not just those who raise their hands. Everyone should get playing time. Of course, when you call on students who haven't volunteered, they may be shell-shocked. Encourage them. Reword your question if needed or replace it with a more basic question. Put the best face on what the student says and try to get to what they were trying to say even if they haven't stated it very clearly. (I've done this many times in class, and it is often received like a life preserver by a drowning man.) Try in every way to get student thinking out in the open so that it can be examined and improved.

The entire learning environment is really all about improving the thinking process itself in individual students and not just pouncing on the immediate products that those students produce. Pouncing on the products shuts down thinking. Put another way, students shift from playing intellectual offense to defensive postures when we prematurely critique their products or put undue stress on them. Your goal in class is "to teach a way of thinking." You want to promote thinking, not terminate it.

Addicted to Explanation

Perhaps the most significant evidence of the effectiveness of thinking is the ability to formulate an answer to the question that has been driving the thinking. Explanation is the process of answering a question through an appeal to principle-based logic. When you satisfactorily explain, you have gone as far as the discipline permits you to go in accounting for the phenomenon in the question. Explanation is, in some sense, the goal of your thinking. There is a great sense of accomplishment when we arrive at explanation. Peter Lipton goes so far as to say that "We are addicted to explanation, constantly asking and answering 'why' questions."[39] Our addiction to answering "why" questions goes back to our early childhood when we were intent on making meaning of the world outside of us through conceptualization. It is not really surprising then, that when we focus on answering questions through conceptualization, even as adults, explanation once again becomes primary. "Why?" is not just for two- or three-year-olds!

If we develop a logically compelling, intellectually satisfying explanation, we feel that, in some sense, we understand. You recall that understanding is the raison d'être of teaching a way of thinking, of learning the logic of a discipline. Obviously there are levels of understanding, but understanding is a real milestone. I consider it to be the gateway to the so-called higher levels of the revised Bloom's taxonomy (applying, analyzing, evaluating, creating). In understanding we have crossed the line from knowing the "what" to knowing the "why."

Having understanding, you gain the ability to transact real intellectual business. No wonder explanation is something we strive for! When you say you understand, you indicate you know the cause, the reason behind the phenomenon. "The *causal* conception of understanding . . . [maintains that] to explain something is to give information about its causes. . . . [S]o many explanations we give both in science and in everyday life are manifestly causal."[40] Cause-effect explanations are very powerful in problem solving as I indicated in chapter 5, when I developed the idea of principles as causal. Explanation also allows us to make immediate inferences as well as the ability to anticipate longer-term consequences. Finally, "the construction and evaluation of competing explanations is one important route to the discovery of causes. If our explanatory practices give us this sort of information it is unsurprising that they play such a large role in our cognitive economy."[41] This is where things get really exciting and rewarding for your students! There's also a tremendous side benefit. Mortimer Adler doesn't overstate the case when he says that "[understanding] is unconditionally durable. Unlike verbal memories, something understood does not need to be exercised

---

39. Lipton, "What Good Is an Explanation?" 1.
40. Ibid., 8.
41. Ibid., 19.

in order to be retained. This, then is the kind of learning that lasts for a lifetime."[42]

Maximum learning occurs when students are kept in the role of learners actively grappling with a compelling question. Teachers are never more helpful to their students than when teachers serve as exemplars of reflective analytical thinking. These two seemingly opposed realities are brought together through Socratic discussion where focused questioning by the teacher calls forth and directs the processes of conceptualization and principialization in the student. That's where we're headed in the next chapter.

---

42. Adler, *Paideia Program*, 182.

Chapter 8

Ask, Don't Tell

> Thinking within disciplines is driven, not by answers, but by essential questions.[1]
>
> LINDA ELDER AND RICHARD PAUL

"Questions define tasks, express problems, and delineate issues. They drive thinking forward. Answers, on the other hand, often signal a full stop in thought."[2] How do answers stop thought? Answers have an air of finality. The experts have spoken and the job of the student is to write down their answer, not to quibble about how the experts arrived at their conclusion. Answers are tidy, but questions are messy. Questions imply that there is more to be done. Who wants to get tied up with tasks, problems, and issues if the authoritative answers are already available?

Students typically come to us expecting to be spoon-fed factual content with minimal to modest effort on their part. The force-feeding regimen is a ritualized drill designed to get the greatest volume of factual information into the student over the course of the semester. Unfortunately, "Spoon-feeding in the long run teaches [students] nothing but the shape of the spoon."[3]

Facts were originally discovered as answers to compelling questions through a process of disciplined thought, but contemporary instruction barely acknowledges the process. Today's curriculum delivers answers to questions that no one is asking. In some such classrooms, a student who ventures to ask a substantive question is out of order. When the teacher asks, "Are there any questions?" every student knows the answer is "No,"

---

1. Elder and Paul, *Miniature Guide*, 3.
2. Ibid.
3. Forster, "Spoon-feeding," 21.

always "No." Students arrive in your classroom and mine needing intellectual resuscitation. Linda Elder says we need to give them "'artificial cogitation' (the intellectual equivalent of artificial respiration)."[4] The phrase "artificial cogitation" is a particularly apt metaphor because the goal of artificial respiration is getting the patient to breathe on his own, and the goal of our instruction is to get students to think on their own. We want to power thinking, not stop it; and we power thinking through questions. To change the metaphor, questions are the engines of thought; so "artificial cogitation" is a bit like pushing a car to start it. The teacher uses questions to "push" the student until he sputters to life and starts generating questions of his own. This may be a daily occurrence for a while, maybe even quite a while, until individual students recognize that they don't need you to push them. When that happens, they are on their way to becoming autonomous learners.

Changing Your Mind About Questions

Decades ago following my first semester of full-time teaching at the college level, I had a performance review from my dean based on my course evaluations. "Your students like you and respect you, but some of them are not entirely convinced that you know your stuff," he said. In response I said, "I've tried to be thoroughly prepared for each class session. Is there any reason they gave for questioning my competence?" The dean answered, "Several of them said you weren't very straightforward when they asked you a question. It seems you tended to respond to a question with a question. Some of them wondered whether you did this to stall for time until you could come up with an answer."

At that point in my teaching career I hadn't developed an intentional approach to using questions strategically like what I'll advocate in this chapter. My reason for asking questions tended to center only on clarifying the students' questions. I wanted to be certain that I understood what they were asking before I started answering. This is a good reason for asking questions. You want your response to be tailored to the question so that you don't waste your time (and the students') telling them something that they already know. You want your response to start in the right place and address the specific confusion that prompted the question. I asked clarifying questions so I could answer the real question that was being posed.

However, giving good, specifically targeted answers is not the primary goal of teaching. The best thing you can give to a man who asks for a fish is not a fish but a working knowledge of the process of fishing. Similarly, the

---

4. Elder, "Role of Questions in Teaching."

best gift you can give to your students is not an answer (the product of your thinking) but a better working knowledge of the process of thinking that will lead them to the products we call answers.

This is not a new insight. Josiah Fitch in 1879 said:

> The whole sum of what may be said about questioning is comprised in this: It ought to set the learners thinking, to promote activity and energy on their part, and to arouse the whole mental faculty into action, instead of blindly cultivating the memory at the expense of higher intellectual powers. That is the best questioning which best stimulates action on the part of the learner; which gives him a habit of thinking and inquiring for himself; which tends in a great measure to render him independent of his teacher; which makes him, in fact, a rather skillful finder than a patient receiver of the truth."[5]

Imagine that you have somehow just now been transported to a microbiology classroom somewhere in the U.S. where content about antibiotic use and misuse is being presented. *You know what you've learned in this book about how people learn, so you're filtering this experience through that grid.* You are seated on the back row of the classroom and you're not even sure if the students or the teacher can see you. Definitely no one is interacting with you. Students are in their seats, the bell has rung, and a standard informative lecture is underway.

Here's what you are hearing in the first twenty minutes: *Antibiotics were first used in the early 1940s. The first antibiotic discovered was penicillin, and initially it was administered only by injection. We have discovered many additional antibiotics since the 1940s and created many chemical modifications of those we have discovered. The most prolific period for discovery of new antibiotics ended about 1970, and the pace of discovery has slowed considerably since then.*

At the same time antibiotic prescribing has skyrocketed since the early 1940s, when antibiotics were primarily used to treat serious battlefield wounds. Presently the CDC estimates that antibiotic use in the U.S. may be as high as four out of every five Americans in a given year.[6] *Multiple estimates indicate that 50 percent of all prescriptions in the U.S. are inappropriate or unnecessary.*[7] *Many of the antibiotics prescribed are modified types created since 1970. The shift in prescribing is a reflection of a growing problem with antibiotic resistance. At least two million people per year are infected with an-*

---

5. Fitch, *Art of Questioning*, 91.
6. Anonymous, "Antibiotics Prescribed."
7. Anonymous, "Antibiotic Prescribing."

tibiotic-resistant bacteria in the U.S., and resistance to virtually every known antibiotic has been discovered. Indeed at least twenty-three thousand people died in 2013 from infections that would have been treatable in the 1970s when antibiotic resistance was a relatively minor problem.[8]

These are fact-laden paragraphs. To be fair, these are probably the take-home messages from the lecture (no one could endure such an information-dense lecture for very long!). The additional content of the class period beyond these messages was just factual filler, however. What is striking here is that the basic problem is, at best, only hinted at. The content screams the big question, "How has the promise of antibiotics been squandered?" The student experience in this classroom, however, didn't engage the big question. Students in this classroom were beset with wave after wave of facts. No doubt these are interesting facts in their own right, but this situation clearly has higher stakes than a game of *Trivial Pursuit*.

A little reflection reveals that all of these facts are the result of serious thought and investigation by knowledgeable professionals. The facts are answers to questions, but the questions have disappeared. The facts are now mere products on display; nowhere is there even a discussion of the thinking process by which others learned these things. What were the questions that propelled their thinking? What are the current questions that drive the thinking of professionals? Can the students vicariously partner with professionals in their thinking? Are there actions students should take given these realities? How should a student interact with his physician next time the student has an office visit for treatment of an infection? The questions just keep on coming . . . IF they aren't smothered by an avalanche of answers.

Not an Inquisition

The place to start is for you, the teacher, to use questions as an intentional part of your instruction. Don't reserve questions just for review or summation activities. Intersperse them throughout your class periods. While you are getting comfortable with questions, use them at least for diagnostic purposes. You want to find out what your students know—preferably what they understand, misunderstand, or don't understand. Ask questions of clarification so that you understand exactly what the student is saying. That's just part of being a good listener.

Speaking of being a good listener, give the student who is answering your question your undivided attention. Maintain eye contact, but don't stare her down. Lean forward a little toward the student. Give positive,

---

8. Anonymous, "Antibiotic Resistance."

affirming body language that says you want to understand her. Don't cross your arms. Don't read your notes or look out the window while she is talking. Insist that other students also accord her similar respect. The general tone of the class should be conversational—the opposite of a spontaneous oral examination in front of her peers. Make her feel safe and put the best face on any responses she gives. To reinforce the importance of her contribution, you might sometimes ask another student to summarize the answer she has given. Reformulate the summary (or the answer) as necessary for accuracy, but be tactful and gentle as you add, subtract, or make substitutions.

Misuses of questions are certainly possible. Low-level questions of fact should be avoided. Students either know or don't know the answer to a fact question. Additional questions piled on top of an unanswered fact question will most likely just produce frustration in both the questioner and the would-be answerer. A not too uncommon extreme to be avoided is to pepper a student with multiple, related questions and leave him feeling assaulted and unsure which of your questions he is supposed to answer. This also occurs when questions are posed with insufficient wait time. In one study in an elementary school classroom it was observed that "students were confronted with a new question every twelve seconds. In this kind of inquisitorial atmosphere, questioning can actually discourage class discussion."[9]

Worthwhile questions probe understanding, but those are the very questions that require you to patiently wait for an answer. Formulation of a suitable response to a thought-provoking question requires processing time. Your sense of time and the student's sense of time will be vastly different. Most teachers answer their own questions in about two seconds. Don't answer your own questions! Reformulate the question to a more basic question if ten to fifteen seconds of wait time doesn't garner an answer. Rarely, you can direct the question to a different student after the wait time produces no answer. If you do this, assure the first student that you'll return to her a bit later (and then do it). By the way, this also signals that "I don't know" responses are unacceptable. You'll have to communicate this to students at the beginning of your course when you unveil the rules of engagement for your class. All students are members of a learning community, and they have responsibilities to the community. Do not limit your questions to those who raise their hands or recognize those who tend to blurt out answers. Don't allow anyone to dominate the conversation.

Occasionally it is a good thing to end class with a thought-provoking question so that students can chew on it until the next class period. This is more helpful for "crockpot thinkers" (more than for "microwave thinkers"),

---

9. Christenbury and Kelly, *Questioning*, 9.

because it allows for individual differences in background knowledge and processing time. It also generates higher quality responses. Be certain if you end class this way, that you start the next class period dealing with the question and possible answers. This communicates that you expect engagement with class outside of the class period. In the age of LMS (learning management systems), it is useful to allow for asynchronous responses to your questions by posting questions online and allowing hours or days for student responses to your post. Class time is more attuned to near synchronous responses to questions.

Connecting the Dots

Questions can be used to diagnose understanding; but, more fundamentally, questions are the engines of thought. You want students to engage in question answering (and eventually question generating too) because questions propel thinking. Working out an answer to a question propels us straight into the working layer of the logic of a discipline.

The working layer of logic is inhabited by assumptions, facts, and our existing conceptual framework. In attempting to answer a question we become especially engaged in the process of concept assimilation. To assimilate a concept is not the same as concept creation (which we did lots of until we were about three). As adults we are typically involved in trying to find a home for a new concept among our old familiar concepts. Someone introduces us to a new idea, and we try to find a place for it. There is no mental equivalent to a garage where things are stored willy-nilly. There must be a logical home for each concept, or it gets kicked to the curb for disposal.

To find this logical home, we wrestle with the unwieldy idea and try it out in relation to other ideas that we are already secure in understanding. The first strong linkage to the new concept is satisfying, but it's not enough. We explore other possible relationships too because mature thinking is highly branched and connects in unexpected (but very logical) ways. This is what Ken Bain calls "mindfulness." Knowing that we don't inhabit a private universe, our understanding is going to have to make peace with the conceptual frameworks of others who are dealing with the same reality. This happens through interacting with their questions and their assertions about the way they see this concept. "I'm constantly creating new categories surrounding the event or object, and I'm aware that someone else might create other categories that could challenge mine. I imagine seeing, using, understanding, comparing, and contrasting in whole new ways, and always

I wonder what I don't know that might upset my applecart of thinking. . . . In short, I'm thinking deeply about it."[10]

Logical grappling with a concept while trying to connect it is intellectually demanding and, ultimately, very satisfying. Each of your students is personally involved in this logical connecting, and each one feels that he has come up with the conclusion. The conclusion is not imposed on him from outside, but it is a product of his own thinking. The conclusion "makes sense," so it is memorable. It is he who has achieved understanding (on some level), and that means that he can explain to someone else the reason for the linkage he has made to other concepts. If the concepts are like dots, he's trying to connect the dots. He connects dots using lines, but the "lines" between concepts in his brain (and in his concept maps) always have logical propositions "written" on them. When the student is trying to connect one concept with another, it is hard to know where to start. Unlike in 'dot-to-dot' pictures, the dots are not numbered. It is not obvious which of the old dots he's going to connect to this new dot. There are lots possibilities, and this is not something anyone else can do for him.

Suppose for instance that a student is flying for the first time in leaving college for a holiday break. Perhaps he is trying to make sense of having to have a boarding pass and a government issued photo ID to get past the TSA checkpoint. He has already purchased a ticket online and reserved a seat in the process, so why is there this additional red tape? (Let's leave the inspection of carry-on luggage out of it.) How could a teacher facilitate the student's conceptualization? *Facilitation is best accomplished by means of questions.* Here the teacher might ask some of these questions: Why is there a checkpoint set up? Who is authorized to be in the part of the airport past the checkpoint? Why are other people excluded? How can you prove that you have business in that part of the airport?

The teacher cannot successfully impose his personal conceptual associations on his student. He can't transfer his understanding. He can only guide the student *through questions* to consider more plausible and less plausible target concepts and *through questions* steer the student to evaluate the logic of his propositional links.

As with a good driver's ed instructor, the student is behind the wheel even though the journey would be safer and more time-efficient if the instructor took the wheel. The purpose of driver's ed is to produce skilled drivers, and that can't happen unless neophytes get instruction that makes sense to them. If they are obeying instructions only while the instructor is in

---

10. Bain, *What the Best College Students Do*, 73-74.

the car, it may become tragically evident once they get their driver's license what they really do and do not understand about driving.

Writing Questions That Facilitate Thinking

If, by now, you're persuaded that asking good questions is essential to facilitating learning, the difficulty becomes one of "How do I learn to write good questions?" This is a valid concern. If you are coming from a teaching as telling background, it should be assumed to begin with that your default mode is to ask questions about what you "told" your students. Such questions are generally factual recall questions. But remembering is not the goal of teaching—understanding is. Memory is a byproduct of understanding. Writing questions that test understanding is a major thrust of chapter 9. What I'll give you in this chapter is an approach by which you can successfully formulate questions that will *facilitate student thinking*.

Simply put, questions that facilitate thinking are questions that intentionally focus attention on the elements of logical thought. These elements are the same for all academic domains, though the specifics of each vary enormously. The elements of thought are point of view, motivation, appropriate questions, assumptions, information, conceptual frameworks, explanation, and implications/consequences. Therefore you need to learn to write questions in each of these categories.[11] As you become increasingly self-aware in employing the logic of your discipline, you will simultaneously be growing in your ability to ask questions that will stimulate and clarify thinking in your students. Becoming a clear-thinking teacher will pay dividends in the classroom.

Core Logic Questions

The first group of questions you should learn to write are questions about elements of the core of logic. It is easy to overlook these questions and to jump right to questions about the working layer, but that is a mistake. The clarity of thinking will inevitably be compromised if your questions don't help students to confront directly the point of view they are reasoning from, the motive behind their thinking (what they hope to accomplish with it),

---

11. Paul and Elder, *Thinker's Guide to Socratic Questioning*. Contains additional information about Socratic questioning and many examples of specific questions that probe the elements of thinking. My categories in this chapter are substantially the same as those of Paul and Elder with the exceptions noted in chapter 3 of this book.

and the questions that can properly be answered from this chosen vantage point.

Elder and Paul observe that with a complex conceptual question there are many ways in which the question can be approached. "In this case, standard definitions do not settle the question, but rather open the argument. Divergent points of view can be brought to bear on the definitions stretching them this way or that."[12] Because multiple *points of view* can legitimately be adopted on many questions, it is crucial that the students know what point of view they are going to reason from and what motivates that choice. It can be very confusing to students when the point of view shifts during a discussion. If you elect to adopt a different point of view, make sure that is made explicit and that you don't drift into another point of view. If a student shifts to a different point of view during a discussion, you might simply say, "Are you intentionally looking at this from the point of view of Y? Remember that our discussion to this point has been based on the point of view of X." You might follow with, "How do you think this change of point of view might be helpful in addressing the question?" (*a question of motivation*).

Remembering that thinking is always driven by questions, help students to focus on the question that is currently on the table. You might ask, "Is this the right question to start with or is there a more basic question that we need to answer first?" This is called *questioning the question*. The wrong question can lead to disastrous consequences in the profitability and clarity of the discussion that follows, so make sure you are focusing on the right question. If the discussion demonstrates that the question is not clear to the students, you might ask how the question can be reworded. Similarly, if a student offers an answer that is only tangentially related to the question on the table, you might ask, "What question does that help to answer?" This recognizes the contribution while at the same time signaling that the discussion should be based on logical connection and not just free association.

Working Layer Questions

Logical discourse can always move back and forth between core logic, working layer, and the output layer; but a significant amount of the discussion time should usually be spent in the working layer. Resist the temptation to minimize the working process and to jump to answers prematurely. Your goal in asking questions is not to answer them with the greatest possible time efficiency. Rather your questions are intended to drive a process of *student thinking*. A majority of the time your questions should be facilitating

---

12. Elder and Paul, *Miniature Guide to Essential Questions*, 12.

conceptualization while also exploring what the student is assuming and what facts support a particular line of reasoning. These are the elements of the working layer.

You can be a significant help to your student by helping him recognize what he is basing his reasoning on that he is taking for granted. Perhaps the assumptions are justified in a different domain of thought, or perhaps they are impossible to prove. Whichever is the case, it is always helpful before the reasoning proceeds very far to recognize that all reasoning assumes something. That includes the reasoning your student is embarking on. By all means *question assumptions* so that they are at least acknowledged.

Previous reasoning by others in the discipline has yielded a body of factual information that is generally accepted. Good reasoning *usually* doesn't contradict factual information. I say usually because supposed facts are not always true; and, over time, some are removed from the body of information. Factual information generally serves as evidence for or against a line of reasoning. Questions that ask for examples or evidence are *information questions*. Another name for these is empirical questions, which "are questions primarily answered through determining facts. . . . Empirical questions fall into two categories: those for which the answer has already been determined, and those not yet settled. . . . Both depend on facts. . . . Many questions are not exclusively empirical, but have an important empirical dimension."[13] With few exceptions the original question that started this line of reasoning (back in the core) is not answered simply by coming up with the appropriate fact. That is to say, even with questions for which the answer is already known (probably the majority of your questions), you don't want just to unearth the answer. Your goal is to stimulate thinking, and thinking uses facts primarily as evidence pro and con for a line of reasoning.

Because conceptualization is the heart of reasoning, the majority of your questions should be conceptual questions. Conceptual questions aim for a deep understanding of the concepts (ideas) and principles (foundational propositions) that are intrinsic to answering the original question. Along the way to answering the bigger question you need to make certain that ideas are being handled appropriately. Some *conceptual questions* are as simple as gaining clarity about the meaning of words in generally accepted use.[14] "What do you mean when you refer to 'intellectual property'? Would

---

13. Ibid., 15.

14. Wilson, *Thinking with Concepts*, 11. "We must not make the mistake of thinking that answering questions of concept is a matter of 'defining one's terms', and that we should begin by producing a definition of 'science', 'democracy', etc. For the whole point of asking such questions is that the definition of these words is unclear: or we might rather say that they do not have definitions, but only uses."

looking at information on a cell phone you have just found qualify as 'espionage'?" Just because the answer is found in generally accepted usage does not make these trivial throwaway questions. When students are permitted sloppy use of terms, the concepts that underlie the terms are distorted or corrupted. Such intellectual dithering does not produce a clear picture.

Along the way to getting students to answer a complex conceptual question, you will frequently need to ask simple conceptual questions that deal with word usage. The complex conceptual question is clarified by seeking a clear sense of how the underlying concepts are being employed, but that is only a beginning. Questioning can often profitably drive toward finding the central concept or principle or by highlighting conflict or even apparent (or real) contradiction between two ideas. Probing questions can be just what the student needs to address a misconception that he harbors. Conceptualization is sabotaged when the student's foundational concepts are flawed, and exposing these flaws requires good questions that the student has probably never asked himself. Cognitive dissonance is desirable in this case, and you are in a position to create it with your questions if you understand the common misconceptions that students hold. I'm not talking about your becoming an interrogator grilling your victim—that atmosphere will elicit intransigence from the student on the inside at least and maybe on the outside as well. You're probably familiar with the folk wisdom in "A man convinced against his will is of the same opinion still." You don't want this to become a battle of the wills but rather a conversation with your assuming the role of an interested absorbed listener. You demonstrate the depth of your listening by the depth of your questions. If everything about the conversation says that you want to help the student, her desire will normally be to cooperate—to help you help her. This is as good as it gets. You are the ally of the student helping her toward personal flashes of insight that occur within her own brain. The flashes are hers, and she owns them; but you facilitated the flashes through your skilled questioning. I say questioning because the most effective help is not one insightful question but a series of them.

Output Layer Questions

The final group of questions concerns the outputs of thinking. One output is an explanation in which we utilize principles in the form of cause and effect relationships (or otherwise account for a phenomenon) to answer the original question. The other output is the ability to predict short-term implications and long-term consequences. Implications and consequences take the form of "if (explanation), then ___." The output layer actually generates another round of questions rather than just smug answers to be memorized.

These outputs are powerful outcomes generated especially through robust conceptualization. *Questions of explanation* often take the form of asking the student questions about the *relationship* between concepts. You are trying to catalyze the quantum leap in understanding that occurs when the student creates robust conceptual *frameworks*. You are particularly asking questions that facilitate the student articulating propositional relationships between concepts. Strive to help her make those propositions as strong as possible—cause and effect when that is realistic. Strong propositions are often principles. Explanation is an answer, but there may be different possible answers to a question. Elder and Paul call these "Questions of Judgment (conflicting systems)—Questions requiring reasoning, but with more than one arguable answer. These are questions that make sense to debate, questions with better-or-worse-answers."[15]

To have good judgment is akin to wisdom, and wisdom (sometimes defined as "pursuing of the best ends by the best means")[16] is certainly the ultimate in the panoply of academic outcomes. Wisdom looks down the road for the implications and consequences of taking a particular position. *Questions of implication* involve asking students for immediate logical implications based on the assertion they are making in the form of "If ___, then ___." What immediately follows from the position they are taking? This is pure deductive logic. Sometimes the implications are significant enough that the student realizes that where his position leads invalidates his own thinking. He is not willing to own the implications of his line of reasoning, so he analyzes it as defective in some way. This is enormously helpful as it is one of the places where metacognition surfaces explicitly.

Questions about consequences are not as straightforward as implications, but students need to realize that "ideas have consequences."[17] Encourage your student through questions to follow the trajectory of his thought forward in time. This is a useful exercise but hard to do without some guidance. How does one extrapolate the obvious immediate deductive implications? Perhaps there is already some evidence available for where a particular course of action can lead? If so, direct him through questions to ponder whether a particular case is parallel. To what extent is the case informative? In what ways does it differ? Don't impose your own foresight as the answer. None of us can see into the future, and the prophecies of

---

15. Elder and Paul, *Miniature Guide to Essential Questions*, 9.
16. Hutcheson, *Inquiry Into the Original of Our Ideas*.
17. Weaver, *Ideas Have Consequences*.

experts can be as badly flawed as those of amateurs.[18] As with questions of implication, when the student recognizes the logical consequences of his position, he may be forced to rethink his position because of his discomfort with the consequences. Help students recognize that they are conducting "thought experiments" when they do this. All good and wise thinking tries to anticipate consequences before committing to a course of action.

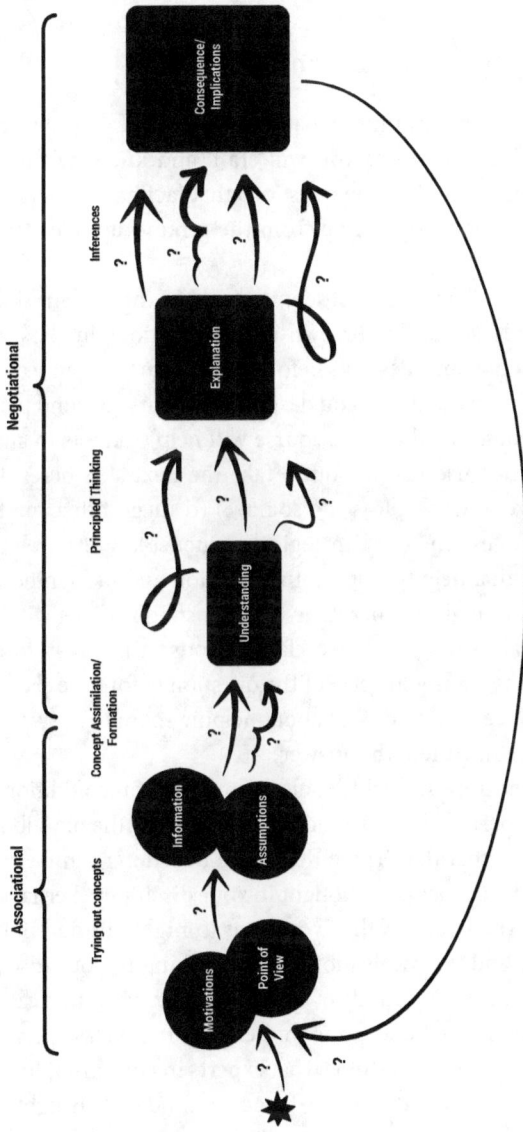

18. Failure of experts to foresee the collapse of the Internet tech bubble, the housing bubble, the Great Recession of 2007, etc.

The diagram on the previous page shows the driving role of questions in moving thinking forward toward answers (explanation). Questions can be about any of the elements of logical thought, and questions ultimately generate new questions, creating an infinite loop. Understanding begins to crystallize at the level of principle formation, and explanation emerges as a consequence of principialization.

Learning to Fly

The clarity of your own thinking about the logic of your discipline will directly inform the questions you will craft, and knowing this should be a great encouragement. Writing questions that facilitate understanding is not a skill that you have to develop from the ground up like learning to play Quidditch![19]

Just as you would for a student who is trying to gain skill at reasoning, you should scaffold your own use of questions in class. Initially you should write out your questions beforehand as part of your lesson planning. In chapter 6 I suggested that you design your course around perhaps six big compelling questions that your course will help students to answer. I hope you did that because I want you to take the next step here. (If you didn't write any big questions, please do so now.) I'd suggest that you take the first of those big questions (first in logical sequence), and develop a series of subquestions that help to unpack the question and its significance. Put the subquestions in logical order. One of these subquestions will be the question on the table for one or two class periods. It is a help to the students even if this is as far as you get. Put the question before the class explicitly so that they can see that class is all about helping them to answer the question (rather than telling them the answer).

A further improvement would be to plan some additional questions for each class period. These would be derived from the big subquestion that is driving class that day. These derivative questions can be crafted to explore any of the elements of thought in your discipline. Perhaps for the first class period when you do this, you want to highlight questions regarding point of view and the motivation of the thinking in your discipline. These directly determine what kinds of questions your discipline can ask and the kind of answers you'll end up with. Perhaps a few class periods later you can highlight through questions what experts in your discipline assume and major relevant facts that have to be accommodated in light of the question that controls the day. Conceptualization questions can ramp up shortly

---

19. Anonymous, "Quidditch."

thereafter and take a prominent role in most class periods. This is but one possible way to practice gaining facility with questions.

To be perfectly honest, I must tell you that a percentage of your questions will misfire. What I mean is that students may not know what you are asking, or your question might lead to responses that are not at all what you had in mind. This happens to everyone. Don't let it bother you. Learn from the student responses how they take your question. Be humble and don't take yourself too seriously. Be prepared to question your own question by asking a more basic question. If that doesn't work, abandon that question for that class period and move on.

As you gain the ability to preplan questions that work reasonably well, the next step is to take the risk of generating questions "on the fly" during the class period. This isn't as hard as it sounds if you think of yourself as an engaged reflective listener participating in a conversation. What do you not understand about what the student said? Ask questions of clarification. Ask for an example. Pursue the line of reasoning actively, but do it through questions. Perhaps you think the student has misunderstood—then question his fact base, question his sources, question his conceptualization, question the logical sequence of his ideas. Perhaps you think the student has a skewed perspective—question his point of view, question why he has chosen to look at things this way instead of another way, question whether he is aware of another perspective and, if so, question on what basis he has dismissed it.[20]

Flying Solo: Socratic Questioning

In chapter 7 I introduced the Paideia group's three-column approach to teaching. The three columns were instruction (didactic teaching), coaching, and seminars (Socratic questioning). Although the Paideia representation portrays Socratic questioning as something apart from coaching, I don't believe that it is. On closer examination Adler and Van Doren came close to agreeing, for they said, "Seminars can be used to reinforce coaching in a variety of ways. When well-conducted, seminars involve coaching in the arts of reading, of speaking, and of listening."[21] And, I would add, coaching in reflective analytical thinking. Socratic questioning is an extraordinarily effective way to coach.

Socratic questioning is intimidating to most teachers. Teachers tend to view Socratic questioning as the province of a gifted few whose combination of incisive intellect and razor sharp rhetorical skills allows them to

20. Elder and Paul, *Miniature Guide to Essential Questions*, 22-23.
21. Adler, *Paideia Program*, 30.

mesmerize an auditorium full of students. The mythology surrounding this kind of teaching is that you need to have to a verbal black belt before you enter the arena, I mean the classroom. I assure you this is not true. Coaching by means of Socratic questioning is within the reach of every teacher.

Socratic discussion is a valuable tool to have in your tool box. You can use it periodically in ten-to-twenty-minute bursts, it can be used for an entire class period to discuss a particular idea, or (more rarely) it can dictate the form of an entire course. I'd like you to warm to the idea of eventually using it about a quarter of the time in at least one of your courses. The more you use it, the more you will find it to be a powerful way to help students learn.

"[Socrates] called his method of teaching something like midwifery because he viewed it as assisting the labor of his companions in giving birth to ideas."[22] A midwife is often viewed as a coach in the labor and delivery process. Like a coach, the midwife knows a lot about the process she is coaching. She is not the one trying to give birth, but she is trying to facilitate the birth process. As an intellectual coach (midwife), you are trying to help your students through the sometimes trying conceptualization process; but it is they who must ultimately birth the ideas.

Two of the major problems that block thinking in students are vagueness in thinking and faulty conceptualization. Moving students through such blocks is where Socratic discussion shines. John Stuart Mill (the father of utilitarianism) said of his own education at the hand of his father:

> The Socratic method . . . is unsurpassed as a discipline for correcting the errors and clearing up the confusions incident to the *intellectus sibi permissus* [mind left to itself], . . .The close, searching *elenchus* [debate] by which the man of vague generalities is constrained either to express his meaning . . . or to confess that he does not know what he is talking about; the perpetual testing of all general statements by particular instances; the siege in form which is laid to the meaning of large abstract terms, by fixing upon some still larger class-name which includes that and more, and dividing down to the thing sought—marking out its limits and definition by a series of accurately drawn distinctions between it and each of the cognate objects which are successively parted off from it —all this, as an education for precise thinking is inestimable."[23]

---

22. Ibid, 16.
23. Mill, *Autobiography*, 38-39.

In the interest of clarity and precision I need to distinguish what Mill experienced from what I'm proposing. Mill was subjected to the Socratic Method, also known as the Elenchus or Socratic Debate. The spirit of such inquiry was centered on leading a participant to contradict himself so that the questioner in the debate could "win." Mill and other intellectuals have thrived in such a challenging atmosphere, but I think it is unnecessarily polemical and threatening to most students. That is why I and others use instead the phrase Socratic discussion. The tone of the discussion is that of a conversation with the questioner modeling a sympathetic engaged listener and not Torquemada.

I don't think this modification weakens the effectiveness of Socratic questioning in the slightest, and it is egalitarian rather than intellectually elitist. As a teacher you want to help create intellectual fitness in all of your students rather than through intellectual combat selecting those that are already the fittest. Socratic discussion puts you in the position of modeling your expert thinking in real time. Don't stumble over the word *model*. Modeling doesn't mean you have to be the quintessence of a thinker, a dominating intellect. You just need to be competent, humble, and gentle as you guide the discussion by means of your questions rather than through assertions. Instead of hovering over a discussion as a towering intellect ready to hurl down thunderbolts like Zeus, you actually get into the middle of student perplexity. As thinking encounters fog, uncertainty, and even cognitive dissonance, you are there, not to give answers but to model what a reflective analytical thinker does in such a situation. In the process you show students the power of strategic questioning—a power that they too can develop. Through modeling you help students to embrace perplexity as an inevitable part of analytical reasoning, and you help them grow in their competence as question askers.

In preparing for a Socratic discussion you should preplan the major questions. These will end up being strategic in the discussion, but you'll have to make up a significant number of additional questions "on the fly" to keep the discussion headed in a profitable direction. Don't let the reality that you can't script the entire time spook you. It would be very artificial if you had scripted in advance what you would ask as a follow-up to every conceivable response to the previous question. Operating from a script would keep you from really listening and asking appropriate follow-up questions. Use your preplanned questions to launch the discussion and again periodically as they fit in at various branch points in the conversation.

There's one last preparatory point before we try to preplan a Socratic discussion. Mill commented above that he was obliged by the Socratic Method to either express himself "or to confess that he does not know what he is talking about." This could be an opportunity for a negative putdown; but in the supportive atmosphere of a Socratic discussion, it is a simple expedient to unearth what is inside. "In . . . conversation, many of us have been startled to hear ourselves making a statement or expressing an opinion that we did not know we actually believe until we *heard* ourselves speak."[24] Having to answer a question gets a student's thinking out where we can all see it. On the other hand it is also true that "the person who says he knows what he thinks but cannot express it usually does not know what he thinks."[25] To help the student discover this requires gentleness and a supportive atmosphere, but it is a kindness for a student to realize what he doesn't know. Ignorance can be cured!

Preplanning a Socratic Discussion

Let's walk through a practical example of the preplanning process you would use to generate questions. The topic will be the one we visited as a negative example of teaching by telling early in this chapter. What we experienced there was an information dump full of answers rather than driven by questions. We concluded then that the central question should have been "How has the promise of antibiotics been squandered?" I'm using this question because most of us have been prescribed antibiotics and because the factual information is already available in this chapter. A Socratic discussion is not a place to build a fact base. If the facts aren't already there, the questioning just elicits opinions rather than "justifiable belief." Preceding this discussion you would assign some reading like the three articles that were referenced on this topic early in this chapter. Students should be told that the articles are just the starting point for reasoning but that they will be accountable for analytical reading of the articles (see chapter 7). The Roman numerals I, II, and III on the next two pages represent respectively the core, working layer, and output layer of thinking.

---

24. Christenbury and Kelly, *Questioning*, 1.
25. Adler and Van Doren, *How to Read a Book*, 49.

I. A. *Appropriate Questions (Central Question & Nested Subquestions)*

How has the promise of antibiotics been squandered?
    What did the discovery of antibiotics promise?
        What is an antibiotic?
            How does an antibiotic work?
                What do antibiotics work against?
                      Do antibiotics work as well as they once did?
                          How do antibiotics lose their effectiveness?
                              How has the promise been squandered?

B. *Motivation for the Thinking*

To decide what appropriate antibiotic prescribing looks like.

C. *Point of View (Multidimensional Question with Multiple Points of View)*

Microbiologist

Patient

Physician

Public health worker

II. A. *Assumptions*

All infectious diseases that can be treated should be treated.

Antibiotics will always be available.

(Microbiologist) Antibiotic resistance occurs naturally whether or not antibiotics are used.

B. *Information*

CDC/WHO statistics on antibiotic resistant strains of various disease agents

Case studies showing the emergence of antibiotic resistance

Personal experience with failed antibiotic prescribing

International perspective showing that antibiotics are available without prescription in some countries

C. *Concepts/Principles*

> Antibiotics always target vital aspects of the infectious agent that are not shared by the human host (selective toxicity principle).
>
> Mechanisms of antibiotic resistance
>
> Antibiotic resistance genes
>
> Mechanisms for transferring antibiotic resistance genes
>
> Culturing infectious disease agents
>
> Identifying infectious disease agents
>
> Antimicrobial susceptibility testing
>
> Serious infectious disease
>
> Necessary duration of antimicrobial treatment

III. A. *Explanation*

> Antibiotic therapy needs be appropriately informed. This is done by culturing and identifying the infectious agent and by testing the susceptibility of the agent to specific antimicrobials. The prescription should be for an agent that data strongly suggest will give a successful therapeutic outcome.
>
> Antibiotic therapy should be reserved for significant infections.

B. *Implications*

> Antibiotic use always constitutes artificial selection for antibiotic resistance genes.
>
> Antibiotic resistance is bound to emerge in infectious organisms.

C. *Consequences*

> More frequent use of a specific antibiotic decreases the length of time that antibiotic will remain therapeutically useful.
>
> The magnitude of current antibiotic prescribing cannot be sustained and, unless drastically reduced, will result in a postantibiotic era in which most infectious diseases will once again be untreatable.

Conducting a Socratic Discussion

To write out the entire dialog of a Socratic discussion would be tedious, and it would make a very long chapter. I do want to give you some practical sense of how a discussion would be conducted, so I'll start the discussion and give you glimpses of a few places that the discussion might go. In the process you'll notice that I have you asking some questions that aren't in the list above. Notice that these additional questions are a natural consequence of you really hearing what the student is saying and responding in a helpful way.

You: Today we're going to be discussing the question "How has the promise of antibiotics been squandered?" This question was formulated as a result of reflection on the sources that you were assigned to read. You're welcome to reference factual information from those sources, but otherwise I want you to do your own thinking. Let's start with a simpler question and build toward an answer to the central question. The simpler question is "What did the discovery of antibiotics promise?" Sarah, how would you answer that?

Sarah: Before antibiotics were discovered infections could not be treated. I mean you would try to make the patient comfortable, but you couldn't really treat the cause of the infection. The use of the first antibiotic in treating infections was viewed as nearly miraculous.

You: That's good historical perspective. So, follow-up question, Sarah. Whose perspective are you looking at this question from?

Sarah: I guess from the medical viewpoint. From the viewpoint of a person who wanted to help the person who had an infection.

You: Excellent. Maybe later we'll explore other points of view, but let's stick with the perspective of a physician for now. One more question, Sarah. What does the word *promise* as in "the promise of antibiotics" cause us to focus on besides the accurate historical perspective you gave us?

Sarah: I guess it means "how could things be better in the future as the result of the discovery of antibiotics?"

You: That's right. Another way of saying this is that the discovery of antibiotics was a potential game changer. Ted, what was game changing about the availability of antibiotics?

Ted: People didn't need to die as a result of infections.

You: Was that a common occurrence, Ted?

Ted: I believe so, based on the articles we read.

You: What were the most common causes of death before 1940? Does anyone know? [silence]

You: What are the most common causes of death today?

Ted: Things like cancer and heart disease.

You: Ted said he believed that people often died of infections before there were antibiotics available to physicians, and he was right. Were cancer and heart disease the major killers before 1940?

Melissa (volunteers): I think the major killers were infections.

You: Why do you say that?

Melissa: Because babies and children get lots of infections so they have lots of chances to die.

You: I think you're on the right track, Melissa. Is there any evidence that you know of that lots of children died?

Melissa: People had lots of children and many of them died during childhood.

You: What statistic would reflect this?

Sid (volunteers): Life expectancy. People live to be a lot older now than they did a hundred years ago.

You: Is that true in every country?

Sid: It's not true of some countries. I think it is not true in countries where the water is not clean and people don't have enough food.

The conversation continues. Let's pick up the discussion a bit later.

You: Sophie, how do we look at the use of antibiotics differently from the way patients and physicians looked at them in the early 1940s?

Sophie: They were rare back then, but they are common now.

You: That's true. Why are they common now, Sophie?

Sophie: Because they are easy to get.

You: Is that another way of saying they are common?

Sophie: I guess so. What I meant was that any drugstore carries them and most of us have taken one.

You: OK. Becca, how do you get an antibiotic? Can you just go to the drugstore and buy one?

Becca: My uncle who lives in Thailand can do that. Here we have to have a prescription sent to the drugstore.

You: Adam, why you do you think a prescription is required in the U.S. but not in Thailand?

Adam: To make it harder to get an antibiotic here.

You: Why would we want to make it harder to get an antibiotic, Adam?

Adam: To make sure you really need one?

You: How can someone determine that, Adam?

Adam: A doctor could take a look at you to see if you are really sick.

You: So how sick do you have to be before you get a prescription for an antibiotic? Zach, why don't you answer that?

Zach: Pretty sick, I guess.

You: Zach, when would it be the right call for an antibiotic to be prescribed for a patient?
Zach: When it could help fix the problem the patient has; otherwise it's a waste.
You: What kinds of problems can an antibiotic help with, Zach?
Zach: With infections, I think.
You: That's right. What causes an infection, Emily?
Emily: All kinds of things, bacteria, germs, that kind of thing.
You: Are those alive, Emily?
Emily: I think so, yes.
You: So what is the antibiotic supposed to do to the cause of the infection, Emily?
Emily: Kill it, I guess.
You: Does that sound dangerous, Emily?
Emily: (laughs) To the germs, for sure.
You: Emily, if the antibiotic failed to kill the cause of the infection, what would happen?
Emily: I guess you'd have to go back and get a different antibiotic.
You: What might have happened while you were taking the wrong antibiotic? Has anyone had that experience?
Tyler: I did about a month ago. I got a lot sicker while I was taking an antibiotic and eventually I got a prescription for a stronger antibiotic that worked.
You: Why did your physician start with a weak antibiotic, Tyler?
Tyler: I guess he thought it would work, but it didn't.
You: Is there any way a physician could know in advance whether an antibiotic will work, or is it just a guessing game?
Amanda: If he grew a culture of the infection, he could try antibiotics out on the culture to see what would work.
You: That's an excellent approach. How often is it used? Did Tyler's physician use it?
Tyler: My doctor didn't take a culture.
You: Why do you think culturing and testing of antibiotics isn't used more often? Becca, why don't you answer that one?
Becca: It takes time to do the testing.
You: That's true. While the physician is waiting for test results, what should he do for the patient, Becca?
Becca: Make the patient comfortable, but they should wait to prescribe an antibiotic until the test results tell them which one to use. Otherwise they are guessing.
You: That makes sense. Will the patient be happy with the wait?

Tyler: My mom definitely would not be happy. She expected to have a prescription in her hand when the doctor was finished looking at me last month.

You: So are there multiple points of view from which we should look at the question?

Here's another fork in the road and you can decide where to go from here in a way that will get your students thinking about the big question, "How has the promise of antibiotics been squandered?" *Squandered* is a strong word, so be prepared for some strong reactions, e.g., from the children of physicians. Make certain, however, that emotion plays only a supporting role in the discussion. Explanations should be generated through logical reasoning and supported by evidence. Also, don't allow any student to dominate the discussion.

One thing that this example highlights is that I seldom use the preplanned questions exactly as written. Writing them is not a waste of time, however! Preplanned questions guide the questioning even though I often used them on the fly to generate related questions. The tone of the discussion needs to show that the discussion leader is really listening, and the best way to do that is to interact with the actual responses of the students with your preplanned questions in the background. This example also demonstrates that not every opportunity to move the discussion in a particular direction is taken. Don't worry about this and don't second guess yourself at these decision points. Socratic discussion is a sequence of questions intended to drive the discussion deeper than it would otherwise go. Socratic discussion is coaching in thinking that helps each student explore possible next questions, depth of understanding, connectedness of concepts, evidence, point of view—in short the whole of the logic of your discipline. Make certain you spread the questioning around. Involving as many students as possible creates a clear sense that we're reasoning as a community of thinkers and that every student is responsible to contribute, and ultimately to own the conclusions. In the event you get to a point in the discussion where you don't know what kind of question should be asked next, I've provided a Socratic GPS in Appendix 4.

When the discussion has reached a satisfactory end-point, it is helpful to the students to summarize the major explanatory principles derived along with the major implications and consequences of these principles. Students should be able to do this for the class. These are not to be memorized. Rather, with these in hand, students should be able to work backward to reconstruct the line of reasoning that produced these conclusions. They should recall major supporting evidence, differing perspectives, and things assumed and otherwise do justice to the multifaceted nature of the discussion.

Options, Do You Have Options!

If the prospect of conducting even a short Socratic discussion still seems daunting, you can work yourself into a position of using this tool eventually by just using questions in any form in your classroom. Because thinking is driven by questions, not answers, any step you take in this direction is a positive development. The more you use questions, the more you will discover their power, and the more comfortable you will become using them.

The emphasis of the previous chapter culminated with active learning strategies. Such strategies catalyze a marked improvement in student learning as we documented there. When you view yourself as a coach rather than as a didactic transmitter, you recognize that students in your course should be playing the game (doing the thinking) rather than watching you play the game or, worse yet, listening to you recount stories from when you and others played the game. Asking questions and waiting for student answers is inherently an active learning strategy.

If you are trying to escape from teaching as telling through lecture, the easiest transition is to move to interactive lecture. In the interactive lecture you lecture, but you interrupt your lecture frequently to ask questions that your students answer. I don't mean that you give your same old lectures punctuated with student involvement. You are now teaching a way of thinking and your lectures need to reflect the *thinking process* of an expert and not just the products of expert thinking (aka "content") that the typical lecture emphasizes. That means that your lectures are going to have to go through a major overhaul as you move to principle-based instruction in your classroom. Punctuating this kind of lecture with questions is a significant step forward as long as the answers students give affect where your lecture goes.

When you consider how you are going to ask questions in the interactive lecture format, you have multiple options. One option is to orally ask one student the question and interact with what she says while trying to make it applicable to the whole class. Another option is to stop and give a brief quiz to the whole class. An attractive option is to poll the class. In a poll you ask a question (usually just one), and students respond within a minute or two using a polling website and their cell phones (or using flash cards with one letter choice on each flash card or even using a certain number of fingers displayed to indicate an answer). The purpose of these polls is to get each student to commit to an answer and then to use the response patterns of the class to determine their degree of understanding so that the teacher knows whether she can move on or whether more instruction is needed.

Approach	Questions	Answers	Student-Generated Thinking	Teacher-Generated Thinking	Content Focus	Didactic	Dialog
Pure Lecture	Rhetorical/peripheral	Teacher	Incidental and later	Central	Central	Pure	Minimal via interruption
Interactive Lecture	Episodic/encouraged	Teacher and/or student	Encouraged	Central	Moderate	Moderate to low	Moderate via invitation
Polling	Teacher	Students	Central	Planning poll questions	Variable	Variable	Teacher to student catalyzed by polls
Think-Pair-Share	Teacher sets starting question	Students	Central	Exercise planning	Secondary	Briefly as needed	Standard operating procedure
Case-based	Teacher and students	Students	Central	Selects case and resources	Secondary	Rarely	Varies: moderate by teacher, to student only

Approach	Questions	Answers	Student-Generated Thinking	Teacher-Generated Thinking	Content Focus	Didactic	Dialog
Socratic Discussion	Teacher and students; disciplined, sequential, central	Students	Central	For discussion planning and guidance	Secondary	None	Standard operating procedure
Group Investigation	Teacher and students	Students	Central	Planning or approving topics	Secondary	None	Mostly between students
Flipped	Indirect via performance tasks	Student performance on tasks	Task oriented	Task planning	Moderate	Mainly out of class; briefly as needed in class	Episodic; based on performance difficulties
Just-in-Time	Teacher and students	Students	Central	Planning modified by student achievement	Secondary	Through out-of-class activities	Mostly between students

Approach	Questions	Answers	Student-Generated Thinking	Teacher-Generated Thinking	Content Focus	Didactic	Dialog
Peer Instruction	Primarily by students	Students	Central	Set starting question and monitor discussion	Secondary	Rarely and in short bursts	Mostly between students
Problem-based	Primarily by students	Students	Central	Planning problems	Secondary	None	Mostly between students
Conceptual Workshop	Students	Students	Central	Exercise planning	Secondary	Rarely	Mostly between students
Open-ended Seminar	Students	Students	Central	Exercise planning	Secondary	None	Mostly between students

Another tactic that can be used from time to time in any kind of classroom (including the interactive lecture) is to do a collaborative activity. One favorite form of this is called "Think, Pair, Share." In this activity you pose to the entire class a question that requires significant thought. You give students a minute or two to think individually about the question and then ask them to talk to a neighbor (pair). After a few minutes of discussion, you then ask a pair of students to share their thinking with another pair. This should expose them to new ways to think about the question or at least new ways to support the reasoning. At this point you as the teacher can call on a few groups to get a sense of the diversity of thinking on the question. Some teachers use what they hear to launch into a short round of Socratic discussion while others use it as a springboard to a brief lecture. There is no one right way to do it. If the truth be told, students enjoy diverse approaches as long as there is some predictability to the class structure. If there is absolutely no pattern, some students feel a loss of control that is harmful to learning.

Perhaps, since you are drastically rethinking your lectures, this is as good a time as any to throw them out and start with a fresh approach. That is definitely in the spirit of crafting the optimal learning path for students. I offer the table on the previous page as a way to evaluate some of the major options. The more radical options are farther down in the table. Some of the options can work nicely together; for example, interactive lecture can include polling, think-pair-share, case-based learning, and Socratic discussion. On the other hand, some of these are stand-alone options. Such is the case with problem-based learning, for instance. Just-in-Time Teaching is frequently practiced with Peer Instruction. Certainly some of these options are probably not familiar to you, so I've included additional information in the footnotes.

This table can help you put the primary focus on active learning, with the students doing the thinking and the thinking driven by questions. The ultimate goal of producing autonomous learners aims to produce students who know how to ask probing questions that direct their own personal inquiry. To that end, some of the approaches (e.g., conceptual workshops) have students as the primary generators of questions. The content column frequently lists a secondary focus on content—this is another way of saying that the emphasis on the products of the thinking in the field is secondary to the thinking process that produced them.

See these notes for more information:

Case-based[26]

Group Investigation[27]

Flipped Classroom[28]

Just-in-Time Teaching[29]

26. Case-based learning tells us students are working within cases as the major focus, but not what they are responsible to do with those cases or how many cases there are or how the cases relate to each other. Go to Anonymous, "Case-based Learning." At this resource you'll find the following: "We have also found the method [case studies] to be extraordinarily flexible. We have seen it used as the core of entire courses or for single experiences in otherwise traditional lecture and lab courses. Moreover, cases can be presented in a variety of formats and taught in a variety of ways, ranging from the classical discussion method used in business and law schools to Problem-Based Learning and Team Learning, with their emphasis on small-group, cooperative learning strategies."

"Case-based learning can be used to illustrated [sic] particular issues or, as in problem-based learning (see later), it can be used throughout a course to address the whole syllabus, the cases being carefully selected so that the contents [sic] areas that are to be addressed are represented and sequenced in the logic of the build-up of knowledge." Biggs and Tang, *Teaching for Quality Learning at University*, 139.

M. Srinivasan, "Comparing Problem-based Learning with Case-based Learning," 74-82. "Case-based learning (CBL) uses a guided inquiry method and provides more structure [than PBL] during small-group sessions."

27. Group investigations are large-scale projects (like semester-long lab projects) where the topic of the investigation is assigned or approved and parameters are established before the investigation begins. Students have great liberty in how to conduct the investigation, but they are responsible for answering certain basic questions and for gathering sufficient evidence (often through experimentation) to support their conclusions. Group papers or individual papers may be written. An oral presentation of the conclusions of the project allows for specific questioning regarding the reasoning process used to formulate conclusions. This questioning may be through Socratic discussion.

28. A Flipped Classroom can mean many things. I use it as it is currently practiced in the K-12 arena. Typically students watch lectures outside of class (sometimes explanations by organizations like the Khan Academy are assigned), and classroom time is focused on the student being engaged with performance tasks (formerly called homework). The teacher circulates through the class helping individual students with the tasks and occasionally making brief presentations to the class to correct problems that are surfacing. The flipped model is based on the work of Jonathan Bergmann and Aaron Sams, *Flip Your Classroom: Reach Every Student in Class Every Day* (Arlington, VA: International Society for Technology in Education, 2012).

29. Novak and Patterson, "Introduction to Just-in-Time Teaching," 3-23. This work indicates that originally JiTT (Just-In-Time Teaching) was developed for nontraditional students. The developers "were striving to help students structure their out-of-class efforts and to get more out of precious in-class student-instructor face time.... The key idea of JiTT pedagogy is to develop an intentional, direct linkage between in-class and out-of-class activities via preparatory web-based assignments ... that generally require

Peer Instruction[30]

Problem-based Learning[31]

Conceptual Workshop[32]

Regardless of the teaching strategy that you employ, you need to carry on a conversation with your students to find out what they are thinking. Asking questions of your students is a fundamental approach that catalyzes a give-and-take that advances thinking. It also gives both the teacher and the student insight into the thinking that is going on. Both the student and the teacher need feedback if thinking is going to continue to move forward. Feedback is just another name for assessment, and assessment is really nothing more than vigorous healthy communication. That is the topic of the next chapter.

---

students to read, view, or do something and answer related questions," p. 5. JiTT is based on thought-provoking questions about the web assignments.

30. Peer instruction as practiced by Eric Mazur involves students discussing and persuading each other during class, similar to pair-share. Groups are responding to a teacher question but are questioning each other in their small groups as they grapple with a thought-provoking question. Mazur, *Peer Instruction*. Also see Lasry, "Peer Instruction: From Harvard to Community Colleges." Peer Instruction in class is frequently paired with JiTT outside of class. See Jessica Watkins and Eric Mazur, "Using JiTT with Peer Instruction," 39-62.

31. Biggs and Tang, *Teaching for Quality Learning*, 151-53. "Problem-based learning (PBL) reflects the way people learn in real life; they simply get on with solving the problems life puts before them with whatever resources are on hand," 151.
"The problem, or a series of problems, is where learning starts and, in going about solving those problems, the learner seeks the knowledge of disciplines, facts, and procedures that are needed to solve the problems. The traditional disciplines do not define what is to be learned, the problems do," 152. PBL is typically done in the context of group learning because the problems are too large to solve as an individual. PBL was originally developed by medical schools. See also M. Srinivasan et al. cited above for case-based learning.

32. Finkel, *Teaching with Your Mouth Shut*, 96-98. This teaching approach was developed by Finkel and Stephen Monk in the early 1970s. "It started as an attempt to promote more active learning for students in . . . large lecture classes" Conceptual Workshop is a phrase coined by Finkel in the 1990s. This is a type of group inquiry in which students divide into small groups and work for extended periods on a sequence of teacher-generated thought-provoking questions that catalyze activities in the group. Groups periodically present what they have come up with to the rest of the class. The teacher helps students by listening in on discussions and intervening only when necessary to get the students unstuck.

Chapter 9

Speaking Truth in Love: Assessment as Communication

Without assessment, there is no path to excellence.[1]

JOHN HARTOG III

The mere mention of assessment immediately causes the minds of students and faculty to race to the intellectual game known as grades. I say it is a game because it is an event where there are winners and there are losers. The stakes for losers can be high—failing a course, loss of scholarships, parental disapproval, narrowing of career options, wasted time, additional debt, and so on. There is a tacit recognition that the game is supposed to be about intellectual attainment—learning. Most students work for grades, and learning is a nice side benefit—if it happens at all. The reality is that the game is mostly about finding out what the referees (faculty) are looking for and trying to please them since they hold most of the power. The faculty referees respond that they too can lose their jobs or get bad performance reviews, so they try not to make waves.

Most faculty referees attempt to make their calls in predictable ways, but they have loosened up considerably over the years about what constitutes a "foul." Fifty years ago faculty in all disciplines included marking for spelling and grammar as they evaluated papers written for academic domains outside of professional writing. Very few do such markings (or count them against the student) these days. Spelling and grammar must be truly atrocious before they are marked in a nonwriting class. Faculty, then, are similar to the referees in college basketball. Fifty years ago no physical contact between players was permitted. Today the amount of physical contact that may be allowed by

---

1. Hartog, "Avoiding God's Disqualification."

basketball referees is something that has to be determined by the players in the first minutes of play because so much discretion is given to the referees. Are the referees going to call a tight game or "let the players play?" Players adjust accordingly. Students in a course use the first few quizzes and/or the first test to feel out their teacher, to see how things are going to be called this semester. Most faculty know how they are expected to call the game, but infrequently a student encounters a teacher who didn't get the memo.

"Assessment sometimes appears to be, at one and the same time, enormously expensive, disliked by both students and teachers, and largely ineffective in supporting learning."[2] Certainly faculty spend a substantial amount of time marking papers and calculating grades, and most find it the part of their job that they like the least. Faculty also recognize the significant likelihood that the grades they assign will antagonize students. A typical faculty response has been to loosen up on grading standards so that as of 2006 an A was the most common grade (43%) on college campuses, followed by B (34%) and C (15%).[3] Obviously this trend renders an A or a B significantly less informative than either was decades ago. Some have sarcastically called this the Lake Wobegon effect.[4] Grade inflation serves to strongly disincentivize striving for excellence. Why work so hard when a lot of other students who don't work half as hard will get the same grade?

As important as these issues are, I think it will be very helpful if we take ten steps back and return here later in the chapter. The most stunning part of the critique of assessment should be that it is "largely ineffective in supporting learning." Student learning is what animates this book and, I hope, your desire to teach. Your job as a teacher is to be an intellectual coach, not referee, judge, jury, or executioner in the grading games. You want your students to be successful, and you have done everything possible to structure your course to maximize student learning. You are there to facilitate their growth as learners. You are an ally, not an adversary. You will do everything reasonably possible to facilitate student flourishing. In the realm of assessment, that means that you major on feedback rather than giving grades. For that to be reality, you're going to have to take a deep breath and stop grading "everything that moves."[5] Well, maybe that's not you, but that was me. Until fairly recently my assessment was mostly about giving grades. I wanted students to succeed, so I gave them lots of assignments, which meant lots of grades in my grade book, which

---

2. Gibbs and Simpson, "Assessment Supports Students' Learning," 9.

3. Rojstaczer and Healey, "Where A Is Ordinary," 2.

4. Keillor, "Above Average." "Lake Wobegon where . . . all the children are above average."

5. Gibbs and Simpson, "Assessment Supports Students' Learning," 6.

meant lots of data points, which equals accurate determination of their final grade. At least, that's how I used to look at it.

The more you put yourself in the role of a learner, the more you realize their need for practice *without grades*. They need some practice shots without comment and then a few more shots accompanied by pointers on how to do it better—but still no grades. Learners need tons of feedback and lots of encouragement. They need direction, not grades, for a reasonable period of time. Learners also need something else: they need context. Imagine how meaningless it would be to practice basketball shots as an individual without knowing anything at all about the game of basketball. What would motivate you to keep going? More to the point, how would you ever learn that (except for free-throw foul shots), your shots are going to be done as you transition from dribbling to the act of shooting or from receiving a pass to shooting? David Perkins has memorably illustrated this part of learning in his book, *Making Learning Whole*, in which he argues effectively that learners need to "engage [in] some accessible version of the whole game early and often."[6] Your course design should provide for regular student practice with this "junior version" of the game.[7]

Feedback for Flourishing

Student flourishing connotes a blossoming of potential—perhaps potential that the student didn't even know he had. Assessment is a tool to promote flourishing, not a penalty whistle waiting to be blown. Assessment links the promises of intellectual development that you made in the course learning outcomes to the sweaty practice learning sessions and beyond to the real games (authentic learning scenarios). Assessment is the core of coaching. Coaches constantly observe their players in order to diagnose strengths and correct weaknesses. A good coach isn't poised to pounce on every wrong move, or her players would be fearful of performing in front of her. Players who hold back in practice are resisting coaching. The tone of the coach during practice is positive, like she's offering advice instead of criticizing. She's not judging the players; she's assisting them by means of her expertise, and that takes the form of regular feedback, especially when players are engaged in an intrasquad scrimmage, a junior version of the real game that can be halted and restarted as needed. Coaching opportunities are much more limited in real games, but even there the coach is still diagnosing with the aim of maximizing the development of individual players and of the team.

6. Perkins, *Making Learning Whole*, 9.
7. Ibid., 16.

The kind of assessment that I'm calling feedback is technically called formative assessment. Formative assessment is designed for student flourishing; it is intended to maximize the rate and depth of student growth in learning. Generally feedback is ungraded or low stakes.

> Formative assessment can be any assessment that . . . promotes students' learning. Many refer to this type of assessment as 'for' learning. . . . It is formative because it gathers evidence that helps teachers better meet the learning needs of students . . . it can greatly enhance . . . the speed of student learning.[8]

A large meta-analysis of previous research in the field of assessment by Gibbs and Simpson in 2004 focused on how learning can be enabled through assessment. They list ten conditions that improve the quality of learning. Three of these have to do with tasks that appropriately engage students in playing "the whole game." Seven of the ten have to do with the importance of feedback to learning. The current emphasis on grading to the detriment of feedback should be a major attack point in our efforts to improve learning. Feedback is a severely underutilized tool that has extraordinary power when it is used properly. Since we are focusing in this book on higher-order learning within the logic of a discipline, regular feedback is required to prevent novice learners from floundering and abandoning the learning quest due to discouragement and disillusionment.

Here are Gibbs and Simpson's observations about the way feedback should be structured to support optimal learning:

- Sufficient feedback is provided, both often enough and in enough detail.
- The feedback focuses on students' performance, on their learning, and on actions under the students' control.
- The feedback is timely in that it is received by students while it still matters to them and in time for them to pay attention to further learning.
- Feedback is appropriate to the purpose of the assignment and to its criteria for success.
- Feedback is appropriate, in relation to students' understanding of what they are supposed to be doing.
- Feedback is received.
- Feedback is acted on by the student.[9]

8. Buchanan, "Fitness Bands Can Teach Us," 1.
9. Gibbs and Simpson, "Assessment Supports Students' Learning," 12-25.

If you've been successful in putting yourself in your student's shoes in the last few chapters, you can appreciate their need for feedback to support them and direct them. Logical thinking in a new domain of thought is likely a daunting expectation, especially to neophytes who are typically rewarded for mere factual recall. Your students need directing (not hand holding), but how can you manage the task, especially if you have large classes? You want your feedback to help them to find and stay on the path to excellence. Feedback has traditionally involved written comments following an evaluation of a student's written work. Who has the time to write comments (especially detailed comments) on all of the papers, especially with the number of students you have?

Feedback Allies

Take heart, the task is not as Herculean as you fear! There are numerous ways to help your students get the systematic feedback they need without your becoming a basket case. You have allies who can help your students get the objective evaluation they need about the quality of their thinking in a timely manner, feedback that includes concrete directives that allow them to improve the quality of their thinking.

You can be your own best friend in this cause. You can help yourself immensely by communicating clearly before students enter a learning scenario. Students need to clearly understand what you are after, and many times they don't. Most students want to please you (at the very least because you hold the power of grades), but they simply don't understand what you want from them. More than likely you've written the instructions to a paper or a project using concepts that are clear to you, but not to your students. Communication is a fine art, and here is another instance of misguided faith in teaching by telling. To make certain you communicate your expectations clearly, you might conduct a brief Socratic discussion about the concepts in the assignment instructions. You might have a Q & A session about the paper or project in which you highlight and illustrate your expectations.

Consider showing students multiple graded examples of anonymous past student work on similar projects. Ideally the examples of student work would be evaluated with a scoring rubric, the same rubric you're going to employ when you evaluate the work of your current students. Giving students the rubric in advance directs their work in its formative stages rather than being a hidden tool for grading that they see only when it is too late. Make certain through the gallery of examples (excellent, good, unacceptable) that students thoroughly understand the basis on which their work will be evaluated as they see the rubric being used, the grade assigned, and the specific comments you made in your evaluation.

Another way you can help yourself while you help your students is to give brief targeted feedback on small chunks of a paper or project. If you wait until the paper or project is done to give feedback, your feedback will likely be overlooked because the grade is all that is important to many students at that juncture. For large papers and projects, it's also a challenge knowing how many comments to make and what to leave alone. Consider simplifying the process for yourself and your students by having them submit, well in advance of the due date, the first four paragraphs, the first major developed point, or some other early indicator of the quality of their work. Having a small amount to read and comment on will help you to be more timely and more focused in your comments. Target one or two central attributes of the thinking here, perhaps the quality of the thesis statement and/or the structure of the supporting arguments. Your feedback will be a "heads up" for your students to see if they have really understood what you were asking for. It may well change the direction of their efforts on the rest of the assignment to better align with your expectations. Communication is all the more important as you move from a content-driven model into a principle-driven model in which you explicitly evaluate the quality of their thinking within your discipline.

After this early contact with a student paper or project, you might require students to write a paragraph or two telling you concretely what they changed when they revised the submission because of your feedback. They should also tell you how this altered the way they approached subsequent phases of the paper or project. Their reaction to your feedback should be part of the grade given at the end because the feedback was given primarily for their benefit, not yours. If they never acted on your feedback, that reflects poorly on their commitment to growth as a learner.

An unexpected ally is technology. You have to be only modestly technologically competent to significantly multiply your efforts at providing timely feedback. Have students submit their work to you as pdf files. Many schools have learning management systems (LMS), and you can construct a dropbox that receives these files and creates a time stamp for each. Even email attachments can be a boon. For small classes, I simply construct a folder for a class in my email client and have students email pdf attachment files. I put them in the folder on my computer. When it is time to give feedback on submissions, I open the file and give my feedback electronically using a pdf annotation tool[10]. Because there tend to be patterns in the kinds of

---

10. Pdf annotation can be done with options within the leading pdf reader programs

errors students make, comments can be saved in a separate file and you can copy and paste appropriate comments from this master file. Make certain the comments are appropriate, and write additional explanation where it is needed. After a few semesters this comment file can be pretty rich, but don't rely strictly on boilerplate comments. Save the annotated version of the student pdf file, and email a copy back to him or her. The saved version is your record of what you said, so name the file in a way that keeps this straight.

In the previous chapter we dealt with conducting polls as a means of bringing questions into the classroom. Once the poll is closed, your interaction with the poll results can be used as a type of feedback. Sometimes this can be quite direct. You can use class time to go through each possible answer and explain why it is or is not the best answer. If you wrote an appropriately thought-provoking poll question, you'll be giving feedback on the thinking process to the entire class at once. Interacting with the poll results might take the form of a Socratic discussion where students discuss the merits of various answers. The poll might be an entrance point to scaffold and direct the thinking that students will be asked to do during that class period through collaborative activities. Those activities provide a type of feedback.

Learning management systems provide a rich set of tools to promote feedback. I like to use online self-assessment quizzes to help students practice on the kinds of multiple-choice higher-order thinking questions they will be taking during my large classes. Online quizzes can be constructed to give feedback on relatively small chunks of material: one or two quizzes per class period's assignments. Students should take this like a normal quiz looking at all the possible answers and successively ruling out answers until they are left with the one best answer. For each possible answer to a quiz question I have written several sentences of detailed feedback that explain how the student should have reasoned in light of the evidence and ideas they should know from the assignment. As a student chooses an answer, he is told whether that is the best answer and why or that it is not the best answer and why. Some answers are outright wrong, some are weak answers, and some employ common thinking errors such as misconceptions. I encourage students to keep answering until they come to the right answer but that the reasoning process behind the answer is what they should be emulating. Conscientious students work through the feedback for each answer to each question. This feedback took a substantial amount of time to write, but it only had to happen once. It relieves me of the burden of explaining to

---

including Adobe Acrobat Reader and Preview. In both of these programs there are annotation features that enable you to highlight text and to write comments.

each puzzled student how they should have been thinking. As time permits following in-class quizzes I like to go through the same reasoning process, briefly, for each answer to each question. As I do this online and in person for the whole class at once, I'm helping them grapple with "a way of thinking" that goes far beyond getting the right answer.

Practice tests with feedback for each question can also be made available online. Repeated practice testing is one of the most powerful strategies known for correcting thinking errors. These practice tests shouldn't be trivial recall questions or questions that you will be asking for credit in slightly restated form. If all of your test questions probe the thinking process, then practice in grappling with the relevant reasoning is immeasurably helpful in growing as a thinker. If, on the other hand, the questions test mere recall, practice in retrieval of information is useless to learning to think and sends the wrong message to your students about what you value. I've found that most practice test questions provided by publishers are fact-recall questions. I explicitly distance myself from these questions by telling students that these are not the kinds of questions that will appear on the test that I will be giving them.

Another technology-enabled option for feedback is online discussion. In a large nonmajors course that I teach, discussion is the major basis for the online part of the course grade. Having interacted with ideas in online readings and targeted web pages, students take self-assessment quizzes and, eventually, participate in online discussion with other students in the class. A rubric details how the discussion will be graded and is available to the student before he enters the discussion. Entry to the discussion is by way of a two paragraph post about the ethical question that is driving the discussion. Students cannot see the discussion until they have articulated their personal position on the question and submitted it. Once they enter the discussion, students will encounter a variety of different perspectives. Over time their post will elicit discussion and they must enter into that discussion and see it to a logical end. As students interact with one another's posts they are providing feedback and provoking thinking. The quality of the thinking in their interaction with each other is part of their grade for the discussion. Often the online discussion precedes Socratic discussion in class. The feedback that students have gotten from their peers in the online discussion helps the quality of the Socratic discussion in class to be on a significantly higher level than it might otherwise be.

Creating Autonomous Learners

Online discussion provokes peer feedback, which may sound like a poor substitute for feedback from an expert. Actually, it is amazingly beneficial. Peer feedback is the basis for Eric Mazur's "Peer Instruction," where students teach other students in the classroom by communally interacting with a question (see chapter 8). Mazur has found that this kind of feedback is actually more effective than the feedback he gives. He explains:

> When one student has the right answer and the other doesn't, the first one is more likely to convince the second—it's hard to talk someone into the wrong answer when they have the right one. More important, a fellow student is *more likely* to reach them than Professor Mazur—and this is the crux of the method. You're a student and you've only recently learned this, so you still know where you got hung up, because it's not that long ago that *you* were hung up on that very same thing. Whereas Professor Mazur got hung up on this point when he was 17, and he no longer remembers how difficult it was back then. He has lost the ability to understand what a beginning learner faces.[11]

I'm not suggesting that your students don't need your expertise—after all, you created the course. However, students can be effective allies in correcting poor thinking. If students internalize the standards of clear thinking that you've designed the course around, they can use those standards to confront the thinking of other students and, most importantly, their own thinking. When a student is proficient at evaluating his own thinking, he is an autonomous (self-directed) learner. This is the goal of your course and of the entire educational process. Lifelong learning occurs because the learner has figured out how to teach himself and he enjoys learning and the personal growth that it brings.

Royce Sadler in a watershed paper in 1989 articulated the means by which autonomous learners are produced. "The learner has to (a) possess a concept of the *standard* (or goal, or reference level) being aimed for, (b) compare the *actual* (or current) *level of performance* with the standard, and (c) engage in appropriate *action* which leads to some closure of the gap."[12] Your primary and indispensable role is to clearly articulate and interactively aid the student in conceptualizing the intellectual standards of clear thinking. Merely telling her what the concept is won't cut it. The student is going to have to be led through formative experiences to create her concept of the

---

11. Lambert, "Twilight of Lecture," 23.
12. Sadler, "Formative Assessment and Design," 121.

intellectual standard which is substantially parallel with yours. Once she has internalized the standard, she must see how to evaluate the actual level of performance (part b) in comparison to the standard. Evaluation is not automatic once the standard has been internalized. Evaluation is a learned ability. It is situationally learned. She walks with you through evaluations (in the form of feedback) that you conduct in all of the ways we've talked about above. That's a start, but to get really good at evaluating, she needs to practice evaluating and have her evaluating evaluated—by an expert—until she is really good at it.

Good evaluation uncovers gaps in performance. Gaps in performance at this stage (the feedback stage) are not going to be assigned grades. Performance gaps need to be addressed through corrective actions that the learner can still take. These corrective actions would be definite steps in correcting, redirecting, and deepening thinking. These are steps that you've been modeling through your actions and confronting students with through the structure of the class.

Faculty who don't share the evaluation load with their students are cheating their students. One of Sadler's insights that has still largely not been realized is that "the instructional system must make explicit provision for students themselves to acquire evaluative expertise."[13] If you have felt that using students to help you in formative evaluation (feedback) is taking advantage of the students, and providing inferior feedback, I hope you are persuaded that it is exactly the opposite. The question is this: "How are you going to integrate the development of evaluative competence into your course?" How are your students going to gain this experience and get feedback about how to do it better?

One possible approach to developing expertise in generating gap-closing feedback is to have students give each other feedback using the very rubric that you will use. When a partially completed paper or project is submitted to you, have each student submit it also to another student (of your choosing). Have students give feedback to the student author and to you. You can evaluate their peer evaluation (as part of their grade on the project). This should be pretty straightforward since you evaluated the same student submission using the same tools. I've found peer evaluations to be generally helpful. Occasionally a student is overly generous or overly critical but this can be dealt with through training with relevant submission exemplars and through grading their feedback. By the way, while students are early in their training as evaluators, it is good not to grade their evaluations while they gain confidence and accuracy. Trained peer evaluators can shoulder

---

13. Ibid., 143.

some of the load that would have been yours later in the semester. Seasoned peer evaluators who have completed your course can even help to mentor students next time your course is offered.

Through the process of evaluating the thinking of their peers, students are developing the ability to find gaps in their own thinking. Being able to evaluate the quality of one's own thinking and to use definite strategies in improving thinking is metacognition. Effective learners are good at metacognition, while defective learners aren't good at evaluating or correcting their thinking. Defective learners tend to be overconfident going into a test and not even to recognize during the test that their thinking isn't on target. As a result they are shocked with the low test grade they get. I've heard hundreds who said, "I don't know how I did so poorly on the test. I really knew the material." I usually gently point out to such students that we have different definitions of what it means to "know." Their use of "the material" also generally belies a content focus rather than learning to think within the logic of the subject. They "didn't see it coming" because they hadn't learned how to think about their own thinking and bring it under their control. Help your students to take charge of their thinking. Don't allow them to feel that thinking ability is static and they just don't have what it takes. I am a firm believer in the necessity of hope to motivate students through adversity. Hope comes through improving one's thinking and we can all grow as thinkers. Students in this situation need intensive care, and a student mentor might be just the ticket, for both the mentor and the mentee.

Assessing Thinking

A consideration of the concept of metacognition tells us that learners have to be trained to evaluate their own thinking. What hope is there then for outsiders like teachers or peers to properly evaluate the thinking of others? This is not trivial since I've stressed in this book that you should "teach a way of thinking." If you teach a way of thinking, you should also assess a way of thinking. You can only assess thinking indirectly. "Learning is a *process*, not a product. However, because this process takes place in the mind, we can only infer that it has occurred from students' products or performances."[14]

Your syllabus will announce learning outcomes that most students should be able to achieve. Those outcomes target the ability of the student to think about a discipline-specific principle in a certain way. Verbs in outcomes are precisely chosen to denote the ability of the student to analyze, evaluate, explain, and so forth, in terms of the principle. Thinking most

14. Ambrose, *How Learning Works*, 3.

directly exhibits itself through verbalization. Perhaps the purest form of assessment is the oral examination in which there is give-and-take between the evaluator and the one being assessed. Here body language, facility with words, response time, logic, evidence, and the like can all be examined in an interactive manner. Questions can be reformulated and answers likewise reworded so that there is clear communication between both parties. It is probably for this reason that the final exam for doctoral degrees is an oral examination.

Ken Bain tells the story of a calculus teacher who tried to nurture one of his students all semester. The student was diligent, but he had failed all the major tests in the course. The student had consistently sought help and always seemed to understand calculus concepts when he came to his professor's office for help. The professor was mystified by the student's test performance. Nearing the end of the semester and a standardized departmental cumulative final, the student came by for help again. His professor used his rapport with the student to gently probe the student's understanding of calculus. The more he probed, the more impressed he was with the depth of this young man's understanding. At the end of almost two hours he told the student that he should relax, because the professor could assure him at least that he had passed the course based on the spontaneous oral exam he had just taken. He told the student to take the final exam the next day for fun to see what he got. The professor meanwhile would try to determine what sort of a passing grade to assign. Remarkably, with the pressure off, the student got a B+ on the final.[15]

Oral exams frequently induce stage fright in the student being examined. The rapport between teacher and student and the subtlety of examining the student spontaneously without announcement seem to have defused the test for the student above. In any case, oral exams are resource intensive since only one student at a time can be examined, so teachers generally look elsewhere for assessment that measures attainment. Traditionally such assessment is called assessment "of" learning. In educational jargon, it is called summative assessment and it results in the assignment of grades. The implication of this terminology is that such assessment measures only the *results* of previous learning. I disagree. At least for assessment that is designed to measure thinking (learning for understanding), the very engagement of the student with the assessment process produces additional learning. A good test, for example, should be a learning experience by means of which additional conceptual richness is created. And what of an authentic learning experience in the form of a paper or a project? Surely evaluation by the teacher

15. Bain, *What the Best College Teachers Do*, 135-36.

has the potential to enrich the learner, at least to the extent that diagnostic and developmental feedback is shared and not just a grade assigned.

I think it is clear that assessment is not an exact science. You are forced to measure the quality of thinking indirectly through the products produced by the thinking process. You infer something about the quality of the thinking through the assessment of products. It is likely that the quality of the products depends on which products you assess and is especially dependent on how well you communicated your expectations in advance of assessment. In addition, the very act of assessing changes the quality of the products produced, as is clear in the case of test anxiety. Why do some music students freeze and forget their piece when confronted with a public recital? Why is it that some people are good test takers and some are not? More importantly, how well do tests measure the quality of thinking? Are there better products than tests that more accurately predict success in the real (nonacademic) world?

Authentic Learning

A meta-analysis of 150 separate studies on the question of whether course grades and test grades predict success in the adult world concluded that "the studies demonstrated low positive relationships between academic aptitude and/or grades and accomplishment."[16] There is a much stronger relationship between grades on papers and projects and adult performance.[17] This is particularly true when the paper or project engages students in authentic learning, i.e., thinking that produces the kind of products that practitioners in the field are involved in producing. This is not at all surprising. Alignment of learning tasks and learning outcomes with present projects/concerns in the field motivates students and prepares them for "the real world." It is perhaps testament to the isolation of most academics that such alignment is still rare.

I've proposed throughout this book that you "teach a way of thinking." Thinking within a logical domain produces products in the form of explanations that answer questions and give practitioners the ability to look for implications and to forecast consequences. Authentic learning simply demands that students use their thinking for real world purposes and not for practice in "transcendental high-jumping."[18] So, for example in a

---

16. Baird, "Do Grades and Tests Predict Accomplishment?" 3.
17. Gibbs and Simpson, "Assessment Supports Students' Learning," 7-8.
18. Mencken, *Mencken Chrestomathy*, 302. Mencken uses "transcendental high jumping" to refer to teaching.

nonmajors science course, I decided that it wasn't going to be helpful to nonmajors to learn a smattering of science concepts chosen by a committee. Instead, the course is driven by a narrative that involves students in coming to informed views on a handful of controversial issues (e.g., attempts to create synthetic life). They do this through examining primary sources that embody multiple viewpoints on each issue. The aim is to involve the student in thinking about intriguing real-world questions at a sufficient depth that basic science concepts are learned on an "as needed" basis. In the process of engaging with the questions that drive the course, the students are expected to discuss online and in classroom Socratic discussions so that they arrive at logic-based ownership of their conclusions. I aim to produce informed citizens who are conversant with some of the issues of our day for which a knowledge of science is a requirement. In the process of working through multiple issues they also learn a strategy by which they can investigate other issues. In short, they learn to think like a biologist.

Another example of authentic learning is found in a business writing course that I'm familiar with. The creator of this course for nonmajors contrasts traditional assignments and authentic learning.

> When I taught a Business Writing course to university juniors and seniors, I believed I had two choices: teach the course 'in the abstract' or teach it 'in the wild.' I could introduce a set of theoretical ideas and skills, and assign artificial projects that would be easy to compare and grade. Or I could improve the students' Business Writing thinking and skills through genuine assignments. I couldn't bear the thought of teaching my students information that was disconnected from their lives and likely to hit the trash can. So I chose the second path.
>
> As a result, my students had to write a résumé and cover letter for an actual job opening, and they had to include copies of their research on the company that listed the opening. They also created a live LinkedIn profile. In a group project late in the semester, I asked them to choose a local business, and then work together to identity and create a report that would actually benefit the company. Over the semesters I taught the course, these reports helped restaurants and one-of-a-kind stores identify new marketing strategies or ideal operating hours, and led to real initiatives undertaken by the university itself to improve amenities like bicycle storage and car-sharing services.
>
> By the time my students finished the course, they had not just learned the principles of Business Writing; they had created several assignments that had to respond to the more complex

challenges of real life, and that were now producing real-world results.[19]

Stanley Fish at the University of Illinois at Chicago created a truly revolutionary freshman writing course for nonmajors that was based on this thesis: "Students can't write clean English sentences because they are not being taught what sentences are." Fish doesn't mean that students aren't being *told* what sentences are, but that they don't *understand the logic* of sentence structure. His approach is as straightforward as it is revolutionary. Over the course of the semester groups of students have to create a language. The language must be "complete with a syntax, a lexicon, a text, rules for translating the text and strategies for teaching your language to fellow students. . . . [I]t must be capable of indicating the distinctions—between tense, number, manner, mood, agency and the like—that English enables us to make." Fish says the groups are always successful, and in the process they learn the logic (not mere patterns) of the relationships between sentence components (with components now being not just parts of speech but rich language concepts). The students learn how "to spot the formal breakdown of someone else's language [and] to prevent the formal breakdown of their own."[20] Learning the logic of English through the creation of another language is a revolutionary application of authentic learning. It says that grammar is not a set of arbitrary rules, but the application of a logic. Grammar is "a way of thinking."

Authentic learning is not a gimmick to keep students interested in the course. It is a fulfillment of the promise you are making in teaching your students to think like a historian, an accountant, a nurse, a writer, or whatever. Thinking like a historian, for example, means the student is going to gain some facility with how a historian thinks. This begins with the questions that historians engage with, and it leads to the kinds of answers that historians find satisfying. Instead of hearing only about the conclusions of historians, students in a "thinking like a historian" course are involved in the thinking process—they are immersed in historiography. Certainly the students in a lower-level history course are amateurs, but they need to be involved in playing at least a junior version of the real game of history. They need to look at sources and learn how historians evaluate them. In the process they need to learn some of the principles of historiography and to apply them to producing a product where the thinking process is brought to bear on writing history or in evaluating the history that others have written. Of necessity the students in such a course would cover less content (names,

19. William L. Gray, personal communication with author.
20. Fish, "Devoid of Content."

dates, etc.), but they would gain something much more valuable—a way of thinking. This is not to say that content becomes unimportant, but it is subservient to learning the principles of history and the process by which historians use those principles to answer questions.

I've used examples of nonmajors courses to drive home the point that "a way of thinking" is not just something you attempt to teach majors. Majors should have significant aptitude for the way of thinking that is their major, but every student should be able to try out for a semester (or two) various ways of thinking. Students will not be equally good at practicing each way of thinking, but they will become better all-around thinkers through this approach. They will also likely find fascination in unexpected places and uncover abilities they didn't know they had. Finally, they will learn to appreciate the thinking done in every domain of human thought. Developing such a regard for the thinking of others is surely part of becoming an educated person with appropriate intellectual humility.[21]

Effortful Study

Intellectual growth in your students is predicated on the environment you've created with its authentic learning scenarios, plentiful feedback, and periodic grading providing an appropriate level of challenge. It is your job to create challenges that are just beyond the current reach of your students. The rub is that you don't have just one student whose ability is well known to you. What is just out of reach for one student may be completely out of reach for others and well within reach for yet others. Part of the way you address these disparities that would threaten to overwhelm some students is to provide additional optional levels of support and feedback for students. These can take the form of scaffolding through optional detailed instructions, additional examples posted online, opportunities for extended self-assessment, interaction with student mentors, optional help classes, and so forth. For exceptional students you might consider a substitution that allows them to explore innovative options or intriguing topics (within the existing course structure) that would provide additional challenge and enrichment.

It is no secret that assessment in the form of grades drives achievement. Very few students would continue to persevere in your class if there were no grades. All students know that grades have consequences, and those consequences should be important to them. While you don't want students to be strategic learners who are motivated entirely by grades, neither do you want them to be oblivious to the feedback that they get from their grades

---

21. Paul, *Critical Thinking: What Every Person Needs*, 652.

and the reality that the transcript of their grades is a record that will follow them all of their adult lives. I've previously acknowledged my tendency to be overly focused on grading, but it is also possible for a teacher not to employ the power of grades wisely. Some teachers do not provide enough graded assignments and tests to drive the development of their students. (Courses in which the only grades come from a midterm and a final exam come to mind.) Many of these same faculty also don't provide sufficient challenge in the assignments that they do make. Their courses are known as "an easy A." While providing abundant risk-free feedback is laudable, eventually there must be a reckoning in the form of grades for what the student has accomplished. Grades are necessary and not entirely evil.

The motivating power of grades can elicit performances the student did not realize he was capable of. John Stuart Mill captured this memorably when he said "a pupil from whom nothing is ever demanded that he cannot do, never does all that he can."[22] Students frequently find they have underestimated what they can do, especially when the task is learning to think and not simply memorizing content. Thinking invariably produces mental sweat in the form of frustration, but the learning environment you've constructed provides resources to help the student deal with the frustration. Raising a student's horizons so that he learns to maximize his potential is a great kindness. I have had hundreds of notes from students over the years thanking me for the level of challenge that I provide in my courses. As a student, there is nothing quite so satisfying as looking back from an intellectual mountain peak that you did not think you could climb.

Subjective Grading

Much of the pile of grading that threatens to bury teachers, especially as the semester nears a close, is subjective grading. Some professionals in the area of assessment object to the term "subjective" because they think it smacks of capriciousness and lack of reproducibility in the grading. If two experts independently give roughly the same evaluation of the submission, then the evaluation is no longer subjective, but objective, according to this line of thinking. Personally I view this as unhelpful hair splitting. Subjective evaluation needs to be as precise as possible; but even if I personally go back and grade the same assignment much later when my memory of the first evaluation is completely gone, my evaluations will probably agree only by plus or minus half of a letter grade. In contrast, a well-written, multiple-choice

---

22. Mill, *Autobiography*, 45.

objective question will continue to have the same best answer no matter how many times the question is graded or by whom.

Organizations that create and administer national standardized essay tests recognize the problem of reliability when evaluating answers on essay and other free response questions. Human evaluators of answers to these questions must be content experts, but they must also be trained in the use of the scoring rubric and their effectiveness must be certified using standard training essays. When the same essay is evaluated by two trained experts, there may indeed be a significant variation in the score given.[23] Some evaluators are consistently more severe than others, and some are consistently more lenient. For this reason, on high stakes national tests, each answer is evaluated independently by two different people to look for significant disagreement that would require a third independent evaluation. What does this say about subjective grading in your course that is done by you alone? How reproducible is your grading? How unbiased are you in your evaluations? In back-to-back semesters as a freshman, I received mostly C's in my first semester writing course and all A's my second semester (from a different teacher). My first semester teacher found no spelling or grammar errors and gave me no direction about how to improve my writing. My second semester teacher loved my writing. Perhaps you have had similar dismaying experiences with subjective grading. Besides lenient and severe grading, an official publication of the Educational Testing Service (ETS) lists six other "Common Human-Rater Errors and Biases" ending with "Rater Drift."[24] Most of us who have graded a large stack of papers have wondered whether we are staying consistent as we move through the stack. Some of us have a tendency to mark more and more severely as we move through the papers, while others have the opposite tendency. I sometimes regrade an early paper just to check myself.

As an aside, let me briefly acknowledge the growing use of machine-grading (i.e., computerized evaluation) of free-response items by major national standardized testing organizations. This is a growing practice by all of the major players. The Collegiate Learning Assessment (CLA) has, until recently, consisted only of free-response items in a problem-solving context. Studies of their computerized Automated Essay Scoring (AES) found that the automated system "agreed better with human experts than

---

23. Lucas, "Multiple Marking," 78–84. In this study forty-four essays were scored holistically using a 1-6 scale. Each essay was graded by six different scorers. The results were that "only one of the 44 scripts [essays] in the sample were [sic] awarded the same mark by all markers; 12 scripts had a range of one mark, 19 a range of two marks and 12 a range of three marks." (82).

24. Zhang, "Automated and Human Scoring of Essays," 2.

humans agree with each other."[25] Currently about 10 percent of the CLA submissions are graded by trained human evaluators and compared with automated grading to check the automated system and to provide a larger data base of expert evaluation to train the automated system. The existence of such systems makes faculty drool in anticipation of the day when they will be free from the drudgery of subjective grading, which fills so many of their nights and weekends. As of this writing computer code capable of subjective grading is available free from EdX (a major MOOC), but you'd have to be a programmer to use it. Second, the training of the software grader requires hundreds of expert-graded submissions. That's where things stand as of now.

This is not a broadside at assignments that require subjective evaluation. I believe that such assignments are crucial in engaging students in authentic learning that resembles what experts do when they are thinking within the logic of their discipline. Certainly experts seldom take a multiple-choice test! Authentic learning demands a healthy portion of papers and projects that must be subjectively assessed. I'm just asking you to be realistic about the assessment task. Recognize the lack of reproducibility of even your own subjective grading. Don't convey a sense of precision in your grading (e.g., 39.7 out of 50 possible points) that can't be defended. This criticism extends to grading in general and I'll revisit the issue in more detail later in this chapter.

Rapid subjective expert evaluation is fairly accurate (roughly on par with the grade you'd assign after significantly more detailed evaluation). This means that your gut reaction to a paper or project from just a few minutes of browsing will likely be fairly accurate. I've long taken advantage of this by doing a quick evaluation that yields a presort of the papers or projects into piles corresponding to letter grades. That means I could "grade" the papers rather quickly based on my gut reaction. That would confirm the worst fears of students that their work is evaluated flippantly and arbitrarily. That's just the first pass through the papers, however. I then methodically evaluate each submission using a rubric to see if I should promote, demote, or leave the submission in the same pile. Perhaps a quarter of the time the submission changes piles based on evidence accumulating in the rubric that I failed to see in my cursory examination. Filling in the rubric keeps me focused on what I told the students and provides substantial feedback to the student author with a minimum of effort on my part.

A well-crafted evaluation rubric is an invaluable part of your design of a paper or project. You should thoughtfully design a rubric *before* you

25. Steedle and Elliot, "Efficacy of Automated Essay Scoring," 8.

assign the paper or project. Doing so will help you to communicate your expectations with clarity before students start their work, and it will help you to intentionally align the learning scenario with your course learning outcomes. I'll walk you through the process of writing a rubric and provide a concrete example. A footnote[26] will point you to additional resources to help you gain proficiency in writing rubrics.

A rubric is written for each assignment. Take the time to write a few sentences to define what you want the student to do, including basic guidelines for the learning task you have set for the student. The rubric itself takes the form of a table. The first column breaks down the learning task into a series of components (or attributes) to be assessed. The remaining columns represent a series of performance levels for each component of the task. Notice that you are not rating students against each other, but in comparison to a consistent set of task components. You could just leave the resulting boxes empty and use this as a checklist, but I recommend instead that you fill in each box with a detailed concrete description of what that level of performance looks like for each component.

Here's an example. The task you have set for students is to analyze a set of sources to prepare for an online discussion of "just war." Task Description: "Write a two paragraph (200 word minimum) position on this thesis: "The war in Iraq was (or was not) a 'just war' given what was known when the United States invaded Iraq in 2003." Here are some more instructions to the student: "This is not a mere opinion piece. You should demonstrate a significant understanding of the concept of 'just war' as articulated by Augustine and Thomas Aquinas and as the concept has evolved in modern times, including its use in justifying the Iraq War. You should grapple with moral contradictions implicit in your position. You must interact with the reasoning of your fellow students as they respond to your post and you should carry on a serious online conversation with them until the discussion thread reaches a logical conclusion."

---

26. Anonymous, "Create Rubrics."
Anonymous, "Developing Rubrics."
Anonymous, "Rubrics".
Anonymous, "Learning Outcomes."
The first reference is very straightforward, practical, and short. The second contains a multitude of links to other sites (on the last two pages). The third is a thoughtful piece that deals with rubrics extensively within what the author calls "authentic assessment." The final link above is to a national site housed at the University of Illinois; it deals especially with the linkage of rubrics to learning outcomes.
A free online tool for constructing rubrics is available at: Anonymous, "Rubistar." A helpful fairly recent book is Stevens and Levi, *Introduction to Rubrics*.

	Excellent 3 points	Average 2 points	Needs Improvement 1 point	Unacceptable 0 points
Understands "Just War" (2X)	Exceptional use of logical argument in developing the concept beyond quoted sources.	Satisfactory logical development of the concept beyond quoted sources.	Superficial enlargement of the concept beyond quoted sources. Possibly some gaps in logic.	Quoted sources without elaboration.
Applies "Just War" (2X)	Thoughtful consideration of the concept in reference to the moral ambiguities of the Iraq War.	Satisfactory application of the concept to the moral ambiguities of the Iraq War.	Basic application of the concept with minimal engagement of the moral ambiguities.	Expressed an opinion not rooted in the sources.
Interactive	Interacted substantively with two other posts. Actively pursued a conversational thread to a reasonable conclusion.	Interacted substantively with two other posts.	Interacted substantively with one other post.	Did not interact with other posts or was superficial in his interaction.
Use of Language	Exceptionally clear communication. Good grammar and spelling.	The overall message is apparent but suffers from some lack of clarity. There may also be some problems with grammar and/or spelling	The overall message is not entirely clear because there is significant ambiguity. There may also be significant problems with grammar and/or spelling.	The overall message is not clear and/or it is illogical. There may also be major problems with grammar and/or spelling.

Notice how clear the direction is for students before they enter the discussion. (You might quarrel with the "unacceptable" column on the basis of insensitivity, but you can't argue against the clarity of its communication of expectations). In scoring a contribution, you would mark one column for each component of the learning task. This could be through circling the appropriate box or by selecting the proper rating in an LMS. An LMS will calculate and report a total score automatically once a discussion has been evaluated. In an LMS the scoring feedback is available when you decide (after the discussion is closed and probably only after all contributions have been assessed). Various components can be weighted differently. Since this course has been set up to "teach a way of thinking," you've made the understanding and application components twice as important (2X) to the score as the other two components. After you score student contributions, this rubric will be a rich source of feedback for individual students.

Testing Teaches

I believe all of the positive things I said about authentic learning tasks a few pages back. But I don't agree with some who think that authentic learning leaves testing out of the picture entirely. Good testing evaluates the particulars of a student's thinking in unique and helpful ways, much as Socratic discussion provides powerful analysis of the quality of the students' thinking in oral discussion. Test questions should be constructed to lead students into situations in which they are forced to interact with your questions and your logic just as they interacted with you in Socratic discussion. Papers and projects sometimes allow the student a chance to finesse her way around something she isn't competent with and to compensate in other ways. It may never be apparent to the teacher or the student that these deficiencies exist if the scope of the paper or project is broad enough. In contrast, a well-constructed test allows the teacher to take the logic of the discipline apart and to ask questions about the component parts in very specific and intentional ways. It allows the quick construction of new authentic learning environments asking students to apply their understanding to situations they have not faced previously. "It is probably not extravagant to say that the contribution made to a student's store of knowledge [conceptual understanding] by the taking of an examination is as great, minute for minute, as any other enterprise he engages in."[27] A student is not just telling what he knows as he answers test questions. Instead he is simultaneously clarifying conceptual relationships, evaluating propositions, solving problems, and a

27. Stroud, *Psychology in Education*, 7.

host of other thinking exercises that are elicited during the test, because of the test.

I need to make a qualification to what I just said. Thinking develops during a test if the test is constructed to provoke and measure thinking. That's a big "if." Most college tests are tests of factual recall. They are tests of content recall rather than tests of thinking competence. Teaching as telling leads almost inevitably to testing as the student telling the teacher what the teacher said. Testing-as-recall is as useless as teaching-as-telling.

For a test to fulfill its pedagogic function, you will need to become proficient in writing questions that diagnose the *thinking* of your students rather than merely their ability to remember. Many faculty would object at this point that they do write questions that test student thinking. Objective evaluation of such questions generally reveals that they test the ability of students to remember the products of *your* thinking. In your telling mode you reasoned and came to conclusions that you now expect your students to recognize or reproduce (depending on the kind of test question).

Essay questions are sometimes held up as the gold standard of test questions that provoke reflective thinking. Since there is nothing but a blank page or a blank blue book, surely the ability to fill the page or the book with coherent content means that the student has mastered the relevant ideas. To the contrary, such writing generally confirms that the student has come close to memorizing what you said. He absorbed the products of your thinking rather than generating his own thinking. He knew that what you wanted to hear was your own thinking, not his thinking. This becomes particularly blatant when students are given a list of examination questions that they should be prepared to answer. The actual examination will utilize a subset of these questions. Sadly, I know of cases where this was the practice for doctoral "comprehensive" examinations that were ostensibly measuring the ability of the candidate to *think* within the logic, concepts, and principles of the discipline.

If this critique of university testing sounds harsh, consider some evidence that supports it. Paul Ramsden, formerly Pro-Vice Chancellor (for Teaching and Learning) at the University of Sydney, Australia, pointedly says, "It is scarcely surprising to find numerous examples of university examination questions . . . that can actually be answered without any understanding at all of the fundamental principles which the lecturer says he or she is testing."[28] The lack of alignment between tests and lectures is something students quickly pick up on. As one study revealed, "While theory was presented and discussed in class, none of it appeared on the exams,

---

28. Ramsden, *Learning to Teach*, 183.

and students learned to treat the material as digressions."[29] There was a rude awakening for Eric Mazur of Harvard in 1990 when he decide to use a conceptual test of physics (The Force Concept Inventory) for the first time. The results were brutal: "his students had not grasped the basic ideas of his physics course: two thirds of them were modern Aristotelians. 'The students did well on textbook-style problems [Mazur says because] they had a bag of tricks, formulas to apply. But that was solving problems by rote. They *floundered* on the simple word problems, which demanded a real understanding of the concepts behind the formulas.'"[30]

Writing Higher-Order Thinking Questions

The difficulty of writing test items that require higher-order thinking was graphically illustrated in a study of test items submitted by faculty who had previously participated in nationally recognized professional development workshops. These were experienced faculty averaging 13 years of classroom experience from a broad cross-section of public and private colleges and universities. Fifty faculty submitted a total 9713 questions intended for use on tests or quizzes in introductory biology courses. Two trained evaluators independently rated all of these items according to the classic Bloom's taxonomy. The results were appalling: 93 percent were at Bloom's level 1 or level 2, 6.7 percent were at level 3, and 0.3 percent were at level 4–6.[31] In the classic Bloom's taxonomy level 1 was called knowledge (later revised to remembering) and level 2 was comprehension. To comprehend is often interpreted as the ability to describe in your own words or to provide an example. Bloom's level 3 involves the use of a concept in a new situation.[32] This study classified 93 percent of all of the submitted questions as lower-order. The study participants were not trying to produce lower-order questions, but that is what they produced.

Questions that test higher-order thinking are difficult to write, but they can be extraordinarily useful in provoking and diagnosing higher-order thinking. Let me be clear about the motivation for writing such questions. Higher-order questions are not an elitist trap to increase course rigor, keep grades from inflating, and make the instructor feel smug. Higher-order questions are designed to develop (first) and assess (second) the kind of discipline-based thinking your course is designed around. To serve up lower-order learning

29. Jacobs and Chase, *Developing and Using Tests Effectively*, 6.
30. Lambert, "Twilight of Lecture," 23.
31. Momsen, "Just the Facts?" 437.
32. Crowe, "Biology in Bloom," 369.

(LOL!) questions is to gut your course and fail to deliver on your promises. Your course learning outcomes promised to engage students in higher-order learning and, therefore, you have to assess higher-order learning.

Before you can write questions that test higher-order learning, you'll need to have a clear sense of what higher-order learning is. To review, the standard classification was published in 1956, the work of a committee chaired by Benjamin Bloom.[33] Bloom's taxonomy was revised by another committee in 2000. This is the revised taxonomy:

> remembering—understanding—applying—analyzing—evaluating—creating.[34]

The revised taxonomy is an improvement in some respects, but in my opinion it is still ambiguous and misleading. Count me among those who believe that there are really only two classifications: lower-order and higher-order thinking. I believe that remembering (the supposed entry level) is typically a counterfeit for real learning. Remembering should be the result of higher-order learning rather than a standalone that is sought for its own sake and proves nothing (lower-order "thinking"). For me understanding (properly understood!) is the gateway standard. True understanding is the essence of higher-order thinking. To understand is profoundly different from mere remembering. To understand is far more than being able to repeat in your own words or summarize what you have heard. To understand means that you have taken ownership of an idea. As the owner you can use the idea in a variety of different ways: by being able to explain why the idea is significant and powerful, by the ability to apply the idea to a new situation or predict what will happen in a new situation, by being able to take the idea apart (analyzing), by critiquing it (evaluating), by using the idea in concert with other ideas (synthesis or creation, depending on the originality of the formulation). I'm not convinced that these manifestations of understanding are in any kind of logical hierarchy or progression as even the revised Bloom's taxonomy maintains.

My position frees you from painstaking analysis of the questions you write. The fundamental issue is whether the student understands the idea. The question you write may ask the student to do a variety of things to demonstrate the extent of her understanding. What the question will not do is ask her something she can answer because she read it or heard it somewhere (maybe from you). One further observation is that faculty may confuse a variety of other things as evidence of a question being higher-order. In a

---

33. Bloom, *Taxonomy of Educational Objectives*.
34. Anderson, *Taxonomy for Learning, Teaching, and Assessing*.

study involving a group of faculty attempting to write higher-order questions, things such as the perceived novelty or difficulty of the question or the time required to answer the question were taken as prima facie evidence that the question was higher-order.[35] A higher-order question might be novel or difficult or time-consuming to answer, but those attributes are incidental and not intrinsic to the question being higher-order.

Alignment

There should be a tight alignment between your course learning outcomes and the kinds of questions you write. As an example, consider the following sample of thinking skills listed in a book aimed at helping faculty write instructional objectives:[36]

Analysis—Student Identifies

- Assumptions
- Causes
- Central issue
- Contradictions
- Fallacies
- Inconsistencies
- Inferences

Synthesis—Student Formulates

- Concepts
- Equations
- Explanations
- Hypotheses
- Predictions
- Principles

---

35. Lemons and Lemons, "Questions for Assessing Higher-Order Cognitive Skills," 47–58.
36. Gronlund, *How to Write Instructional Objectives*, 51.

These learning outcomes point you directly to crafting experiences where the student (not you) is involved in doing these very things. One of those kinds of experiences would be in the realm of testing. When writing questions in which the student demonstrates facility with analysis, you ask him to examine the components of an argument, a data set, a graph, a scenario, and so forth with a view to examining the relationship and function played by the components. This can be done either through free-response (including essay) questions or through multiple-choice questions. In contrast, asking the student to formulate something through synthesis can be done only through free-response questions. The nature of the case in multiple-choice questions is that the student is selecting from items you have crafted rather than manufacturing his own. This is the only systemic limitation of multiple-choice testing. Multiple-choice questions can be a powerful tool in developing and evaluating higher-order thinking in all of its manifestations except for the process of synthesis or creation.

Some faculty dismiss multiple-choice questions as mere "multiple guess" and express a belief that nothing can match essay testing. Certainly crafting a few good essay questions is simpler than writing forty or fifty high quality multiple-choice items. However, the time saved here is partially lost in the time required for the subjective evaluation of the essay responses (including writing a significant grading rubric). Well-written multiple-choice questions can be machine-graded and reused year after year (as long as test security is maintained). Time is invested up-front for multiple-choice questions and on the grading side (in perpetuity) for essay questions. There is a place for both kinds of questions, but there is little support for the idea that an essay test is inherently superior to other forms of testing. Although multiple-choice questions are susceptible to guessing, essay tests are susceptible to bluffing in the form of padding and evasive sentence structure where the writer is not certain of her facts or the appropriate application of a concept.[37] An essay test allows the student to have wide latitude in the organization, marshaling of evidence, logical argumentation, and so forth of his essay, while the multiple-choice question requires him to choose from alternatives that you've purposely crafted. He can't skirt the issue in a multiple-choice question by writing an answer he likes better.

To assure alignment of your test questions with your course learning outcomes, make certain that each question you write engages with a big idea or principle that you identified in your learning outcomes. (To be clear, you would never ask a student to simply recall the principle as you stated it.) The question you write will typically focus on a concept (idea) closely

---

37. Jacobs and Chase, *Developing and Using Tests Effectively*, 118-19.

related to a big idea or principle. You may write multiple questions on this concept (or the related principle) depending on the emphasis you gave it in class. Indeed multiple-choice tests in particular can be enriched through the use of clusters of questions that probe a strategic idea in multiple ways at various levels of sophistication. Try to maximize the number of questions on a multiple-choice exam that emphasize the interconnectedness rather than the isolation of concepts. Finally, to avoid unnecessary stress on the student during testing, you should put the questions in a logical order and not jump around.

Once you've identified an appropriate principle (big idea) and an associated concept, you must decide how you want the student to demonstrate his understanding. A few possibilities include the ability of the student to do the following:

- recognize an equivalent restated form of the concept or principle
- recognize an application of the concept or principle
- recognize the consequences of the idea
- recognize logical flaws in an argument
- apply the concept properly (preferably in a real-life setting)
- analyze a data set for patterns
- predict effects from the cause(s)
- interpret cause-effect relationships
- justify a strategy that employs the idea
- solve a problem
- critique a strategy or interpretation

Everything that I've said so far about the alignment and intentionality of your questioning in the previous paragraph applies equally to free-response and multiple-choice questions. The rest of this section, however, will focus exclusively on multiple-choice questions.

Strategic Crafting of Multiple-Choice Questions

Taking into consideration what I've just said about alignment, the next step is to write a clear and compact question stem. Typically the question stem poses a problem that the answer solves. Ask the question as directly as possible and don't pad the question with extraneous information. Follow the question by writing the answer that you intend the student to choose. (Be certain in the test instructions that you ask the student to identify the best answer rather than the correct answer. You'll see why shortly.) You then want to construct plausible answers that are not the best answer. Traditionally these are called distractors.[38] The richest source of plausible distractors comes from a knowledge of student responses to this kind of question. This might come from asking a similar question in free-response form in previous semesters and collecting wrong answers. Additional distractors can be

- student misconceptions[39]
- verbal/definitional errors
- computational errors
- procedural errors
- cause-effect errors
- twisted logic

Factual errors including:
- inverted relationships (cart before the horse)
- inaccurate marshaling of supporting facts
- inaccurate restatement of an idea
- factually correct statements that don't really answer the question
- factually correct statements that are significantly weaker than the best answer

Try to write four plausible distractors (in addition to the correct answer) whenever possible. This reduces the impact of student guessing. Never write throwaway distractors even for the sake of test humor. Once you have written the question, the answer, and all of the distractors, take the time to write out in a version for yourself the reasoning by which you declare an answer wrong, weak, or the best answer. This reasoning is the kind of thing you would actually deploy in a self-assessment exercise for students. This exercise also helps to keep you from asking a question with multiple "best" answers. Such flawed questions can create conflict with students and may undermine your credibility if they occur frequently. If you and another

---

38. Anonymous, "Testing Resources." Contains many helpful resources for writing tests and test questions available as pdf files under the "Writing Better Tests" section at the URL listed in the bibliography.

39. Anonymous, "Writing Distractors." Contains many good resources for identifying misconceptions and using them in writing test item distractors. Secondary education level science of all types is represented.

faculty member can partner in transparently critiquing each other's questions, you can avoid ever deploying many of your flawed questions.

If it sounds like trickery to write out distractors that you know past students have found plausible, remind yourself that you are trying to diagnose and develop thinking in your students by means of assessment. Thinking errors tend not to be original any more than the symptoms of childhood diseases are original. Patterns help you diagnose root causes much more readily than would be the case if every student were unique in his thinking difficulties. You want your students to be thinking clearly enough that they can root out misconceptions and various thinking errors that have bedeviled previous students. You aren't laying a trap for them any more than the school nurse who gave me my first vision test in third grade was trying to trick me. I felt bad when I failed the test, but really good when I got corrective lenses that showed me how deficient my vision had become. The test set me on a path by which my previously unrecognized vision problem was corrected. Your test is likewise designed to diagnose and develop thinking. That is the spirit in which you write your questions.

Since the BP Deep Water Horizon oil spill in the Gulf of Mexico in the summer of 2010 is well known to most people, I'll use a few examples of multiple-choice questions about the event to contrast questions that reward memory with those that reward reasoning. Try to categorize each question as you read it.

1. Although nearly 5 million barrels of oil were released into the ocean in the BP oil spill, a large amount was also captured by various means. Approximately how much oil was recovered?

A. 800,000 barrels

B. 500,000 barrels

C. 100,000 barrels

D. 80,000 barrels

E. 50,000 barrels

This is a standard factual recall question. Notice that memory trumps thinking in this question. Depending on what a student knows about this event, he might be able to eliminate certain answers as implausible, but the question can best be answered by pure recall. (The answer is A, by the way).

2. Federal scientists were reported as saying, "[T]he BP spill is by far the world's largest accidental release of oil into marine waters."[40] The spill was estimated to be about 5 million barrels. In comparison the Exxon Valdez spill was put at 11 million gallons. Why is the BP spill considered the largest?

A. The Exxon Valdez spill was the result of a mechanical failure.

B. The BP spill spread more widely and more quickly.

C. The BP spill was relatively near heavily populated areas

D. A barrel contains 42 gallons.

This demands a close reading of the question and a recognition that the question stem employs an inappropriate comparison. The BP spill is measured in barrels and the Exxon Valdez spill is measured in gallons. (The answer is D and requires a bit of analysis).

3. BP had no strong incentive to accurately report the magnitude of the spill. Scientists working for the federal government were called in to independently verify the rate at which oil was leaving the well. The reason for calling in outsiders was

A. The statement itself shows a strong antibusiness bias.

B. BP was given a chance to make the assessment and their results were dubious.

C. The government wants to take over the oil industry just as they took over the auto industry.

D. The Clean Water Act levies fines on a per-barrel-spilled basis.

BP at the time of the spill and thereafter was pilloried in the press for its negligence. The public learned quickly to distrust BP's estimates of the extent of the spill because the numbers they provided regarding the extent of the spill rapidly escalated over a period of days. That makes B look very attractive. A and C might be tempting to people in special interest groups, but they are not supported by the passage of time since the event or by responsible journalism of the time. The actual best answer is D (which is

---

40. Robertson and Krauss, "Gulf Spill Largest of Its Kind."

factually correct) because it means the government itself is a major stakeholder in the accuracy of the estimate. This would be true even if BP's estimates had been more accurate. This question tests the ability of the student to evaluate evidence and to reason carefully within the evidence.

I mentioned above the idea that questions generally should call for the single best answer. Occasionally, however, it is helpful to write some questions where you ask the student to mark all correct answers. This serves as a corrective to the "process of elimination" method of answering questions where the student settles for an answer because he has ruled out every other possible answer and not because he is persuaded that what is left is the best answer. If you ask questions where there may be more than one correct answer, put these in a separate section of the test with new instructions that indicate this attribute is shared by all questions in this section and then reinforce this in your directions (e.g., this applies only to questions 34-40). If you ask questions where there may be more than one correct answer, mix in a few questions in this section which actually have only one correct answer to see if students are convinced that there is only one correct answer. Here's a sample question with multiple good answers:

4. The oil released by the BP spill did not produce the level of ocean or shoreline contamination that was initially feared. Which of these explains the relatively mild environmental damage and the relatively short duration that contamination persisted? (Mark ALL correct answers.)

  A. Unprecedented amounts of chemical dispersants were used.

  B. The oil was a lighter type than what is found in wells in other locales.

  C. The Gulf has warm temperatures and an abundance of oil-degrading bacteria.

  D. Much of the oil was released as subsurface plumes on the ocean floor.

All of the answers are correct. Notice that this kind of question requires students to be sure about the answer(s). If they are conservative and mark only the answer(s) they are certain of, they will receive a deduction for answers they should have marked. On the other hand, if they are aggressive and mark answers that might be correct (but aren't) they will receive a deduction for the extra wrong answers. Because of the additional difficulty of marking only the correct answers, I strongly recommend that you give partial credit on questions where there is more than one correct answer. For example here there are four correct answers to the question. If the entire question is worth one point, each correct answer would be worth 1/4 pt. (Likewise each incorrect answer or unmarked correct answer counts as minus 1/4 pt.). These questions can generally still be machine-graded and then you just have to hand-grade those that the machine counted as wrong because they didn't match the key exactly.

Enriching Objective Questioning

There is no reason that objective questioning should be a straitjacket. Objective testing is designed to diagnose and develop the thinking of your students. Thinking within your domain is a very rich multifaceted thing, and your testing should be too.

Consider writing questions that test the following:

- appropriate analogies (this is to ___ as ___ is to ___)
- calculations
- comparisons (semiquantitative)
- conceptualization using incomplete concept maps
- data analysis based on a research study
- logic
- passage-based or case-study-based reasoning
- relationships (between ideas or structures)
- sequentiality
- others[41]

I'll develop a few of the more innovative types of test questions listed above in a bit more detail.

Semi-quantitative comparison questions take this form:

Mark A if the item in column A is greater, B if the item in column B is greater, and C if they are about the same.

---

41. Examine standardized tests such as the GRE, MCAT, LSAT, CPA exam and other tests in your area. Study materials for these exams are available online and for purchase. Practice tests are typically available free or for a nominal cost. Another rich source of question types is by the National Board of Medical Examiners, "Constructing Written Test Questions." Another resource that is particularly strong in the sciences is the two volume set by Tobias and Raphael, *The Hidden Curriculum*.

A	B
5. number of civilian casualties WWII	number of civilian casualties Iraq War
6. blood pressure in arteries	blood pressure in veins
7. ten year total of time writing and grading an essay question	ten year total of time writing and grading a multiple-choice question

These questions can profitably be used when no figure is cited, but competence with course principles and their application should lead to a justifiable sense of a basis for the comparison. This is a very versatile and easily written kind of question that should be used to probe thinking about complex issues as they surface in comparisons. (The answer to all three questions is A.)

Conceptualization

Unless you have a lot of time in which to conduct an exam, it is likely unfair to ask a student to construct a concept map of a topic during the exam. A helpful substitute, which is particularly appropriate for entry-level students, is for you to draw a concept map in which a few concepts are not labeled and/or a few propositional links have not been labeled. Unlabeled concepts or propositional links can have a question number referring to the missing element. You can make this machine-gradable by providing a short matching section of options to be used as answers. You might also ask for a cross-link that could be drawn in the existing map and provide potential answers from which to choose to indicate a cross-link that would be justified. Of course, such questions can also be answered as free-response questions.

Logic Questions

Mark *A* if only statement A is false.

Mark *B* if only statement B is false.

Mark *C* if both statement A and statement B are false.

Mark *D* if both statements are true but are not related by implication.

Mark *E* if both statements are true and statement B is implied by statement A.

8A. Totally electric cars currently have a range that is limited by their batteries.

8B. Battery technology must improve before electric cars are widely accepted.

(The answer is E.)

Relationships

Mark *A* if A is part of B.

Mark *B* if B is part of A.

Mark *C* if A is produced by B.

Mark *D* if B is produced by A.

Mark *E* if none of the above apply.

9A. Blood

9B. Plasma

(The answer is B.)

Learning Through Assessment

The purpose of all assessment in your course is to help students to gain proficiency in the thinking that characterizes your discipline. Feedback should be plentiful, but measurements that result in grades are also needed. In a real sense this is simply higher-stakes feedback designed to help the student measure her proficiency as a thinker. Higher-stakes feedback provides motivation to the student who knows that "this one counts" and who therefore prepares more conscientiously.

I am a firm believer that all learning is cumulative. My entire life has been a process of intellectual growth based on previous learning. Learning isn't about exposure to truth, but about truth changing your conceptual frameworks. The way you think should be undergoing constant remodeling that allows for better informed judgments and a deeper capacity for appreciating the wonders of our universe. Consistent with this view is a commitment to cumulative final exams.

I tell my students that placing the highest stakes assessment at the end of the course as a sort of exit interview is a kindness. Students have had the entire semester to get used to what it means to "think like a ____" and the final exam is the ideal time to try to measure their proficiency. A cumulative final also forces students to integrate their learning from the entire semester. Revisiting concepts the student never quite mastered and working to understand those ideas based on an end-of-semester perspective helps him to tidy things up intellectually so that his conceptual frameworks are reworked right through the final.[42] I generally make the cumulative final exam count 20-30 percent of the course grade. That means that no student can afford to coast at the end of the semester. Positively speaking, a final exam of this magnitude gives a student who had a slow start or some deep potholes in his semester the chance to clear the record with a strong performance on the final exam. I go further and tell students that if their computed final grade ends up in a border-line situation between two letter grades, I will use their score on the final to tell me what to do. If they make the higher grade on the final, they get the higher grade. I do this in good conscience because I've put enormous effort into writing a final that has a balanced handling of the concepts of the entire semester. The final requires students to analyze, evaluate, predict, critique, explain—in short it requires them to "think like a ____."

Many students respond to this challenge magnificently. Those who adapt to the structure of the course have learned through the semester how to think, and I'm not going to pull a bait and switch on the final. There are no tricks with a *Trivial Pursuit* of minutiae on the final. One of my nonmajor students in a required science course said in a course evaluation:

> "The tests are purely critical thinking through each question; not blurting out facts and information like most academic testing. I appreciated this because it came by reasoning out the best possible answer and actually using your brain. . . . Critical thinking actually sticks in your head [because] you have to reason and understand the material and . . . come to logical conclusions."

Before we leave the topic of the role of testing in learning, let's take a step back to how you and your students can use test results. This is more frequently done for tests given before the final. (I do keep final exams on file for one year to allow students to review and learn from the final.) Don't miss the opportunity to do a group postmortem on major tests. This can be done in class or you can schedule a special test review session. You can give

---

42. "Regardless of the type of course, students with cumulative finals did better on departmental content tests than students in courses with noncumulative exams." Khanna, "Short- and Long-term Effects of Cumulative Finals."

group feedback on the thinking process behind properly answering each test question. (I usually major on the most frequently missed questions.) As time permits, you can entertain questions from the floor. Don't let the tone of the Q & A become adversarial—you are there to help them profit from this test and to approach the next test more effectively. The test is not on trial either. If a student still believes his answer is correct after you explain your reasoning, he should be invited to see you privately. Don't debate answers with students. If the student's thinking is good and he was misled by the question, take notes about how the question could be changed and whether it perhaps needs to be dropped.

Help students to recognize the enormous benefits that accrue to them as they confront test questions that they missed and learn to ask themselves why they missed the question. There are many reasons for missing a question including failing to read the question properly (and thus answering a different question), test anxiety, poor note-taking or listening skills, defects in logical thinking, and various misconceptions. There are different cures for each of these problems. Students who come to my office to review a test fill out a diagnostic form asking them to analyze the reason they missed each question so that I can help them detect a pattern that we can plan to address in specific ways. Testing really is part of the diagnosis and development of student thinking.

Assessing Assessment

A natural part of the postmortem process on a test is to assess what worked and what needs improvement on the test. You have to get past your innate tendency to admire and defend your test. My colleague Bill Lovegrove has memorably expressed this resistance as "Of course it's a good test—I wrote it." There are formal and informal ways to assess your assessment.

Informal feedback on your test comes through conversations with students who took the test. Remember that you have the "curse of knowledge," and you don't remember what it is like not to know these things. You aren't reasoning about these questions in the same way as your students because of the difference in what you know. You also have what I might call "communication myopia." You know what you intended to say, and you feel as though you said it clearly. This came home to me as I was writing this chapter and received an e-mail from my university about some paragraphs I had written to publicize one of our programs. The e-mail writer pointed out one sentence that he and a fellow publication proofreader were having trouble with. I just couldn't see what *their* problem was!

If you've cultivated the right relationship with your students, they will feel a certain liberty to explain their thinking to you. View this as valuable insight, especially when it is about something you said or a test item you wrote. I've found myself using convoluted reasoning when talking to a student trying to help her understand why the answer I had chosen to a test question was the best answer. When you are in a similar situation and detect this convolution, recognize that at least the question is not as straightforward as you thought. Perhaps the student has a point (or should receive one). Perhaps you've shifted to a defensive stance in regard to *your* question.

Formal assessment of your test is the domain of statistics, but you don't need to be a statistician to employ some basic tests of your test. You simply want to determine which questions work and which ones don't. This is called item analysis. The two major analytical techniques are discrimination and difficulty. You should use these techniques on each test question.

Difficulty is the more straightforward concept, so I'll start there. You know whether the test as a whole was difficult because of the overall grades that students got. If there were lots of low grades and no one made an A, it was a difficult test—probably too difficult, but I'll address that a bit later. First you're going to look at your test one question at a time to see how many students got that question right. If more than 70 percent of your class missed the question, there are likely to be problems with the question.[43] When I say problems with the question, I mean with either the way the question was phrased or the alignment of the question with the way you structured the learning for your class. In the latter case the question may be perfectly fine, but nothing prepared your students to answer it.

Question discrimination is most often viewed as a correlation of a student's overall grade on the test with whether he got a particular question right or wrong. Generally students who did well on the test got questions right. If students who did well on the test tended to get a particular question right, there is a positive correlation. If students who did well on the test tended to miss a particular question, the question is potentially flawed. This becomes particularly evident if we find that the students who did not do well on the test tended to get particular questions right while the higher achieving students tended to miss those same questions. Calculation of an actual discrimination index by hand is labor intensive.[44] Some scoring ma-

---

43. Jacobs and Chase, *Developing and Using Tests Effectively*, 187.

44. Ibid., 183-86. A procedure is outlined that is straightforward. Test papers are put in order from highest score to lowest and then the stack is split in half. You look in the highest half and see how many people chose the correct answer and then repeat for the bottom half of the class. This may provide you with all the information you need, but a procedure for calculation of a discrimination index is also described in detail.

chines provide an automatic calculation of a battery of statistics including a discrimination index. Low index values (0.2 or lower) suggest problems with the item[45] that cause higher achievers to "over think" the question. Such questions should be discarded or rewritten for future administrations of the test.

Distractor analysis is a profitable assessment to make for each test item. If certain distractors are never chosen, they aren't serving any function and should be replaced. This analysis will also help you to determine which distractors were chosen at the expense of the best answer you had intended. Careful examination of such distractors may reveal good reasons that they were preferred (and your question should be altered accordingly) or may indicate thinking errors that you should target in the future.

When you find evidence that a question is fatally flawed, don't hesitate to admit it and to compensate for it. To admit it is to keep the lines of communication open with your students. It is appropriate humility. You are confessing that your best efforts contain some flaws and that you try to learn from your mistakes. Practically speaking, when you make a mistake, you make certain that it doesn't cost your students. I routinely discard questions when 70 percent or more of the class miss a question. My simple strategy is to add those points to everyone's score. If three questions fail the difficulty level test, I add three points to *all* raw scores. I also make it a point to use the distractor analysis to give targeted feedback to the students about the basis on which they should have eliminated certain distractors that were frequently chosen. Sometimes my students explain how they were thinking and it's a revelation that gives me direction in crafting a revised question. Even without such insight, the fact that a strong majority of the class missed the question points to a breakdown in the learning environment or in question writing.

If a significant proportion of your test questions need to be discarded on the basis of difficulty level, there is a likelihood that the remaining questions are no longer a valid measure of the student's learning because they aren't representative. Don't be misled into believing that you can fix the problem by adding thirty points to all of the scores (or something nearly as drastic). This evidence says that you didn't write an appropriate test. Your test was not aligned with what you asked students to learn or your test questions are intrinsically confusing. In such a situation it is best to eat crow and administer an alternative test. Just make certain that the new test is much better than the old one. Make certain that the results of the first test are not just thrown away, however, because that will justifiably anger students who

---

45. Ibid., 185.

did fairly well. You'll have to look at the situation student-by-student and do the right thing. Perhaps you'll give students individually the option of averaging the two tests together or throwing the first test result away entirely. This is a judgment call that I hope you won't frequently have to make.

Philosophy of Assessment

Grades are intended as communication. They communicate to the students who earned them. They communicate to the faculty who may teach these students in the future. They communicate to faculty who are asked to write a recommendation for a student for graduate school or employment. They communicate to employers who are looking to hire expertise. The big question is *what* do grades communicate?

Grades mean different things to different people, and that's unfortunate and very unhelpful. There are at least eight different things that grades might communicate. To be concrete let me use a student who made a 90 percent and received an A- in a class. This could mean she

1. is in the top 10 percent of her class.
2. is in the top 10 percent of all students who have taken that class over a period (e.g., past 5 years).
3. has mastered 90 percent of the content of the course.
4. has mastered 90 percent of the concepts/principles of the course.
5. has facility with 90 percent of the thinking skills taught in the course.
6. has improved more over the semester than 90 percent of the class.
7. has achieved 90 percent of her innate ability.
8. has worked harder than 90 percent of her peers.

Many people, especially outside of academia, take position 1 or 2. To them an A means the student is special when compared with her peers. Most of the peers don't compare favorably. Within academia this view is perpetuated in the bell curve. Diehards use "grading on the curve" to impose a so-called normal distribution on every class. Students are competing against each other for the very few A's that are given in this class. The actual level of achievement required to earn an A varies from semester to semester, but the percent of the class receiving A's does not vary.

Positions 6-8 are sometimes used in elementary school, but seldom in college. Position 6 views improvement as ultimate, so it favors those who start weakly and finish strongly. Position 6 puts students who perform strongly all semester at a disadvantage. In practice it isn't used to directly discriminate against strong achievers but to encourage those who would otherwise be discouraged—to level the playing field. This position has begun to creep into secondary schools. Just this year I read of several high schools that canceled academic honors recognition in favor of a public declaration that "we're all winners." Positions 7 and 8 suffer from a lack of reliable information. How can we know what her innate ability is? How can we know for sure how hard she worked compared to her peers? These schemes are fatally flawed but represent a desire to be helpful and generous to the underdog. Effort and improvement are commendable, but grades must be based on something that is measurable, something that answers the question of attainment.

Since your class is based on teaching your students a way of thinking, what does 90 percent of thinking like a sociologist, or biologist, or writer look like? I think this approach clearly is not as simple or discriminatory as the quota approach in numbers 1 and 2. Positions 3-5 all recognize attainment measured against some body of things to be learned. Position 3 tends toward an emphasis on content. Content tends to be viewed as a body of "stuff" to be remembered. I think perhaps the closest basis that parallels the philosophy behind this book would be a combination of positions 4 and 5. Though a bit clunky stated as separate positions, the combination would define a group of concepts and principles and then involve students in thinking that employs these concepts and principles. An A student is one who excels at thinking in this way as measured by assessment. In principle the entire class could attain this level of competence—you'd be shocked but not displeased if this happened!

In the course that I envision, you're teaching for mastery of "thinking like a ____." You'll have to decide what counts as evidence and assess accordingly. A portion of your summative assessment will be subjective and should be guided by a rubric through which you produce a numerical score. Some of it will be objective and yield numerical scores directly. Normally you would total all of these scores (perhaps weighting some categories as more important) and assign grades based on total points. If you do this, please recognize the somewhat arbitrary nature of cut-offs (like a 10 percent scale). Your course isn't made more rigorous by raising your cut-offs (say to a 93 percent for an A-). Appropriate rigor comes from the structure of your course and the level of intellectual challenge (and therefore potential intellectual growth) that your course offers.

You might consider adding another layer to check (and perhaps tweak) the conclusions that your grand total numbers are leading you to. If you elect to go this route, you'll look at a holistic picture of the student's performance. For this you'll need to subjectively assess the quality of thinking that the students have exhibited (based at least in part on summative assessment) and emphasizing the level they operate at by the end the course. Richard Paul has written a description of what an A and other grades should entail from a college-wide perspective.[46] Paul's performance criteria (with some of my modifications) include these:

1. analyzes questions and problems
2. raises issues
3. recognizes assumptions
4. clarifies concepts
5. weighs evidence
6. is proficient in reasoning and problem solving
7. is sensitive to implications and consequences
8. is committed to careful reasoning
9. thinks precisely and insightfully
10. evaluates his or her own thinking
11. numerical summative assessment data
12. overall intellectual performance

You might consider making this into a rubric that you use to view your assessment holistically in calculating a grade. You can weight the rubric as you desire to emphasize or deemphasize number 11, which is where the number that would normally be used to calculate the student's grade would go. You don't have to use this rubric numerically at all. You might look at the student's grade as numerically calculated and then look at what you would come up with through completing the rest of this rubric (leaving number 11 out). You can then use your professional judgment to justify a grade that takes everything into account. If you elect the holistic option, make certain that you have communicated this in your syllabus.

Taking Its Rightful Place

Even if you don't actually use these twelve criteria to calculate student grades, you should use them to assess a subset of your students to make certain their overall grades reflect an appropriate level of competence in thinking

---

46. Paul, "Grading Standards."

as independently determined using these criteria. If your subjective sense (using these criteria) of how strong or weak a student is as a thinker does not match the numerical grade she earned, you have more work to do. That would be expected, especially in the early semesters of implementing what you've learned in this book. Radical change leaves kinks to be ironed out.

A bit of reflection on the twelve criteria listed above reveals that they largely mirror the components of thinking that were first articulated in chapter 3. We've come full circle. You need to become a clear-thinking teacher who is laser-focused on teaching students your way of thinking by means of the structure of the learning environment you create for them. Assessment is an integral part of the means by which the development of thinking is maximized in students—and in their teachers.[47]

---

47. A concept map in Appendix 5 makes this point visually. Assessment provides only one new concept to a map of course construction. Instead assessment adds connections to existing propositions that ensure intention will become reality. Assessment literally closes the circle.

Chapter 10

Averting Disaster

The justification for a university is that it preserves the connection between knowledge and the zest for life, by uniting the young and the old in the imaginative consideration of learning.... A university which fails in this respect has no reason for existence.[1]

ALFRED NORTH WHITEHEAD

Effective teaching is intrinsically learner centered. The teacher harnesses her expertise for the sake of her students. She thinks deeply about the logic of her discipline, especially the principles upon which it rests. Based on this insight, she imaginatively constructs a learning environment in which students are motivated by compelling questions to discover discipline-specific principles and to use those principles to answer questions and make predictions. Principle-driven thinking is applied by the student in authentic learning scenarios in which the teacher provides abundant feedback and, eventually, graded assessment. Effective teachers, therefore, must master pedagogy consisting of "the science of learning, the science of instruction, and the science of assessment."[2] These three areas constitute the outline of this book. Since 2005 I've referred to these three as the legs of a three-legged stool to indicate their interdependence. Lack of understanding of this interdependence is one of the core problems in education.

In the first six chapters of this book I dealt in depth with *how people learn*, starting with you, the teacher. Chapter 2 focused on becoming a "clear-thinking teacher." Your desire should be to use metacognition to unpack your expertise for the sake of your students. The unpacking process

---

1. Whitehead, "Universities and Their Function," 93.
2. Mayer, *Applying the Science of Learning*, vii.

began by coming to terms with the logic of your discipline. That was discussed in chapter 3. You then move purposefully into the working layer of logic and emphasize the process of conceptualization. That was discussed in chapter 4. Finally, in chapter 5, I showed you how to uncover the powerful propositions called principles. Principles answer questions and are the means by which new problems in your discipline are solved, predictions are made, and new questions are formulated. Chapters 2–5 of this book were aimed at crystallizing what it means to think like an expert in your domain of knowledge. You need to be very clear about thinking in your domain because you want to help your students to think in a similar manner.

Lest I prove guilty of "chronological snobbery,"[3] let me recognize here the clarity of thought about certain aspects of learning in various writers of the past. *The Idea of a University,* a monumental work written by John Henry Newman in 1873, is dense and long winded by our modern standards, but it is regularly full of insight. For example, Newman speaks of "enlargement" in students and anticipates the need for active conceptualization in the mind of the student in a way not unlike that which I've articulated in this book:

> The enlargement consists, not merely in the passive reception into the mind of a number of ideas unknown to it, but in the mind's energetic and simultaneous action upon and towards and among those new ideas, which are rushing in upon it. It is the action of a formative power, reducing to order and meaning the matter of our acquirements; it is a making the objects of our knowledge subjectively our own, or, to use a familiar word, it is a digestion of what we receive, into the substance of our previous state of thought; and without this no enlargement is said to follow. There is no enlargement, unless there be a comparison of ideas one with another, as they come before the mind, and a systematizing of them. We feel our minds to be growing and expanding then, when we not only learn, but refer what we learn to what we know already."[4]

It's not just the importance of conceptualization that Newman recognizes, but he also emphasizes the need to understand principles:

> I say then, if we would improve the intellect, first of all, we must ascend; we cannot gain real knowledge on a level; we must generalize, we must reduce to method, we must have a grasp

---

3. "'Chronological snobbery,' the uncritical acceptance of the intellectual climate common to our own age and the assumption that whatever has gone out of date is on that account discredited." Lewis, *Surprised by Joy*, 207.

4. Newman, *Idea of a University Defined and Illustrated.*

of principles, and group and shape our acquisitions by means of them.[5]

Newman recognizes that principles are generalizations that involve a bigger picture view ("we must ascend") and that they serve to organize and shape our thinking. This is helpful, but it lacks the insight into the process that is needed to actually formulate principles.

Alfred North Whitehead in 1927 focused on using logic to inductively "elicit" principles:

> Imagination is not to be divorced from the facts: it is a way of illuminating the facts. It works by eliciting the general principles which apply to the facts as they exist and then by an intellectual survey of alternative possibilities which are consistent with those principles.[6]

Whitehead's principle "illuminates" (makes sense of) facts. His principles are the result of applied imagination (mindfulness leading to induction). Whitehead's principles parsimoniously eliminate some possibilities (those inconsistent with the principle). This is helpful, but it falls short of defining a process. Many illustrations from other writers could be given of the "diamond in the rough" usage of the term *principle*. Almost invariably a principle is represented as little more than an important idea; consequently, the unique power of principles has been squandered. Take a recent illustration of this from Derek Bok in 2006:

> Students are often unable to think effectively about material in a course or apply what they have learned to new problems and new situations because they have not truly understood the underlying concepts on which the course was based. Some cannot grasp the concepts because they enter the course with faulty preconceptions that clash with the principles they are asked to learn. Others simply do not understand the basic principles. Many professors skip these concepts too quickly.[7]

When the conversation links thinking with "material" or "content" as this one does, clarity has already been sabotaged. We think about ideas, not about "material." Bok here seems to be using "underlying concepts" and "principles" interchangeably. It is important to recognize that some concepts are foundational and thus, more important. Principles, however,

---

5. Ibid., 139.
6. Whitehead, "Universities and Their Function," 93.
7. Bok, *Our Underachieving Colleges*, 115.

are not merely important concepts—they are propositions that explain. I argue in chapter 5 for the primacy of principles in the reasoning process. Principles are refined diamonds of expertise that should be showcased in discipline-specific reasoning. Principles are the essential core of what it means to demonstrate expertise. Experts think, explain, solve problems, and predict using principles—even though most experts can't articulate the principles that they use. For the sake of your students, principles must be explicit to you. The lack of explicit focus on the development and use of principles is one of the central problems in education.

Focusing on Student Learning

The second leg of the three-legged stool that is pedagogy is *instruction* in Richard Mayer's taxonomy. Instruction is a low-level term with a lot of didactic baggage.[8] Instruction is a teacher-centered term. I sometimes refer to the second leg as "clear classroom communication." However, you are not the only communicator in the classroom. The learning environment you've constructed communicates through the learning scenarios in which your students are engaged. Your students are enabled to learn through scaffolding (that you created) and a conversational atmosphere that encourages dialogue. You are aiming for "pedagogic resonance, [which] is the bridge between teaching knowledge and the student learning that results from that knowledge."[9] Resonance is a powerful analogy. When something resonates, it vibrates synchronously with a source. Your expertise is being captured by students who are thinking in parallel with you. The student is the only one who can do his own thinking. Student thinking can be guided, but it can't be forced. The result of your careful guidance and nurturing of student thinking is student ownership of his personal conceptual frameworks, which include the powerful principles of disciplinary expertise.

The best way to think about your role in learning is that you *construct the optimal learning environment* for producing proficient thinkers. You inhabit this learning environment as a coach and not as a player. Chapter 6 was designed to help you get the big picture about how to design such an environment. Chapter 7 then pointed you to student flourishing as your objective and encouraged you not to assume the ability of your students to read, write, and listen analytically. You were also encouraged to mentor

---

8. "Education is a higher word [than instruction]; it implies an action upon our mental nature, and the formation of a character; it is something individual and permanent." Newman, Discourse V, 114.

9. Trigwell and Shale, "Student Learning and University Teaching," 532.

your students in a variety of ways including helping them to learn to study productively. Learning how to think is worlds apart from fact memorization. In chapter 8 you were pointed to the reality that thinking is driven by questions, not by answers. This points to a substantial change in the learning environment from the standard paradigm that made you the "answer man." It is by means of your questions that student thinking is guided and nurtured. Answers from you abort the thinking process. An emphasis on students thinking through compelling questions is a profound shift that most of the educational world has not yet made.

In view of the current dominance of "teaching as telling," it may be surprising that history provides us with some positive counter examples of classroom pedagogy. Hundreds of years before Christ, Plato used the Socratic method to produce autonomous learners.[10] One wonders what happened to supplant the Socratic approach. One theory is that there was a shortage of teachers and thus the lecture developed. Charles Eliot in 1869 at his inauguration as president of Harvard pointedly critiqued the futility of the lecture: "The lecturer pumps laboriously into sieves. The water may be wholesome but it runs through. A mind must work to grow."[11] In chapter 7 we reviewed some of the work of Mortimer Adler and a constellation of educational VIPs in the early 1980s in a proposal they called the Paideia Program. Adler doesn't mince words about "teaching as telling" (didactic instruction):

> The basic pedagogical precept of the Paideia Program is that all genuine learning arises from the activity of the learner's own mind. It may be assisted, guided, and stimulated by the activity of teachers. But no activity on the part of teachers can ever be a substitute and become the sole cause of a student's learning.... Didactic instruction, as it is usually conducted, tends much too frequently and regularly to violate the precept.... [T]he chief difficulty of didactic instruction is to make it the cause of active learning."[12]

Students who personally own disciplinary thinking expertise can demonstrate that reality through assessment. *Assessment* is the third leg of the three-legged stool. Assessment informs both the student and the teacher. Assessment serves to close the circle and assure that substantial learning has occurred in the student. I therefore refer to the third leg as "substantive assessment." Chapter 9 deals with the necessity of focusing on authentic

---

10. Case, "Plato's Premise," 33-40.
11. Eliot, Charles William, *Turning Point in Higher Education*.
12. Adler, *Paideia Program*, 47-48.

learning tasks that are relevant to the real world. Assessment in your classroom needs to be assessment of principle-driven thinking competence and not mere factual recall. Proficiency in higher-order thinking is what students need in order to handle the challenges they will face in their later personal and professional lives. Since you get what you assess, your assessment must have real world relevance. Assessment in higher education rarely hits this relevance target. Higher-order thinking results in understanding, which is "*unconditionally* durable. Unlike verbal memories, something understood does not need to be exercised in order to be retained. This, then is the kind of learning that lasts for a lifetime."[13]

Because assessment is often a mine field that destroys the rapport you have worked so hard to establish with your students, it is important that you major on feedback and minor on grades. Grades frequently antagonize students, so the learning environment you construct must provide abundant feedback to the student in preparation for graded assignments and tests. Feedback is essential for student flourishing as students try out and correct their thinking while gaining proficiency. Feedback also allows you to know how best to guide the student, how to tweak the course during the semester, and how to make next semester even better.

Recognizing the imprecise nature of grading, you realize you can't do better than to separate student performances into rough categories. Notice that I said student performances and not students. You aren't trying to separate the sheep from the goats. You are an educator, and you have failed if most of your students fail to learn from you. You grade against performance standards and not on a quota system. Your real aim is to evaluate the quality and depth of the students' thinking in your academic domain, and you truly hope that all students will perform well. You realize that you can assess thinking only indirectly through the products the student produces. Projects with real-world significance are good predictors of success in later life, but objective testing has a strategic place in *methodically* evaluating the students' thinking by means of carefully constructed questions.

The three-legged stool is a holistic view of teaching and learning. Teachers first focus on deriving the principles that fuel their thinking expertise. Secondly, faculty construct a learning environment in which students are immersed in principle-based reasoning as they pursue essential questions with real-world significance. In this environment, students learn to think as experts in that field do. Third and finally, faculty provide students with regular feedback (some of it graded) on the quality of their thinking.

---

13. Ibid., 182.

A Change in Job Description?

This focus on expert thinking in the service of student learning is at the heart of what it means to teach effectively. Teachers need to be proficient in the expert knowledge of their academic discipline and, at the same time, proficient in their knowledge of pedagogy as I've articulated it in this book. To gain this kind of facility with both kinds of knowledge is the work of a lifetime. Effective teachers don't just pop into a classroom to work their magic. There is a widespread myth to the contrary. The current model of a university faculty member is dominated by the researcher who teaches (or the teacher who does research). The teacher who teaches and does not do research is rare except at some small liberal arts colleges and community colleges. Think about the term *professor*. A professor is one who professes, i.e., makes a public claim to know or believe something. Language morphs in ways that obscure. Much as a doctor (literally a teacher) is really a physician who treats patients but doesn't actually teach, today's professor doesn't do much public professing except (perhaps) in canned presentations before one or two classes per semester and before professional conferences, where she presents her research. Research and research publications win tenure at most schools. Teaching effectiveness is secondary, if it counts at all.

It is instructive to note that this is a fairly recent aberration. John Henry Newman stated the obvious: "To discover and to teach are distinct functions; they are also distinct gifts, and are not commonly found united in the same person. He, too, who spends his day in . . . [teaching] is unlikely to have either leisure or energy to [do research]."[14] Around the same time (1869), Charles W. Eliot, president of Harvard, insisted that "the prime business of American professors . . . must be regular and assiduous class teaching."[15] Change was in the wind, however, and before the end of the "nineteenth century, the advancement of knowledge through *research* had taken firm root in American higher education and colonial college values, which emphasized teaching undergraduates, began to lose ground to the new university that was emerging."[16] This change was driven by faculty who saw opportunities for funding and status, which were subsequently embraced by departments and universities for the same reasons. By 1958 the "new reality [was that] young faculty were hired as *teachers*, [but] they were evaluated primarily as *researchers*."[17] In the 1800s and before, teaching and

---

14. Newman, Preface, xiii.
15. Boyer, *Scholarship Reconsidered*, 4.
16. Ibid., 9.
17. Ibid., 11.

research were carried on by two different institutions: colleges or universities for teaching and research in specialized academies.

The modern research university has badly skewed the role of a university faculty member and the value of his teaching. Nobel Prize-winning physicist and Carnegie Professor of the Year Carl Wieman is a rare exception. Wieman says, "it is hard to imagine that a faculty member could teach expert competence in an area of modern science and technology unless they have been active in the field themselves for much of their careers."[18] Wieman also maintains that "there is no valid way to generally evaluate teaching in terms of student learning, [and therefore] it is pointless to discuss whether or not teaching is appropriately valued and rewarded."[19] I would maintain that your professional academic expertise is more efficiently honed by keeping up with the professional literature (especially through literature reviews) than by troubleshooting experiments that didn't work in your lab. There is certainly a place for scientific (or other academic) research, but working with the vagaries of experiments and graduate students won't leave most of us the kind of time necessary to master pedagogical knowledge. Wieman has formed two large science education research groups to promote good teaching, so it is hard to imagine that he truly believes there is no valid way to recognize good teaching.[20]

Ernest L. Boyer of the Carnegie Foundation sought in 1990 to address this situation by his proposal that there are four interdependent kinds of scholarship. To Boyer these were the scholarship of discovery, integration, application, and teaching.[21] There is room in this perspective for SOTL, the scholarship of teaching and learning. Though defined in various ways, SOTL is exemplified by teaching faculty who creatively *discover* how to optimize learners' thinking within and between disciplines (the latter would be one example of *integration*) and to help students to *apply* their thinking to the solution of authentic problems. Appropriate assessment shows the effectiveness of optimized approaches based on the way the mind learns. In the SOTL sense, teaching faculty can be regularly involved in all four kinds of scholarship. This is the kind of scholarship that needs to be focal

---

18. Wieman, "A New Model for Post-secondary Education."

19. Ibid., 16.

20. Carl Wieman, Science Education Initiative at the University of British Columbia and the Science Education Initiative at the University of Colorado (Boulder). He is currently at Stanford University with a joint appointment in Physics and Education.

Sample papers include these two: Deslauriers, Schelew, and Wieman, "Improved Learning in Large Enrollment Physics Class;" and Smith et al. "The Classroom Observation Protocol."

21. Boyer, *Scholarship Reconsidered*, 17-25.

at undergraduate institutions around the world. "The Teaching Professor" is almost redundant but serves as a necessary clarification in the research-dominated world of higher education. Undergraduate educators need to focus on the kind of scholarship that optimizes student learning, especially learning how to think.

Catalyzing Change

This book has focused on you, the individual teacher. You are the right place to start to change education, especially higher education. Transforming your courses can make a profound difference for your students, enabling them to metamorphose into careful analytical thinkers. But what if your courses were not isolated atolls in a sea of educational irrelevance? What if students at your university were consistently and compellingly taught "a way of thinking" in every course? As we near the end of this book, I encourage you to think on a scale bigger than your own courses. The next step outward would be for you to seek a group of like-minded faculty friends at your school. That's how I started this SOTL journey back in the late 1980s. There were three of us who got together sporadically to talk about our concerns—about what seemed to work and what didn't. Eventually we found some helpful books and we shared what we were learning through them. Having a group of like-minded faculty will be synergistic. You'll all go farther with reforming your classes when you band together. Perhaps you can all attend a conference or a summer institute together. Your growing effectiveness as teachers is likely to pull in other faculty on your campus over time.

In my experience of over twenty-five years in SOTL, the single greatest catalyst for change has been to have a summer institute on campus. We've been able to do this for the past twelve years. Our summer institute takes place over three weeks or longer (dependent on funding). During the summer, faculty work side-by-side with other faculty developing their own expert thinking. Application is immediate as faculty practice teaching a way of thinking on a group of faculty outside their area of expertise. (Outsiders don't know your professional jargon and can't unconsciously fill in the gaps in your teaching). When multiple faculty from the same department participate in the institute, there is synergy during the academic year that usually recruits additional faculty from the same department over time. Eventually the core of like-minded faculty in one department is sufficient to establish a beachhead for change.

When you work on the department level, you are trying to harmonize a way of teaching with the structure of a series of courses. Look at one of the majors (programs) in your department. Is the curriculum defensible in terms of sequentially developing the logic of the discipline at increasing levels of depth or is it more of an ad hoc conglomeration of elective courses that faculty like to teach? Are the foundational courses being taught in a way that establishes what it means to think within the logic of your discipline, or are they "mile-wide inch-deep surveys"? Do these courses "worry... pupils with memorizing a lot of irrelevant stuff of inferior importance?"[22] These entry courses are the place that you should start in the development of your curriculum. My experience is that students who are taught a way of thinking in their first year are disappointed if the experience is not sustained in the later years of their program. This is a good disappointment that fuels improvement right up the line. While I'm on the topic of improvement, over time your enhanced ability as a teacher and constructor of learning environments may well translate into better grades for your students. Be certain that you can defend the basis for the grades to your superiors, who may doubt that you can increase intellectual rigor and grades at the same time (examples of student work on authentic learning projects would be great). If your students' grades do increase in this way, that would not be another example of ubiquitous grade inflation but of increased student motivation and buy-in that legitimately produces a gain in performance that should be rewarded. One way to validate this improvement is through benchmarking your students against some well-recognized external standard (typically a nationally normed test).

Over the past decade plus of summer institutes on my campus, about 40 percent of all faculty have participated. In several departments 100 percent of the faculty have participated for multiple summers. In several of those departments every course has been revised to teach students to think within a discipline-specific logic. In addition courses have been dropped and new courses created to craft a logical and deepening sequence of courses. More recently courses in our university core curriculum have begun to change. For example, nonmajors take an innovative science course designed from the ground up to involve them in thinking like a biologist about current bioethical issues. I don't know how much transformation my university is prepared for, but I do know there is a significant emerging consensus about what effective teaching looks like. We are increasingly focused as an institution on producing graduates who are proficient in critical thinking.

Zooming out to an even bigger picture, I'd like to see the artificial divisions in university curriculum change. I'm dubious that teaching writing separate from another discipline is optimal for students. In such a standard

---

22. Whitehead, "Rhythmic Claims of Freedom and Discipline," 36.

course students end up writing about topics that the faculty know little or nothing about. Consequently papers are judged primarily on the basis of writing mechanics rather than on the basis of the quality of logical argumentation about the topic. The latter is much more important than the former (although mechanics aren't unimportant). I'd like to see instead students writing in several core courses that their writing instructors also attend. These would be courses like the nonmajors bioethical issues course. Writing would be judged by the quality of argumentation, which the writing instructors would also know something significant about (since they are participating in the same class). Students would also meet outside the bioethics issues course with their writing instructor to receive additional guidance about writing mechanics and individual help with the thinking in their papers. A similar argument could be made in regard to communication courses. There is no doubt that every educated person needs to be able to express herself well in writing and orally. Students are normally writing or speaking *about something else*, however, and not about writing and speaking.

Another obvious place that barriers could be broken down is in nonmajors history courses. While there is no doubt a logic of history, history for nonmajors is typically a litany of names, dates, events and places to be remembered (oh so briefly) rather than the rationale with which a historian views this disparate collection. History should be a melding of the philosophy, politics, art, music, science, and so forth of a given period in a way that gives life to events and shows how they *influenced* one another. It should be richly interdisciplinary. A partial realization of this view of history was the forty-episode BBC series aptly titled "Connections."[23] I've asked a number of historians of my generation about this award-winning series, and few have even heard of it. The thesis of "Connections" (subtitled "An Alternative View of Change") is that the science and technology of a period produced innovation that had a profound impact on the subsequent course of history, that could not have been predicted. With this insight about an alternative way to teach history, we're back to chapter 3, where I quoted Richard Paul that "the spirit of critical thinking is 'there is a logic to this, and I can figure it out.'"[24] My two semesters of undergraduate history gave me no inkling that such a logic existed. It is also unreasonable to expect that historians are actually knowledgeable about the diverse collection of people and events that history chronicles. I remember cringing at the way science was handled in my history courses. (I would be agreeable to having a historian talk in my

---

23. Burke, "Connections."
24. Paul, "Critical Thinking: How to Design Instruction."

science classes about the way a historian thinks about pivotal people and events in my domain.)

Interdisciplinary courses should be the norm in universities because of the need to bring multiple points of view to bear on some of the major questions of human existence and of our time in history. I can think of nothing more helpful to promoting integrated critical thought than having these compelling questions addressed by multiple kinds of expertise, each inviting you and enabling you to "think like a _____." Such courses are taught at some schools,[25] but they are still a rarity. It could be argued that the best answers to compelling questions fall between our current academic domains. Perhaps we have to remind people to think outside the box so often because we have educated them to think within boxes.

In thinking about and studying attempts at education reform, I've been intrigued at how many of our cherished notions of how things have always been are actually relatively recent innovations. Take majors, for instance. Derek Bok informs us that majors were originally created in the early 1900s to compel undergraduate students to explore a related set of ideas in depth. Prior to that the emphasis was mostly on breadth.[26] The tables now have turned so that students often become overspecialized as undergraduates concentrating the vast majority of their course work in their major. Bok recommends calling majors "concentrations," and he maintains that the deep thinking goals of the curriculum "can almost certainly be achieved in most fields with little more than the equivalent of a year's study."[27]

There have been many proposals for university reform on a broad scale. John Henry Newman in 1852 wrote a lengthy proposal, *The Idea of a University*, to prototype Catholic universities. Charles Eliot was installed as president of Harvard College in 1869 based on promises of educational reform that emphasized scholarship in teachers. His inaugural address was expectantly called "A Turning Point in Higher Education."[28] Alfred North Whitehead in 1927 wrote a challenging piece called "Universities and Their

---

25. Evergreen State College in Olympia, Washington, has almost exclusively interdisciplinary courses. Many of these courses (they're called programs) are of such proportions that a student can take only one per quarter. Evergreen grants only generic BA or BS degrees and has no majors and no grades ("narrative evaluations" are substituted). Evergreen has no core curriculum but allows a student to follow her own interests in constructing a path to a degree. Evergreen started in the fall of 1971. http://evergreen.edu/home.htm (25 July 2014).

26. Bok, *Our Underachieving Colleges*, 136-37.

27. Ibid., 142.

28. Boyer, *Scholarship Reconsidered*, 4.

Function."[29] Ken Bain in 2004 proposed "The Learning University . . . in which professors and students are engaged in rich intellectual conversations in a collegial environment."[30] Most of these efforts you've never heard of because they didn't make the splash, or the lasting impact, the authors intended. Derek Bok in 2006 was pessimistic about college reform: "What are the prospects for turning colleges into effective learning organizations? Not good, unfortunately."[31]

Thomas K. Lindsay in the summer of 2013 saw a little window of possible opportunity for reform that he called a "slender reed."[32] Lindsay's slender reed is based on a convergence of two things. The first is the Collegiate Learning Assessment or CLA. The CLA (now revised and known as the CLA+) "measures analysis and problem solving, scientific and quantitative reasoning, critical reading and evaluation, and critiquing argument, in addition to writing mechanics and effectiveness."[33] The CLA has repeatedly shown that "the emperor has no clothes"; and scandalous CLA assessment results were the centerpiece of a 2011 book, *Academically Adrift: Limited Learning on College Campuses*. One often quoted extract from that work is that nearly half of all college students tested showed "no statistically significant gains in critical thinking, complex reasoning, and writing skills"[34] after two full years in college. The CLA documents the grim reality that critical thinking is not being developed by most colleges.

The second factor that might catalyze substantial reform is financial. Many colleges have overbuilt and are mired in debt.[35] As a consequence tuition costs will stay at their historical highs for the foreseeable future. What this means to the public is that college is not delivering value.[36] As a result a significant number of students have opted for low-priced local community colleges and more recently distance learning and even free MOOC-based education. All three of these are low-cost or no-cost versions of the content-driven memorization-rewarding status quo. Universities are rightly being asked to justify their existence.

29. Whitehead, "Universities and Their Function," 91-101.
30. Bain, *What the Best College Teachers Do*, 175.
31. Bok, *Our Underachieving Colleges*, 323.
32. Lindsay, "The Likelihood of Higher Education Reform," 236-44.
33. Anonymous, "CLA Overview."
34. Arum and Roksa, *Academically Adrift*, 36.
35. Lindsay, "Likelihood of Higher Education Reform," 244.
36. Anonymous, "Is College Worth It?" "A Majority of Americans (57%) say the higher education system in the United States fails to provide students with good value for the money . . . An even larger majority—75%—says college is too expensive for most Americans to afford."

It is too early to know how all this will play out, but the next decade is bound to hold a number of surprises. What you can control is the quality of what goes on in your classroom. Your courses can be a learning oasis for you and your students. Faculty who survive and thrive in the next decade will be those who can demonstrate the magnificent difference teaching a way of thinking can make in student learning. Teaching a way of thinking can't be done effectively with any imaginable online technology. To learn a way of thinking, students will have to meet you in real-time in a brick and mortar encounter. In that encounter you as a real person with obvious passions will engage them in thinking about questions that are compelling to them. These questions will drive student thinking grounded in the processes of conceptualization and principle formation. You will give your students rich feedback as they idiosyncratically work to answer questions and solve problems through engagement with the logic of your discipline. The value of this kind of college education will be emphatically proven through the durable understanding and the real-world competence students gain in your classes. The ripples that emanate from your classes will go places and catalyze actions you cannot now imagine.

Appendix 1

The Logic of a Chef[1]

Core

Point of View: Looking at food as one of the pleasures of life.

Motivation: Finding pleasure and fulfillment in preparing innovative, tasty, and nutritious food.

Appropriate Questions: What dishes can I prepare with ingredients I already have on hand? What ingredients are in season? How can this dish be improved?

Working Layer

Assumptions: Many naturally occurring plant and animal materials can be used to produce tasty and nutritious food. Chemical changes are needed to convert raw ingredients into tasty food. The chef has the aptitude to learn to cook well.

Information: Ingredient availability, ingredient nutritional contribution, flavor wheel, ingredient substitutions, equipment and facility needs.

Conceptual Framework: Cooking techniques, preplanning the meal, time management of the dish, food sourcing, sanitation, food safety.

---

1. Rob Hansen, personal communication, July 19, 2013.

Output

Explanation: Why did this dish succeed (or fail)? Why do these dishes work together to enhance the dining experience? What can be done to improve the dish (taste, texture, moistness, etc.)?

Implications/Consequences: Understanding the principles of cooking leads to control of the process, which leads to a reliably tasty end result.

Appendix 2

Richard Paul's eight elements of thought[1] compared with my approach

Richard Paul's Elements of Thought	Paul's Comments	Logic of a Discipline*[2] (in this book)	Layer in the Logic Wheel**[3]
Purpose, Goal, or End in View	Whenever we reason, we reason to some end, to achieve some purpose.	Motivation	Core
Question at Issue (or Problem to Be Solved)	Whenever we attempt to reason something out, there must be at least one question at issue, at least one problem to be solved.	Appropriate question to answer	Core
Point of View or Frame of Reference	Whenever we reason, we reason within some point of view or frame of reference.	Point of view	Core

1. Paul, *Critical Thinking: What Every Person Needs*, 29-30.
2. Generally parallel with Paul's elements (exception noted).
3. Applies only to the logic of a discipline as presented in this book.

APPENDIX 2: RICHARD PAUL'S EIGHT ELEMENTS OF THOUGHT

Richard Paul's Elements of Thought	Paul's Comments	Logic of a Discipline*² (in this book)	Layer in the Logic Wheel***³
Empirical Dimension of Our Reasoning	Whenever we reason, there is some "stuff," some phenomena, about which we are reasoning.... We must actively decide which of a myriad of possible experiences, data, evidence, and so forth we will use.	Information	Working
Conceptual Dimension of Our Reasoning	All reasoning uses some ideas or concepts and not others.	Conceptual framework	Working
Assumptions	The Starting Points of Reasoning: All reasoning must begin somewhere, must take some things for granted.	Assumptions	Working
Inferences	Reasoning proceeds by steps called inferences.... "Because this is so, that also is so (or probably so)."	Explanation (answer to an appropriate question). This element is NOT parallel to Paul's inferences.	Output

APPENDIX 2: RICHARD PAUL'S EIGHT ELEMENTS OF THOUGHT

Richard Paul's Elements of Thought	Paul's Comments	Logic of a Discipline*[2] (in this book)	Layer in the Logic Wheel**[3]
Implications and Consequences	Where Our Reasoning Takes Us: All reasoning begins somewhere and proceeds somewhere else.	Implications/ consequences	Output

Appendix 3

Gowin's Knowledge Vee

D. Bob Gowin's Knowledge Vee compared with my logic of a discipline (chap. 3), the process of conceptualization (chap. 4) and a principle (chap. 5).[1] Gowin is in regular or bold font and my approach is in italics.

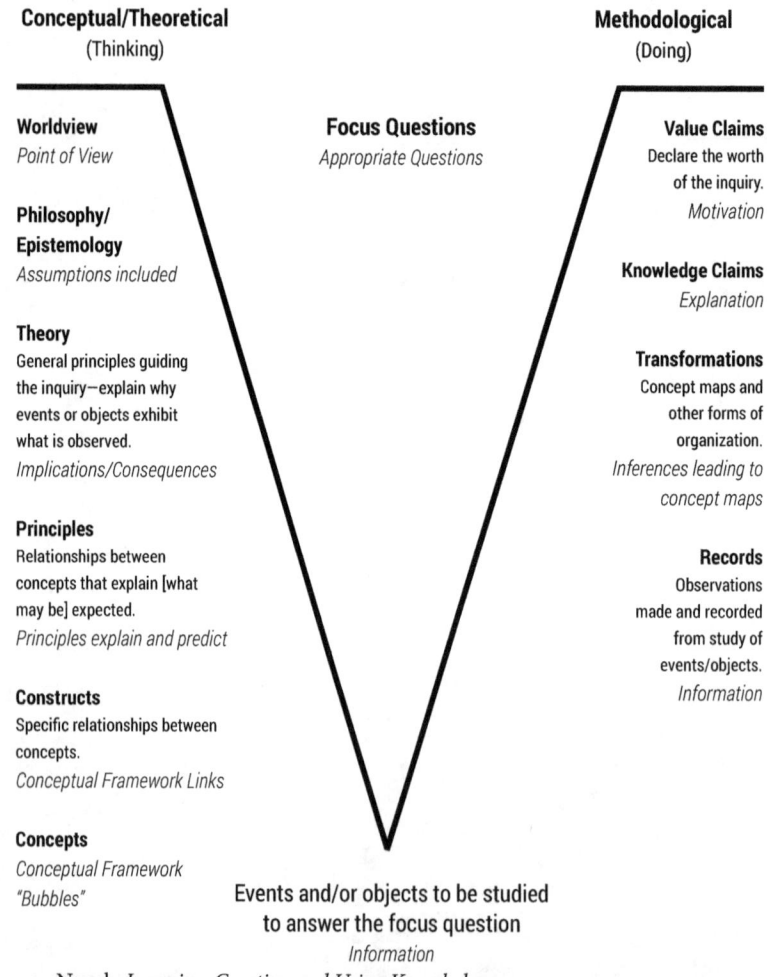

1. Novak, *Learning, Creating and Using Knowledge*, 92.

Appendix 4

Socratic GPS

Appendix 5
Assessment in Course Design

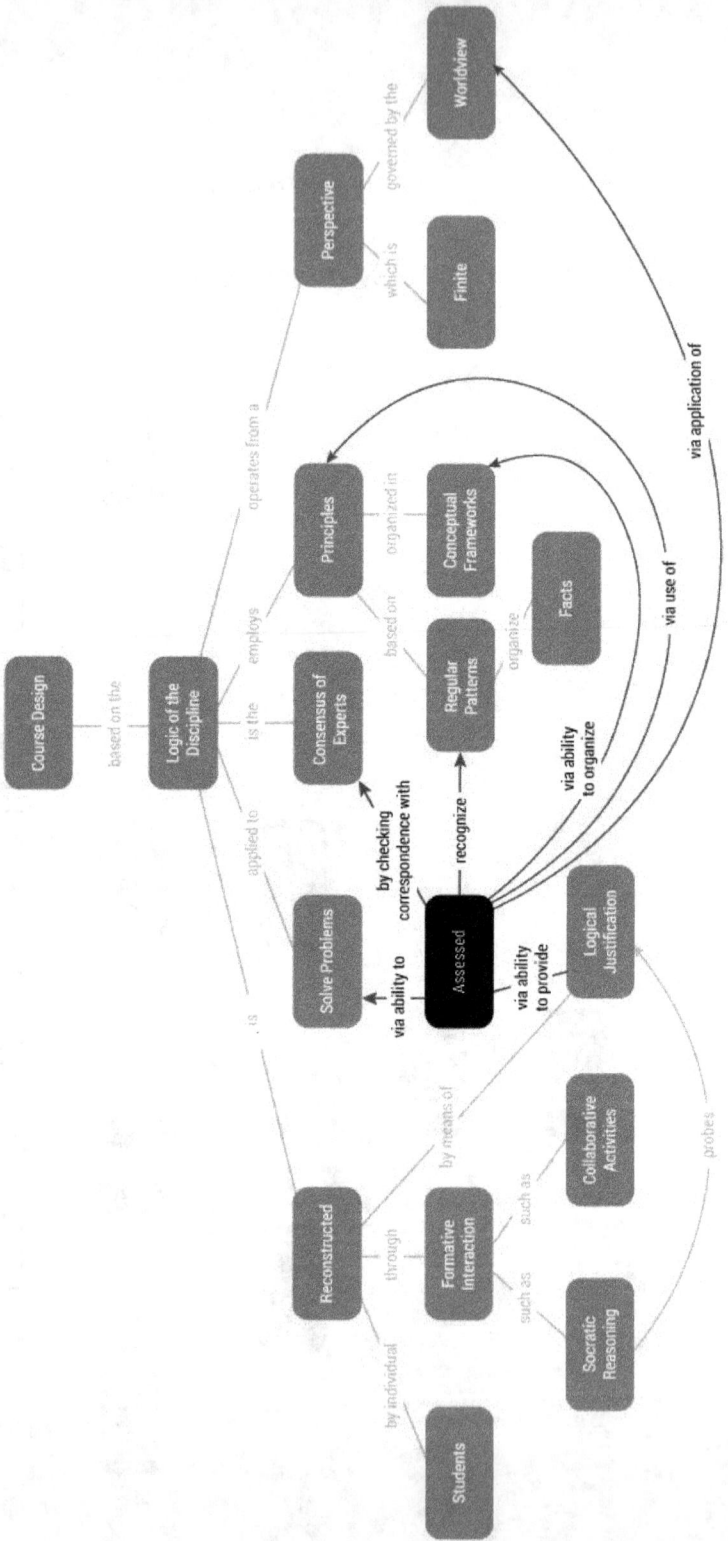

Bibliography

Adler, Mortimer J. *Paideia Problems and Possibilities*. New York: Macmillan, 1983.
———. *The Paideia Program: An Educational Syllabus*. San Francisco: Institute for Philosophical Research, 1984.
———. *The Paideia Proposal*. New York: Touchstone Book, 1982.
Adler, Mortimer J., and Charles Van Doren, *How to Read a Book: The Classic Guide to Intelligent Reading*. rev. ed. New York: Touchstone, 1972.
Alberts, Bruce, et al. *Molecular Biology of the Cell*. New York: Garland Publishing, 1983.
———. *Molecular Biology of the Cell*. 5th ed. New York: Garland Publishing, 2008.
Ambrose, Susan A., et al. *How Learning Works: 7 Research-Based Principles for Smart Teaching*, San Francisco: Jossey-Bass, 2010.
Anderson, L. W., et al. eds. *A Taxonomy for Learning, Teaching, and Assessing: A Revision of Bloom's Taxonomy of Educational Objectives*. Upper Saddle River, NJ: Pearson, 2000.
Anonymous. "20 Dead, 30 Presumed Dead in Quebec Oil Train Crash, Police Say," Fox News (11 July 2013). http://www.foxnews.com/world/2013/07/11/quebec-police-treating-oil-train-derailment-site-as-crime-scene-death-toll/print (26 July 2013).
Anonymous, "Antibiotics Prescribed." http://www.cbsnews.com/news/cdc-4-out-of-5-americans-prescribed-antibiotics-each-year/ (3 July 2014).
Anonymous, "Antibiotic Prescribing." http://www.nejm.org/doi/full/10.1056/NEJMc1212055 (3 July 2014).
Anonymous, "Antibiotic Resistance." http://www.cdc.gov/features/antibioticresistancethreats/ (3 July 2014).
Anonymous, "Archeology." http://www.archaeological.org/education/askexpertsfaq#faq8 (17 June 2014).
Anonymous, "Average Student Loan." http://time.com/money/3581803/average-student-loan-debt-2013 (13 July 2015).
Anonymous, Case-based Learning." http://sciencecases.lib.buffalo.edu/cs/about/ (7 July 2014).
Anonymous, "CLA Overview." http://cae.org/participating-institutions/cla-overview/ (25 July 2014).
Anonymous, "College English Major Pressures." http://americanradioworks.publicradio.org/features/tomorrows-college/english-major/pressures-liberal-education.html (21 July 2014).

BIBLIOGRAPHY

Anonymous, "Copenhagen Interpretation." http://en.wikipedia.org/wiki/Copenhagen_interpretation (13 August 2013).

Anonymous, "Create Rubrics." http://www.assessment.uconn.edu/docs/How_to_Create_Rubrics.pdf (15 July 2014).

Anonymous, "Declining Value." http://www.economist.com/news/united-states/21567373-american-universities-represent-declining-value-money-their-students-not-what-it. (13 July 2015).

Anonymous, "Definition of Generally Accepted Accounting Principles—GAAP." http://www.investopedia.com/terms/g/gaap.asp (13 August 2013).

Anonymous, "Developing Rubrics." http://assess.pages.tcnj.edu/files/2011/06/Developing-Rubrics.pdf (15 July 2014).

Anonymous, "How to Study," Wikihow, http://www.wikihow.com/Study (26 June 2014).

Anonymous, "Investopedia Explains Generally Accepted Accounting Principles—GAAP." http://www.investopedia.com/terms/g/gaap.asp. (13 August 2013).

Anonymous, "Is College Worth It?" May 15, 2011, http://www.pewsocialtrends.org/2011/05/15/is-college-worth-it/ (28 July 2014).

Anonymous, "Lariat." http://en.wikipedia.org/wiki/Lariat. (6 August 2013).

Anonymous, "Learning Outcomes." http://www.learningoutcomeassessment.org/Rubrics.htm (15 July 2014).

Anonymous, "Lessons from Thin Air," *Minds of Our Own*, a video series produced by Annenberg Learner and available at http://www.learner.org/resources/series26.html# (14 August 2013).

Anonymous, "Quebec oil train disaster: 24 bodies recovered so far," *The Guardian* (12 July 2013). http://www.guardian.co.uk/world/2013/jul/12/quebec-oil-train-crash-disaster-24-bodies (26 July 2013).

Anonymous, "Quidditch." http://en.wikipedia.org/wiki/International_Quidditch_Association (7 July 2014).

Anonymous, "Richard Feynman" http://en.wikipedia.org/wiki/Richard_Feynman. (16 July 2013). Refers to Harry LeVine, *The Great Explainer: The Story of Richard Feynman* (Greensboro, NC: Morgan Reynold, 2009).

Anonymous, "Rubistar." http://rubistar.4teachers.org/index.php (15 July 2014).

Anonymous, "Rubrics." http://jfmueller.faculty.noctrl.edu/toolbox/rubrics.htm (15 July 2014).

Anonymous, "'Seattle Underground." http://en.wikipedia.org/wiki/Seattle_Underground (17 June 2014).

Anonymous, "Soccer Fundamentals." http://www.nscaa.com/education/resources/fundamentals (18 June 2014).

Anonymous, "Soccer Tactics." http://www.nscaa.com/education/resources/fundamentals/introduction-to-soccer-tactics-1v1 (18 June 2014).

Anonymous, "Soccer Teaching Model." http://www.nscaa.com/education/resources/fundamentals/a-dynamic-teaching-model-5v5 (18 June 2014).

Anonymous, "Testing Resources." Brigham Young University Testing Center, https://testing.byu.edu/resources?destination=node/105 (16 July 2014).

Anonymous, "The Role of Questions in Teaching, Thinking and, Learning." The Critical Thinking Community, accessed July 22, 2015, https://www.criticalthinking.org/pages/the-role-of-questions-in-teaching-thinking-and-learning/524, paragraph 13.

Anonymous, "Underground Atlanta." http://en.wikipedia.org/wiki/Underground_Atlanta (17 June 2014).
Anonymous, "Use of Time." http://www.bls.gov/tus/charts/students.htm (26 June 2014).
Anonymous, "Value of a College Degree." http://americanradioworks.publicradio.org/features/tomorrows-college/dropouts/value-of-college-degree.html (21 July 2014).
Anonymous, "Worldview." https://en.wikipedia.org/wiki/World_view (19 June 2014).
Anonymous, "Writing Across Curriculum." http://en.wikipedia.org/wiki/Writing_Across_the_Curriculum (25 June 2014).
Anonymous, "Writing Distractors." http://assessment.aaas.org/topics (16 July 2014).
Aristotle, "Teaching and Understanding." http://www.goodreads.com/quotes/392369-teaching-is-the-highest-form-of-understanding (27 June 2014).
Arum, Richard, and Josipa Roksa, *Academically Adrift: Limited Learning on College Campuses*. Chicago: The University of Chicago Press, 2011.
Ausubel, David P., Joseph D. Novak, and Helen Hanesian. *Educational Psychology: A Cognitive View*. 2nd ed. New York: Holt, Rinehart & Winston, 1978.
Bacon, Francis. 1625. http://grammar.about.com/od/60essays/a/studiesessay.htm (25 June 2014).
Bain, Ken. *What the Best College Students Do*. Boston: Harvard University Press, 2012.
———. *What the Best College Teachers Do*. Boston: Harvard University Press, 2004.
Baird, Leonard L. "Do Grades and Tests Predict Adult Accomplishment?" *Research in Higher Education* 23 (1985): 3.
Batdorf, Bradley R. "An Analysis of the Effects of Inquiry-Based Peer Mentoring on the Achievement of College Entry-Level Biology Students." Ed.D. diss., Bob Jones University, 2012.
Bauerlein, Mark. *The Dumbest Generation: How the Digital Age Stupefies Young Americans and Jeopardizes Our Future (Or, Don't Trust Anyone Under 30)*. New York: Penguin, 2008.
Biggs, John, and Catherine Tang *Teaching for Quality Learning at University*. 3rd ed. Maidenhead, UK: Open University Press/McGraw-Hill Education, 2007.
Blinder, Alan S. "Keynesian Economics." *The Concise Encyclopedia of Economics*, http://www.econlib.org/library/Enc/KeynesianEconomics.html (13 August 2013).
Bloom, Benjamin S. *Taxonomy of Educational Objectives: The Classification of Educational Goals; Handbook I: Cognitive Domain*. New York: Longmans, Green, 1956.
Bok, Derek. *Our Underachieving Colleges: A Candid Look at How Much Students Learn and Why They Should Be Learning More*. Princeton, NJ: Princeton University Press, 2006.
Boyer, Ernest L. *Scholarship Reconsidered: Priorities of the Professoriate*. Princeton, NJ: The Carnegie Foundation for the Advancement of Teaching, 1990.
Bradbury, Ray. *The Martian Chronicles*. New York: Simon & Schuster, 1977.
Bransford, J. et al. eds. *How People Learn: Brain, Mind, Experience, and School*. exp. ed. Washington, DC: National Academy Press, 2004.
Brain, Marshall. "How Analog and Digital Recording Works." http://electronics.howstuffworks.com/analog-digital3.htm (5 August 2013).

Brigham Young University Testing Center. https://testing.byu.edu/resources?destination=node/105 (16 July 2014).

Brown, Alton. *I'm Just Here for the Food: Food + Heat = Cooking*. New York: Stewart, Tabori & Chang, 2002.

Bruner, Jerome S. *Toward a Theory of Instruction*. Boston: Belknap Press, 1966.

Buchanan, Karen S. "What Fitness Bands Can Teach Us About Classroom Assessment." *The Teaching Professor* 28 (2014): 1.

Burke, James. http://topdocumentaryfilms.com/james-burke-connections/ (24 July 2014).

Case. Robert Case. "Plato's Premise: Fostering Student Autonomy." *Thought & Action: The NEA Higher Education Journal* 18 (2002): 33-40.

Chec, Thomas R. "Science at Liberal Arts Colleges: A Better Education?" *Daedelus* 128 (1999): 195–216.

Chesterton, G. K. *Heretics*. Rockville, MD: Serenity, 2009.

———. http://www.goodreads.com/quotes/tag/listening (25 June 2014).

Chew, Stephen. "Helping Students to Get the Most Out of Studying." In V. A. Benassi, C. E. Overson, and C. M. Hakala. eds. *Applying the Science of Learning in Education: Infusing Psychological Science into the Curriculum* (2014), 215. Retrieved from the Society for the Teaching of Psychology website: http://teachpsych.org/ebooks/asle2014/index.php (23 July 2015).

———. "How to Get the Most out of Studying." http://www.samford.edu/how-to-study/ or https://www.youtube.com/watch?v=RH95h36NChI (26 June 2014).

Child, Julia. "Cooking." http://www.goodreads.com/author/quotes/3465.Julia_Child (8 August 2013).

Choron, Sandra, and Harry Choron. *College in a Can*. Boston: Houghton Mifflin, 2004.

Christenbury, Leila, and Patricia P. Kelly. *Questioning: A Path to Critical Thinking*. Urbana, IL: The ERIC Clearinghouse on Reading and Communication Skills and the National Council of Teachers of English, 1983.

Ciarcia, Steve. "What Makes an Engineer?" *Circuit Cellar Ink* 213 (2008): 96.

Complete Cook's Country TV Show Cookbook, The. Brookline, MA: America's Test Kitchen, 2012.

Crowe, Alison, et al. "Biology in Bloom: Implementing Bloom's Taxonomy to Enhance Student Learning in Biology." *CBE—Life Sciences Education* 7 (2008): 369.

Dabek, Frank. "'Car Talk' Brothers Address Graduates." *The Tech* 28 (11 June 1999): 9.

Deslauriers, Louis, Ellen Schelew, and Carl Wieman, "Improved Learning in Large Enrollment Physics Class," *Science* 332 (2011): 862-64.

Dickens, Charles. *Hard Times*. New York: Dover Publications, 2001.

Dunn, Joe P. "The Winning Teacher: Metaphors from Coaching," *The Teaching Professor* 6 (1992): 1-2.

Einstein, Albert. "Understand and Explain." http://www.goodreads.com/quotes/271951-you-do-not-really-understand-something-unless-you-can-explain (17 July 2013).

Elder, Linda. "Richard W. Paul: A Biographical Sketch," http://www.criticalthinking.org/data/pages/37/ff640b6d016307b54cad91e5a9d4edfd4f18adb74215a.pdf (25 July 2013).

———. "The Role of Questions in Teaching, Thinking, & Learning," https://www.criticalthinking.org/pages/the-role-of-questions-in-teaching-thinking-and-learning/524, paragraph 13. (22 July 2015).

Elder, Linda, and Richard Paul. *The Miniature Guide to the Art of Asking Essential Questions*. Santa Rosa, CA: The Foundation for Critical Thinking, 2006.

Eliot, Charles William. *Turning Point in Higher Education: The Inaugural Address of Charles William Eliot as President of Harvard College, October 19, 1869*. Quoted in Derek Bok, *Our Underachieving Colleges* (Princeton, NJ: Princeton University Press, 2006), 123.

Eliot. T. S. *Choruses from the Rock*. http://www.brainyquote.com/quotes/quotes/t/tseliot121647.html (12 August 2013).

Emig, Janet. "Writing as a Mode of Learning." *College Composition and Communication* 28, no. 2. (1977): 122-28.

Farber, Jerry. *The Student as Nigger: Essays and Stories*. New York: Pocket Books, 1972. Quoted in Ken Bain. *What the Best College Teachers Do*. Boston: Harvard University Press, 2004, 143.

Feynman, Richard P. "Beauty," http://www.goodreads.com/author/quotes/1429989.Richard_P_Feynman. (15 July 2013).

———. "Nearly Everything is Interesting." http://www.goodreads.com/author/quotes/1429989.Richard_P_Feynman (15 July 2013).

Finkel, Donald L. *Teaching with Your Mouth Shut*. Portsmouth, NH: Heinemann, 2000.

Fish, Stanley. "Devoid of Content." *NY Times*, May 31, 2005. Op-Ed pages. http://www.nytimes.com/2005/05/31/opinion/devoid-of-content.html (24 July 2015).

Fitch, Josiah. *The Art of Questioning*. 9th ed. 1879. Quoted in Kenneth Eble, *The Craft of Teaching*. San Francisco: Jossey Bass, 1988, 91.

Forster, E. M. "Spoon-feeding," Quoted in United Press International and referenced in *The Week*, 11 June 2010, 21.

Frazier, Jennifer. "Falling in Love with Biology." In "The Artful Amoeba: A blog about the weird wonderfulness of life on earth." http://theartfulamoeba.com/2011/05/17/falling-in-love-with-biology/ (17 May 2011).

Fredriksson, Don. *Plumbing for Dummies: A Guide to the Maintenance and Repair of Everything Including the Kitchen Sink*. Indianapolis: Bobbs-Merrill, 1983.

Freeman, Scott, et al. "Active Learning Increases Student Performance in Science, Engineering, and Mathematics." PNAS, May 12, 2014. http://www.pnas.org/content/early/2014/05/08/1319030111.short?rss=1&ssource=mfr.

Gibbs, Graham, and Claire Simpson. "Conditions Under Which Assessment Supports Students' Learning." *Learning and Teaching in Higher Education* 1 (2004-5): 9.

Goldberg, David. "Bury the Cold War Curriculum." *ASEE Prism* 8 (2008): 68.

Gray, William L. Personal communication with author, Greenville, SC, June 14, 2014.

Gray, W. Michael. "Bio 100: General Biology I." Course syllabus, General Biology I, Bob Jones University, January 14, 2015.

———. "Bio 100: General Biology I Study Guide." Supplement, General Biology I, Bob Jones University, January 14, 2015.

Gronlund, Norman E. *How to Write and Use Instructional Objective*. 6th ed. Upper Saddle River, NJ: Prentice Hall, 2000.

Hake, Richard R. "My Conversion to the Arons-Advocated Method of Science Education," *Teaching Education* 3 (Win-Spr 1991): 109.

Hartog III, John. "Avoiding God's Disqualification." Public presentation at Bob Jones University, Greenville, SC, March 24, 2009.

Heath, Chip, and Dan Heath, *Made to Stick: Why Some Ideas Survive and Others Die.* New York: Random House, 2008.

Hutcheson, Francis. *Inquiry into the Original of Our Ideas of Beauty and Virtue* http://www.thefreedictionary.com/wisdom (12 August 2013).

Jacobs, Lucy C., and Clinton I. Chase. *Developing and Using Tests Effectively: A Guide for Faculty.* San Francisco: Jossey-Bass, 1992.

Kalyuga, S. "Cognitive Load Theory: How Many Types of Load Does It Really Need?" *Educational Psychology Review* 23 (2011): 1-19.

Keillor, Garrison. "Above Average." http://www.brainyquote.com/quotes/authors/g/garrison_keillor.html (10 July 2014).

Khanna, M. M., et al., "Short- and long-term effects of cumulative finals on student learning," *Teaching of Psychology* 40 (2013): 180.

Koch, Wendy. "Quebec rail disaster questions safety of oil transport." *USA Today*, (9 July 2013). http://www.usatoday.com/story/news/nation/2013/07/09/quebec-rail-disaster-oil-keystone-pipeline/2503271/ (26 July 2013).

Krathwohl, David R. "A Revision of Bloom's Taxonomy: An Overview," *Theory into Practice* 41, no. 4 (2002): 215.

Lambert, Craig. "Twilight of the Lecture." *Harvard Magazine* 114 (March-April 2012): 23.

Lansing, Alfred. *Endurance: Shackleton's Incredible Voyage.* New York, Carroll & Graf Publishers, 1959.

Lasry, Nathaniel, et al., "Peer Instruction: From Harvard to Community Colleges," *Am. J. Phys.* 76 (2008): 1066-69.

Learner, Annenberg. "Lessons from Thin Air." From *Minds of Our Own*, a video series available at http://www.learner.org/resources/series26.html# (14 August 2013).

Lee, Chee Ha, and Slava Kalyuga. "Expertise Reversal Effect and Its Instructional Implications." In V. A. Benassi, C. E. Overson, and C. M. Hakala, eds. *Applying the Science of Learning in Education: Infusing Psychological Science into the Curriculum* (2014), 33. Retrieved from the Society for the Teaching of Psychology website: http://teachpsych.org/ebooks/asle2014/index.php (23 July 2015).

Lemons, Paula P., and J. Derrick Lemons. "Questions for Assessing Higher-Order Cognitive Skills: It's Not Just Bloom's." *CBE—Life Sciences Education* 12 (2013): 47-58.

Lemov, Doug. *Teach Like a Champion: 49 Techniques That Put Students on the Path to College (K-12).* San Francisco: Jossey-Bass, 2010.

Lewis, C. S. Surprised by Joy: The Shape of My Early Life (Boston: Houghton, Mifflin, Harcourt, 1966), 207.

Lindsay, Thomas K. "The Likelihood of Higher Education Reform." *Society* 50 (June 2013): 236-44.

Lipton, Peter, "What Good Is an Explanation?" In *Explanations: Styles of Explanation in Science.* Edited by John Cornwell. Oxford, UK: Oxford University Press, 2004.

Lucas, A. M. "Multiple Marking of a Matriculation Biology Essay Question." *The British Journal of Educational Psychology* 41 (1971): 78-84.

Madison, Deborah. *Vegetable Literacy.* New York: Crown Publishing Group, Ten Speed Press, 2013.

Mayer, Richard E. *Applying the Science of Learning*. Boston: Allyn and Bacon, 2011.

Mazur, Eric. *Peer Instruction: A User's Manual, Series in Educational Innovation*. Upper Saddle River, NJ: Prentice Hall, 1997.

McCormick, Alexander C. "It's About Time: What to Make of Reported Declines in How Much College Students Study." *Liberal Education* 97, no. 1 (2011). http://www.aacu.org/liberaleducation/le-wi11/LEWI11_McCormick.cfm (26 June 2014).

McTighe, Jay, and Grant Wiggins *Understanding by Design Professional Development Workbook*. Alexandria, VA: Association of Supervision and Curriculum Development, 2004)

Mencken, H. L. *A Mencken Chrestomathy*. New York: Knopf Doubleday Publishing, 2012.

Mill, John Stuart. *Autobiography by John Stuart Mill*. Ed. John M. Robson. London: Penguin Books, 1989.

Miller, George A. "The Magical Number Seven, Plus or Minus Two: Some Limits on Our Capacity for Processing Information." *The Psychological Review* 63 (1956): 81-97.

Momsen, Jennifer L., et al. "Just the Facts? Introductory Undergraduate Biology Courses Focus on Low-Level Cognitive Skills." *CBE—Life Sciences Education* 9 (2010): 437.

Moon, Brian, et al. *Applied Concept Mapping: Capturing, Analyzing, and Organizing Knowledge*. Boca Raton, FL: CRC Press of Taylor & Francis Group, 2011.

Mursell, James "Failure of Schools." *Atlantic Monthly* (1939), quoted in Adler and Van Doren, *How to Read a Book: The Classic Guide to Intelligent Reading*. rev. ed. New York: Touchstone, 1972. xi.

National Board of Medical Examiners, *Constructing Written Test Questions for the Basic and Clinical Sciences*, 3rd ed., http://www.nbme.org/publications/item-writing-manual-download.html (16 July 2014).

Newman, John Henry. *The Idea of a University Defined and Illustrated*. Discourse VI, 134. http://www.newmanreader.org/works/idea/discourse6.html (28 July 2014).

———. Preface, xiii. http://www.newmanreader.org/works/idea/preface.html (24 July 2014).

———. Discourse VII, Stanza 10, 178. http://www.newmanreader.org/works/idea/discourse7.html (21 July 2014).

Novak, Gregor, and Evelyn Patterson. "An Introduction to Just-in-Time Teaching (JiTT)." In *Just in Time Teaching: Across the Disciplines, and Across the Academy. New Pedagogies and Practices for Teaching in Higher Education*. Edited by Scott Simkins and Mark Maier. Sterling, VA: Stylus, 2010.

Novak, Joseph D. *Learning, Creating, and Using Knowledge: Concept Maps as Facilitative Tools in Schools and Corporation*. 2nd ed. New York: Routledge, Taylor Francis Group, 2012.

———. *The Theory Underlying Concept Maps and How to Construct Them*. "IHMC Concept Map Software." http://cmap.coginst.uwf.edu/info/ (31 May 2004).

Novak, Joseph D., and D. Bob Gowin. *Learning How to Learn*. New York: Cambridge University Press, 1984.

O'Brien, Judith G., et al. *The Course Syllabus: A Learning Centered Approach*. San Francisco: Jossey-Bass, 2008.

O'Conner, Patricia T. *NY Times Book Review* of Fowler 3rd ed. Feb 6, 1997. http://www.nytimes.com/books/97/02/16/bookend/bookend.html (15 July 2009).

Omegapowers, "DIKW." https://commons.wikimedia.org/wiki/File:DIKW_(1).png. Graphic released into the public domain.

Oxford English Dictionary. http://www.oed.com.

Pappano, Laura. "The Year of the MOOC," Nov. 2, 2012, *NY Times*, http://www.nytimes.com/2012/11/04/education/edlife/massive-open-online-courses-are-multiplying-at-a-rapid-pace.html?_r=0 (21 July 2014).

Pascal, Blaise. Daily Quotes. "Love." http://www.dailyquotes.us/categs.html?c=love (13 August 2014).

Paul, Richard W. "Critical Thinking: How to Design Instruction So That Students Master Content in a Deep and Thoughtful Way." Park Hotel, Charlotte, NC. January 21-22, 1995.

———. "Critical Thinking: How to Design Instruction So That Students Master Content in a Deep and Thoughtful Way." Park Hotel, Charlotte, NC. January 21-22, 1995. Richard W. Paul Workshop Syllabus, 7.

———. *Critical Thinking: What Every Person Needs to Survive in a Rapidly Changing World*. Rev. 2nd ed. Santa Rosa, CA: Foundation for Critical Thinking, 1992.

———. "College-Wide Grading Standards." http://www.criticalthinking.org/pages/college-wide-grading-standards/441 (17 July 2014).

Paul, Richard W., and Linda Elder, *Critical Thinking: Tools for Taking Charge of Your Learning and Your Life*. Upper Saddle River, NJ: Prentice Hall, 2001.

———. *The Thinker's Guide to the Art of Socratic Questioning*. Santa Rosa, CA, Foundation for Critical Thinking, 2006.

Pepper, John. "Why I Love History." In National History Club, Spring 2008, Issue XII. At http://www.nationalhistoryclub.org/documents/NewsletterFinal.pdf (15 July 2013).

Perkins, David N. *Making Learning Whole: How Seven Principles of Teaching Can Transform Education*. San Francisco: Jossey-Bass, 2009.

Peters, Tom. *Thriving on Chaos: Handbook for a Management Revolution*. New York: Harper Perennial. 1991. http://www.goodreads.com/quotes/tag/confusion (13 August 2013).

Posner, George J., et al. "Accommodation of a Scientific Conception: Towards a Theory of Conceptual Change." *Science Education* 66, Issue 2 (1982): 214.

Postman, Neil. *The End of Education*. New York: Vintage Books, 1995.

Pyc, Mary A., Pooja K. Agarwal, and Henry L. Roediger III. "Test-Enhanced Learning." In V. A. Benassi, C. E. Overson, and C. M. Hakala. eds. *Applying the Science of Learning in Education: Infusing Psychological Science into the Curriculum* (2014). Retrieved from the Society for the Teaching of Psychology website: http://teachpsych.org/ebooks/asle2014/index.php

Ramsden, Paul. *Learning to Teach in Higher Education*. 2nd ed. London: RoutledgeFalmer, 2003.

———. "Studying Learning: Improving Teaching." In Paul Ramsden (ed.) *Improving Learning: New Perspectives*. London: Kogan Page, 1988, 13-14, quoted in Maryellen Weimer, *Learner-Centered Teaching: Five Key Changes to Practice*. San Francisco: Jossey-Bass, 2002, 47-48.

Reed, Richard J. "A Mini-Autobiography" http://www.atmos.washington.edu/Reed/autobio.html (15 July 2013).

Roberts, Terry, and Laura Billings. *The Paideia Classroom: Teaching for Understanding*. Larchmont, NY: Eye on Education, 1999.

Robertson, Campbell, and Clifford Krauss. "Gulf Spill Is the Largest of Its Kind, Scientists Say." *NY Times*, 2 August 2010. Available at http://www.nytimes.com/2010/08/03/us/03spill.html?_r=0 (16 July 2014).

Rojstaczer, Stuart, and Christopher Healey. "Where A Is Ordinary: The Evolution of American College and University Grading, 1940-2009." *Teachers College Record* 114 (2012): 2. Available at: http://www.gradeinflation.com/tcr2011grading.pdf (10 July 2014).

Ross, Philip E. "The Expert Mind." *Scientific American* 295 (2006): 66-68.

Russell, Thomas L. *The No Significant Difference Phenomenon*. Raleigh, NC: Office of Instructional Telecommunications, North Carolina State University, 1999.

Sadler, D. Royce. "Formative Assessment and the Design of Instructional Systems." *Instructional Science* 18 (1989): 121.

Sayers, Dorothy. *The Lost Tools of Learning* (1947), http://www.gbt.org/text/sayers.html (27 June 2014).

Schneck, Daniel J. "Teaching Lessons Learned: Integrated Learning." *American Laboratory* 37 (Sept. 2005): 7.

Sheridan, Richard B. *The Rivals* (1775), https://archive.org/stream/therivals00sheriala/therivals00sheriala_djvu.txt (15 July 2015).

Shingler, Benjamin, and Rob Gillies. "Canada Train Crash: Death Toll in Quebec Disaster Rise to 13, Around 40 Still Missing." *Huffington Post World* (8 July 2013). http://www.huffingtonpost.com/2013/07/08/canada-train-crash-death-toll_n_3563227.html (26 July 2013).

Simon, H. A. "Observations on the Sciences of Science Learning." Paper prepared for the Committee on Developments in the Science of Learning for the Sciences of Science Learning: An Interdisciplinary Discussion. Department of Psychology, Carnegie Mellon University, 1996. Quoted in J. Bransford et al. Eds. *How People Learn: Brain, Mind, Experience, and School*. Washington, DC: National Academy Press, 2004.

Smith, Michelle, et al., "The Classroom Observation Protocol for Undergraduate STEM (COPUS): A New Instrument to Characterize University STEM Classroom Practices," *CBE-Life Sciences Education* 12 (2013): 618-27.

Srinivasan, M., et al. "Comparing problem-based learning with case-based learning: effects of a major curricular shift at two institutions" *Acad. Med.* 82, no. 1 (2007): 74-82.

Steedle, Jeffrey T., and Scott Elliot. "The Efficacy of Automated Essay Scoring for Evaluating Student Responses to Complex Critical Thinking Performance Tasks." http://cae.org/research/category/white-papers-monographs/ (15 July 2014).

Stevens, Dannelle D. and Antonia J. Levi, *Introduction to Rubrics: An Assessment Tool to Save Grading Time, Convey Effective Feedback, and Promote Student Learning* (Sterling, VA: Stylus Publishing, 2005).

Stroud, J. B. *Psychology in Education* (White Plains, NY: Longman, 1946), 476. Quoted in Lucy C. Jacobs and Clinton I. Chase, *Developing and Using Tests Effectively: A Guide for Faculty* (San Francisco: Jossey-Bass, 1992), 7.

Suppes, P., and R. Ginsberg. "A Fundamental Property of All-or-None Models, Binomial Distribution of Responses Prior to Conditioning, with Application to Concept Formation in Children." *Psychological Review* 70 (1963): 139-61.

Quoted in Joseph D. Novak, *Learning, Creating, and Using Knowledge: Concept Maps as Facilitative Tools in Schools and Corporations,* 2nd ed. New York: Routledge, 2012.

Tobias, Sheila and Jacqueline Raphael, *The Hidden Curriculum: Faculty-Made Tests in Science* (New York: Plenum Press, 1997).

Tolkien, J.R.R. *The Hobbit; or, There and Back Again.* New York: Del Rey Mass Market Edition, 2012.

———. *The Lord of the Rings, The Two Towers,* 2002. http://www.imdb.com/character/ch0000152/quotes (16 July 2013).

Trigwell, Keith and Suzanne Shale. "Student Learning and the Scholarship of University Teaching." *Studies in Higher Education* 29 (2004): 532.

Twain, Mark. "Plagiarism." http://www.twainquotes.com/Plagiarism.html. 5 August 2016.

Van Gelder, T. J. *How to Improve Critical Thinking Using Educational Technology,* in G. Kennedy, M. Keppell, C. McNaught, and T. Petrovic. eds. *Meeting at the Crossroads. Proceedings of the 18th Annual Conference of the Australasian Society for Computers in Learning in Tertiary Education (2001).* Melbourne: Biomedical Multimedia Unit, The University of Melbourne. 15 July 2015.

Various, "One Thousand and One Nights." http://en.wikipedia.org/wiki/One_Thousand_and_One_Nights (19 June 2014).

Wahba, Phil "Bell tolls 50 times for Quebec dead in train disaster." Reuters, July 13, 2013. http://www.reuters.com/assets/print?aid=USBRE96A0WS20130713 (26 July 2013).

Watkins, Jessica and Eric Mazur, "Using JiTT with Peer Instruction," in *Just in Time Teaching: Across the Disciplines, and Across the Academy,* ed. Scott Simkins and Mark Maier. Sterling, VA: Stylus, 2010.

Weaver, Richard M. *Ideas Have Consequences.* Chicago: University of Chicago Press, 1948.

Weimer, Maryellen. *Learner-Centered Teaching: Five Key Changes to Practice.* San Francisco: Jossey-Bass, 2002.

"When Computers Leave Classrooms, So Does Boredom." *The Chronicle of Higher Education* 55 (July 20, 2009): A1–A13.

Whitehead, Alfred North. "The Rhythmic Claims of Freedom and Discipline." In *The Aims of Education and Other Essays.* New York: Free Press, 1967.

———. "Universities and Their Function." In Alfred North Whitehead, *The Aims of Education and Other Essays.* New York: Free Press, 1967.

Wieman, Carl. "The 'Curse of Knowledge' or Why Intuition About Teaching Often Fails." *American Physical Society News* 10 (2007): 8.

———. "A new model for post-secondary education, the Optimized University." http://www.cwsei.ubc.ca/about/BCCampus2020_Wieman_think_piece.pdf (24 July 2014).

———. "Why Not Try a Scientific Approach to Science Education?" *Change* 53 (Sept./Oct. 2007): 10.

"Wieman, Carl." Wikipedia, http://en.wikipedia.org/wiki/Carl_Wieman. 12 July 2013.

Wiggins, Grant, and Jay McTighe. *Understanding by Design.* exp. 2nd ed. Alexandria, VA: Association of Supervision and Curriculum Development, 2005.

Wilson, John. *Thinking with Concepts.* Cambridge, UK: Cambridge University Press, 1963.

Zhang, Mo. "Contrasting Automated and Human Scoring of Essays." *R & D Connections* 21 (2013): 2.

Zinsser, William. *On Writing Well: The Classic Guide to Writing Nonfiction*. 30th anniversary ed. New York: Harper Collins, 2006.